IN LIBERTY'S
SHADOW

IN LIBERTY'S
▧ SHADOW ▧

Illegal Aliens and
Immigration Law Enforcement

EDWIN HARWOOD

HOOVER INSTITUTION PRESS

Stanford University   Stanford, California

Hoover Press Publication 331

First printing, 1986
Manufactured in the United States of America
90   89   88   87   86   9   8   7   6   5   4   3   2   1

Library of Congress Cataloging in Publication Data
Harwood, Edwin.
   In liberty's shadow.

   Bibliography: p.
   Includes index.
   1. Aliens, Illegal—United States.   2. Emigration
and immigration law—United States.   3. United States.
Immigration and Naturalization Service.   I. Title.
KF4800.H37   1986   342.73'083   86-10360
                       347.30283
ISBN 0-8179-8311-2 (alk. paper)

Design by P. Kelley Baker

For Susan, my wife. None deserves this dedication more.

CONTENTS

ACKNOWLEDGMENTS

In studying a large and complex organization, such as the Immigration and Naturalization Service, I have necessarily incurred a substantial debt of gratitude. Had it not been for the cooperation of many INS officials, both top- and middle-echelon administrators at the central, regional, and district offices and scores of lower-echelon officers I became acquainted with in the field, I could not have carried out the study. Or to put the matter somewhat differently, although I might have been able to write a book on immigration enforcement based on publicly available statistical information and other source materials, I could not have probed crucial aspects of the agency's operations at the microlevel. An interpretation of agency behavior relying solely on macrolevel statistical data or other published documentary evidence would have been hopelessly incomplete. For example, one cannot know what arrest statistics mean without looking closely at the behavior of the officials who produce those statistics. Moreover, there are many important aspects of agency operations that are not reflected in official statistics or public records at all.

I want to thank the many criminal investigators, border patrol agents, examiners, inspectors, trial attorneys, immigration judges, central office staff personnel, and others I interviewed and whose assistance was crucial in helping me understand INS operations as well as finding my way through the labyrinthine corridors of the Immigration and Nationality Act, a law said to be the most complex federal statute after the tax code.

I would like to thank Commissioner Alan C. Nelson for assuring me of his agency's cooperation in supplying me with essential statistical and other information required for the book. I am especially indebted to Mr. Robert Newman, assistant to the Associate Commissioner, Enforcement, for his assistance in expediting my inquiries, notifying field offices of my visits, and arranging interviews with officials at the central office during my several trips to Washington, D.C.

Because I was assisted by so many INS officials, some of whose names I neglected to record and cannot now recall, I trust that a blanket expression of gratitude will serve in lieu of a listing of each and every officer by name. Not only did these many officers take time from crowded work schedules to answer my questions and permit me to observe them at work, they also talked candidly about the dilemmas facing the agency during the period I was in the field. As a result, I was privy to information that many would have been reluctant to share with most outsiders.

Without their candor, I could not have accomplished my goal, which was to develop a perspective of enforcement operations by looking inside the INS, without the protective public relations gloss all organizations understandably develop to mobilize support for their mission. My responsibility to the many INS officials who assisted my research has always been clear to me: to tell it like it is to the best of my ability, so that readers of the book would have a better understanding of the problems confronting the INS during the period of my study. My duty was to provide as objective an assessment of agency operations as the resources available to me permitted, without partiality toward any party.

I must emphasize that the conclusions and interpretations set down in the chapters that follow are entirely my own. Although INS officials assisted my research by providing statistical and other information and by clarifying agency regulations, terminology, and the like, the conclusions stated in this book are not necessarily ones with which they agree. Nor is the assistance they rendered in responding to my requests for information to be interpreted in any way as an endorsement of the point of view or interpretations set forth in the chapters that follow.

I am indebted to the Sarah Scaife Foundation for providing funding for the field work and to both the Hoover Institution and the Weingart Foundation for providing fellowship support during the two years I spent researching and writing the book. I wish to thank Dr. W. Glenn Campbell, Dr. Dennis Bark, and Dr. John Moore for their assistance in helping to arrange the funding for the study and I thank Dr. Thomas Moore for providing logistical support in his role as director of the Domestic Studies Program.

I owe a special debt of gratitude to a number of my colleagues at the Hoover Institution, who read advance drafts of either articles or chapters of this book; among them were Alvin Rabushka, Annelise Anderson, Peter J. Duignan, and Lewis Gann. They, along with many other Hoover scholars, including Kingsley Davis, Robert Hessen, John Bunzel, Seymour M. Lipset, James Stockdale, Richard Staar, and Mikhail Bernstam, provided helpful insights during occasional conversations on the topic. Numerous other visiting scholars and national fellows stimulated my thinking on immigration policy in the course of the intellectual give-and-take that occurs regularly during the afternoon coffee hour in the Hoover Senior Commons.

I also want to thank Shelly Slade, Don Hernandez, and Pat Montero, students at the Stanford Law School, for assisting me with legal research at various times during the study. Other scholars and legal practitioners from outside the Hoover Institution provided helpful comments and criticism on various chapters, among them Janet Gilboy, Martin Danziger, Donald Huddle, and Philip Martin. I am especially grateful to Peter H. Schuck of the Yale Law School and to my longtime friend and colleague, Franklin Zimring of the University of California Law School, for their informative insights on legal and other issues in immigration law enforcement.

I owe a special debt of gratitude to Naoma Wright, who helped with my correspondence, and to Gloria Watson, who assisted in teaching me how to use Hoover's word processor, which greatly facilitated my productivity. At the end, Gloria provided invaluable assistance in helping me prepare the manuscript for publication. The professionals at the Hoover press gave generously of their time and expertise in helping me to prepare the manuscript for typesetting.

To my wife, Susan, I owe a profound debt of gratitude—for her love and support, not just during this project but through the entire 21 years of our life together.

Finally, I must thank the good friends and relatives around the country who put me up. By helping me save on room and board charges, I was able to carry out more field work than would otherwise have been possible. In Washington, D.C., I spent a total of three to four weeks staying with my good friends of many years, Stan and Marlene Besen. My other good hosts across the country included Margaret and Hurl Churchill; Jim Andrews; Larry Siever; Bob and Shelly Rosenthal; my in-laws, Dr. and Mrs. Morris Rosenthal; and my father and his wife, Mr. and Mrs. E. T. Harwood.

PREFACE

In early summer of 1981, I decided that a study of how the U.S. Immigration and Naturalization Service (INS) enforces the immigration law would be a useful research project. At the time I had only the vaguest notion of what that service did, and I knew next to nothing about the law itself. Like many Americans, I knew that an immigration service existed, that it employed officers at the borders to prevent unauthorized entry into the country, and that it expelled aliens found to have entered the United States illegally. But if pressed, I doubt that I could have gone beyond such sketchy generalities about its functions.

Indeed, until recent years, few native-born Americans would have had much reason to acquaint themselves with the operations of the INS, unless perhaps they had had to assist foreign-born relatives or employees with applications for visas. Today, however, there is increasing public concern over illegal immigration and increasing media coverage of the problem. These developments along with the roiling congressional debates over the wisdom of the Simpson-Mazzoli Immigration Reform and Control Act, the first major legislative overhaul of the immigration law in 30 years, have brought the U.S. Department of Justice's heretofore least visible enforcement agency to the front and center of public attention.

During a visit to California in June 1981 on a pressing family matter, I found time to call on Professor Seymour Martin Lipset, a colleague at the Hoover Institution. I asked whether he thought a research project focused on illegal immigration might appeal to his colleagues. I knew of Hoover's reputation in the field of domestic policy research. I assumed that an application for one of the coveted 12 national fellowships awarded annually would have a better chance of acceptance if it related to a salient domestic policy issue. Professor Lipset agreed that this would be a worthwhile topic to pursue.

Deciding that illegal immigration would be my topic for the fellowship application, I had to decide which aspect of the problem to concentrate on. During the remainder of the summer, I read through the staff report and appendices of the Hesburgh Select Commission on Immigration and Refugee Policy (SCIRP). Established by Congress in 1978, SCIRP was charged with studying immigration and refugee policy issues and reporting its policy recommendations to Congress and the president.

As I read through the voluminous SCIRP study, I was impressed by the abundance of reports on the history of U.S. immigration, the economic and demographic characteristics of immigrants, and other subjects. The evolution of immigration policy and legislation over the years was also covered in substantial detail.

Yet, somewhat surprisingly, research on the operations of the INS, the very agency charged with enforcing the law, was woefully neglected by the SCIRP report. There was one paper by David S. North and Jennifer Wagner, "Enforcing the Immigration Law: A Review of the Options."[1] Although it addressed a number of important issues facing the agency in its efforts to achieve immigration control and wove available governmental statistics on INS enforcement into an illuminating tapestry on agency operations, it had little to say about the microlevel organizational contexts in which officers carry out enforcement activities or the impact of court decisions and local, state, and national politics on INS policymaking.

My choice was simple. I would study the INS's enforcement operations, not just because this was the issue that immigration policy researchers had neglected but because I believed that an understanding of INS's operations was crucial for assessing the likely success of any new legislation.

Assuming authorization could be obtained from the INS, I would interview and observe INS officers while they carried out their various enforcement duties against violators, variously called illegal aliens, deportable aliens, or undocumented workers.[2]

In October 1981, I traveled to Washington, D.C., to discuss my proposed research with staff officials in INS's Office of Planning and Evaluation. I was introduced by their staff to administrators in the enforcement and other service branches, and the wheels were set in motion for obtaining the approval I needed to interview supervisors and officers in several of the 34 INS district offices, where most of the 750 plainclothes criminal investigators having interior enforcement duties were stationed. Later, I would obtain authorization to visit a number of border patrol stations in both border and interior areas. As it turned out, most of my time in the field would be spent with border patrol and investigations branch officers.

Patrol agents and criminal investigators are the officers most likely to make the initial contact with aliens who have entered the United States without inspection or who entered legally but subsequently violated the terms of their visas. Although there are other important participants in the process, including immigration judges, government trial attorneys, and deportation and detention officers, most immigration violators are apprehended in the field by investigators or patrol agents. Indeed, most of those who are caught near the border as entrants without inspection (EWIs) will have no further contact with the service beyond their initial encounter with a patrol agent.

At the time of my first visit to the central office in Washington, the planning and evaluation staff provided me with useful background briefings on the history of the service and some of the current dilemmas facing the INS. They also supplied me with copious in-house research reports, books, and other publications dealing with immigration issues. I left Washington with a bulging travel bag. I had no inkling of the complexities of immigration law at the time. But I would soon come to realize that the legal issues were extremely complex. The case law had grown up within the Immigration and Nationality Act like the leguminous kudzu vines I had seen strangle abandoned shacks in Macon, Georgia, where I taught college. Finding my way through this dense thicket of law would, I soon realized, be indispensable for understanding both the macrolevel policy decisions of the agency and the day-to-day field practices of its enforcement officers.

Even before official authorization for the research had been granted, I was told I could interview INS supervisors in the Chicago district office. In Chicago, I spent two days talking with the district director and several investigations branch supervisors to get briefed on what the investigators did and what the enforcement problems in a large city were like.

I have a striking recollection of one interview in particular. The supervisor in charge of area control operations explained that, to the extent immigration law enforcement was reasonably effective, it was because most aliens were basically honest people. At the time, I didn't understand exactly what he meant. How could enforcing the law depend so crucially on the honesty of those against whom it was brought to bear?

But I came to understand the officer's point quite fully after just a few days with officers in the field. Paradoxically, immigration control depends crucially on aliens' willingness to concede their alienage, that is, their foreign birth. Such voluntary compliance is the sine qua non of law enforcement in a context involving field encounters with hundreds of thousands of violators per year. Without such cooperation, our immigration laws could only be enforced with great difficulty and, indeed, would probably be restricted to just a small percentage of aliens whose violations or potential threat to the society would be judged sufficiently serious to warrant the extensive investigation on the individual's background that would be required. For in the event that aliens who have made an entry, whether legally or illegally, refused to admit to their alienage and deportability, the government would be required to establish both facts in a deportation hearing. If the INS had to make positive identifications on more than just a small fraction of the more than one million deportable aliens now being apprehended annually, the expeditious processing of mass arrests would simply not be possible. The agency does not have the resources to investigate the identities and birthplaces of more than a small fraction of aliens apprehended in the field.

How slender were the straps of the law! Further complicating enforcement efforts is the fact that under our Constitution citizens are not required to carry identification. Nor is there any federal law that requires citizens to talk to immigration officers, although the Immigration and Nationality Act requires that aliens answer questions about their immigration status when approached and questioned by INS officers. As a result, INS officers are much more constrained in the tactics and measures they can use to interrogate suspected deportable aliens than their counterparts in most other democratic societies. Some of the legal and operational dilemmas that confront the INS in the course of field enforcement activities are the result of these unique features of our constitution.

I soon became aware of another important aspect of immigration enforcement. What is noteworthy is the relative leniency with which the immigration law is enforced in most cases. Indeed, although many examples of leniency can be found in other areas of law enforcement, with the more severe sanctions reserved for more serious violators or aggravated cases, immigration law is unique in that the criminal sanctions available under the law are so rarely imposed—even in the case of many aliens who commit immigration felonies. Moreover, even the civil sanction of formal deportation is used for only a very small fraction of those apprehended. Thus immigration law enforcement, although it involves an annual caseload of hundreds of thousands of individuals, is by and large a law in which the criminal sanctions exist mainly in theory. Nor does the public give unequivocal support to the INS. Why this is so is among the important topics explored in the chapters that follow.

ONE

ILLEGAL ALIENS AND
THE AMERICAN POLITY

To the shopworn cliche that the United States is a nation of immigrants must be added the observation that our nation is also becoming home to a second nation of illegal immigrants nestled within the larger polity. Although many deportable aliens have become socially and economically integrated into our society, they are still residing and working in our country in violation of the law. Estimates of the number of illegal aliens presently living in the United States range from 2 to 12 million. Although nobody knows the exact figure, the consensus among most scholars is that it falls somewhere between three and six million.[1]

When the combined legal admission of immigrants and refugees (which amounted to more than 500,000 annually by the late 1970s and topped 800,000 in the single year 1980) is added to the net influx of an estimated 200,000 to 500,000 illegal aliens a year, the combined legal and illegal immigration may well exceed the historical peak level of more than 1 million legal admissions annually recorded in the early 1900s.[2]

That old cliche about ours being a nation of immigrants does more than state the obvious about our nation's demographic history. It also reveals our enduring ambivalence toward those from abroad who seek to participate in our national life. Although we want as a nation to keep the door open, we also want to control the terms of entry and residence. Today, many Americans believe we have lost the ability to set the terms for admission because we have lost the ability to control our borders.

The following chapters attempt to answer the question of why enforcement of the Immigration and Nationality Act (INA) has weakened in recent years. Because a variety of political demands and legal constraints shape

INS's enforcement policies beyond the mandate and requirements of the statute itself, it is important to examine the cultural and political context in which the U.S. Immigration and Naturalization Service (INS), the Department of Justice agency charged with administering the INA, has had to function over the years. A detailed historical account of immigration enforcement is beyond the scope of this book; however, a brief review will serve to put INS's current dilemmas in somewhat better perspective.

HISTORICAL TRENDS IN ENFORCEMENT CONCERN

Immigrants have been coming to the United States illegally ever since the closing decades of the nineteenth century when Congress passed the first restrictive legislation. However, it is only during the last ten to fifteen years that illegal immigration has become not only a major domestic policy issue but a highly divisive one at that.[3] During the era of open immigration in the nineteenth century, aliens simply arrived on our shores, found lodging and jobs, and were assimilated by degrees into the society. Although open immigration led to a variety of social problems, including the growth of congested urban slums and sporadic rioting, illegal aliens did not exist as a policy problem until the 1870s, when Congress began passing legislation to restrict the admission of aliens. Indeed, a legal theory pertaining to alien rights only developed after the first restrictive statutes were finally challenged by plaintiffs. Constitutional constructions were then developed by the Supreme Court to affirm Congress's power to regulate the admission of aliens. The Court reasoned that the United States, as an independent and sovereign nation, is vested with the entire control of international relations and hence "with all the powers of government necessary to maintain that control and to make it effective."[4]

But even after qualitative and quantitative barriers to immigration were passed between the 1870s and 1920s under what Peter Schuck calls the new ideology of "restrictive nationalism," concern over illegal immigrants remained highly selective.[5] While the doors at Ellis Island and other coastal ports of entry were being shut to aliens from overseas, the passage of Mexican and Canadian nationals back and forth across our land borders remained relatively unhindered until 1917. Although the influx of illegal aliens who enter surreptitiously—called *entrants without inspection* (EWIs) by the INS—is almost surely higher now than it was 20 to 30 years ago, it is hard to know whether the incidence of uninspected entries in relation to the total U.S. population was higher or lower in earlier periods. Although major sea ports of entry (POEs) were provided with immigration inspectors, our northern and southern land borders were not well patrolled; nor are they today in most places. What little border control existed during the first quarter of this century arose mainly from a concern to deter the smuggling of Chinese and Europeans (and, after passage of the Volstead Act, alcoholic beverages) much more than from a concern to bar entry to Canadian or Mexican nationals. Indeed, until the Immigration Act of 1917, Canadians and Mexicans had little reason to enter illegally because, in contrast to requirements for aliens from overseas, they did not have to pay the $8 head tax or meet the literacy requirement to gain admission.[6] Although pressures for the expulsion of illegal immigrants oscillated in tandem with economic conditions through much of the twentieth century, perceptions of the illegal alien problem have clearly changed in recent years.[7]

In the early decades of this century, illegal entries by European and Chinese nationals were perceived as the major enforcement problem because the demand for admission continued strong among these groups. In striking contrast, our country's de facto immigration policy with respect to Mexican nationals was very relaxed, possibly because Mexicans had been accustomed to moving freely between the United States and Mexico throughout the nineteenth century, both to work as migrant laborers and to visit relatives living in the United States.[8] Indeed, some scholars have argued that illegal Mexican immigration was actually encouraged by U.S. policy.[9]

One can only speculate on the reasons behind the relaxed policy toward Mexico during this period. Quite possibly, Mexican migrants were not perceived as a cultural or political threat because, unlike the heavy pre–World War I migration of Eastern and Southern Europeans into the cities of the northeast and midwest, the Mexicans were concentrated mainly in southwestern agriculture. Because they had little or no political impact and their cultural values were effectively quarantined by rural isolation, they may not have been viewed as posing the same threat to the newly virulent and often racist Americanism being promoted by nativist political entrepreneurs during the 1920s.

During World War I, Mexicans were invited to enter the United States to help meet our pressing wartime labor shortage. About 75,000 Mexicans entered legally between 1917 and 1921. Many stayed on through the prosperous 1920s, and nobody seemed to mind. Only when the Great Depression arrived in the early 1930s did pressure mount for mass deportations back to Mexico. When Operation Deportation was initiated, tens of thousands of Mexicans voluntarily decided to leave the United States, partly because jobs were drying up and partly because of pressures exerted by local officials and citizens. It is claimed that some legal immigrants and even some naturalized citizens were pressured into returning to Mexico by threats from local officials to cut off welfare assistance. Also, because deportation hearings were summary mass proceedings in the 1930s and were conducted by INS field officers rather than (as is now the case) by attorneys trained in the law, some citizens and lawful immigrants may have been returned in error because immigration officers failed to credit their claims.[10] However, although it appears clear that some U.S. citizen wives and children departed voluntarily with husbands who were Mexican nationals, no documentary evidence exists to assess how many citizens or legal immigrants of Mexican descent may have been involuntarily deported.

This cycle of first an open and then a closed door at the southern border repeated itself again during and after World War II, when the wartime demand for workers led to an official guest worker program that allowed Mexican braceros to enter as temporary workers, along with a more relaxed attitude toward enforcing the law against illegal entrants—at least until the mid-1950s. For example, occasionally when the U.S. Border Patrol encountered Mexicans working illegally in southwestern agriculture, the officers would "dry them out" by taking them back to the border where they would allow them to sign up in the legal program as braceros.[11] Border patrol agents might also occasionally deliver illegal Mexicans they had apprehended on the highways or in town to ranchers who they knew were short of hands.[12] In some parts of Texas, enforcement would slacken off during the planting and harvesting seasons but would tighten up when the ranchers and local town dwellers decided they didn't want the "wetbacks" hanging around.[13]

Nor was Congress unequivocally supportive of strict enforcement. Some lawmakers sympathized with the ranchers' desire for "wet" labor free of the regulatory encumbrances of the contract labor program because the bracero program imposed requirements on ranchers to pay and house the bracero workers according to standards negotiated between the United States and the Mexican government.[14]

Although some scholars claim that the contract labor (bracero) program may have stimulated illegal immigration after World War II and that illegal Mexican entries may have been as high as the 4.5 million legal bracero contracts signed between 1942 and 1964, in those places where it was strictly enforced, the program had an important control feature that is lacking today.[15]

Because ranchers could forfeit their right to employ legal braceros for a season or two if they were caught employing illegals, they had an incentive to screen their work force. The heavier border patrol presence in the southwest apparently aided deterrence because illegal crossers had to travel farther into the interior to get work. In El Paso, for example, ranchers caught using illegal labor were required to post a $2,000 performance bond to be able to continue using legal braceros. Certain district directors—among them Marcus Neely, who was the district director in El Paso in the early 1950s— went by the book. But other district directors might occasionally tolerate ranchers using illegals to pick the cotton crop when braceros were not available in sufficient number.[16]

Because of the bracero program and the more stringent enforcement policies of that era, reasonably effective border control was achieved between the mid-1950s and mid-1960s. Mexicans identified as repeat offenders knew they could be sent to Port Isabel, Texas, for shipment by boat down to Vera Cruz, Mexico, or be sent by train and bus to interior Mexican cities. Many also spent a week or two in detention until their fingerprint checks were sent back by the FBI. However, during the 1960s, the routine fingerprinting of EWIs ended; and by the mid-1970s, the policy of interior repatriation had been phased out because of the high cost of repatriating aliens by air and also, some officers claim, because of pressure from the Mexican government.[17]

The years spanning the early 1950s to mid-1960s represent something of a departure from the situation of the 1930s, when mass expulsions occurred mainly because of the economic depression. In 1954, INS Commissioner Joseph Swing launched Operation Wetback. With the assistance of hundreds of local law enforcement agencies and some other federal agencies, INS expelled close to 2 million illegal Mexican migrants during that year and the one following. Economic concerns may have been one motive behind the operation; the Korean truce had been signed and defense contracts were declining just as veterans were beginning to return to the labor market. On the other hand, there also appears to have been concern in high administration circles that control over the borders was being lost. The more relaxed enforcement policy of the late 1940s had led to the buildup of a sizeable presence of Mexican illegals, especially in southern California. Many officials felt it was time to reaffirm the country's sovereign right to control admissions.[18]

Ten years after the wetback roundup, Congress voted to terminate the bracero program because of growing opposition by Mexican American groups and the AFL-CIO.[19]

This dramatic policy shift cannot be attributed to any cyclical economic woes because the mid-1960s were, if anything, a period of labor shortages. However, localized economic grievances played a role. Mexican Americans living in Texas claimed they were being driven out of agricultural work because the braceros put them at a competitive disadvantage. Concern was also expressed by some Mexican Americans that the upsurge in Mexican illegal immigration was fueling intergroup tensions and leading to an increase in discrimination against Mexican Americans.[20]

Whatever the motivations behind this dramatic change in policy, the termination of the bracero program did not mean that their labor was no longer desired on the U.S. side. As INS statistics clearly show, illegal crossings over the southern border began to accelerate in the late 1960s. Although border patrol apprehensions in the early 1960s were a modest 30,000 to 40,000 a year (and accounted for only about 50 percent of nationwide INS apprehensions), by 1966, the patrol was apprehending 80,000 aliens, of whom 90 percent were Mexican nationals. By 1969, border patrol apprehensions had climbed to 160,000 and by 1972 had topped 350,000.[21] Eleven years later the border patrol arrested, on the southern border, slightly more than 1 million aliens, of whom 98 percent were Mexicans.[22]

Some have argued that the annual ceiling of 120,000 immigrant visas imposed on Western Hemisphere nations for the first time in 1965 also contributed to the rise in illegal entries. However, most INS officers believe the termination of the bracero program was the major factor behind the surge in Mexican EWI crossings from the late 1960s to the present.[23]

ILLEGAL ALIENS: WHO THEY ARE

Illegal aliens come from all over the world today. With the advent of relatively inexpensive commercial air travel, aliens are lured to our shores by the same quest for economic prosperity and political sanctuary that prompted earlier waves of newcomers to immigrate. Over the past half century, the cinema and other mass media have made the American way of life visible to those living in even the poorest backwaters across the globe. And unlike the situation 30 and more years ago when most transoceanic travel was by ship and the number of foreign nationals arriving at U.S. ports of disembarkation was relatively small, today there are approximately 300 million annual inspected entries of individuals arriving at U.S. land, sea, and air POEs, and 60 percent of these involve inspections of aliens.[24]

Because of the dramatic increase in international travel into the United States, INS and U.S. Customs Service inspectors often have only enough time to give passports and other travel permits a cursory glance. They are under pressure to expedite the flow of arriving travelers in order to avoid inconveniencing citizens and authorized alien entrants. Naturally, this increases the odds favoring those who enter with photo-substituted U.S. passports, counterfeit visa stamps, borrowed or forged I-186 border crossing cards (called shoppers cards), and fraudulent I-151 immigrant visa receipts (called green cards even though they are now salmon-colored I-551 immigrant visa receipts). Of the 300 million entrants inspected in 1982, INS and customs inspectors ferreted out only 533,000 inadmissible aliens—one for every 600 border crossers.[25]

In the mid-1970s, the INS conducted a study to determine the number of mala fide (unauthorized) aliens passing through inspections without being detected. Special inspection teams were assigned to selected land and air

POEs. Having all the time they needed to conduct careful checks of documents and oral claims, these teams apprehended an average of twelve to fourteen times the number of fraudulent entrants being caught during routine day-to-day inspections.[26] However, despite the intensive screening done by the special inspection teams, only 1 in every 287 entrants at land POEs and 1 in every 210 at airports turned out to be a fraudulent entrant. A major dilemma facing the INS is that some measures that might tighten border control or achieve more effective enforcement in other ways cannot be implemented without causing inconvenience to the many people who are not immigration violators. Clearly, if the INS force of roughly 1,400 inspectors were to carry out a more thorough scrutiny of all persons entering the country, large numbers of bona fide citizen and alien travelers would be inconvenienced as inspection lines began to lengthen. For reasons to be discussed in Chapter 8, there are political and other trade-offs that the INS must take into account in its effort to enforce the law effectively.

Although the illegal alien population is predominantly Hispanic, with Mexican nationals constituting the largest single nationality, it contains a heterogeneous mixture of nationalities, mainly from the less developed countries of Asia, Africa, and Latin America but also from affluent industrial societies. According to Los Angeles INS officers, working in the United States is apparently a new craze among Japanese youth. In consequence, Japanese youths turn up working illegally as sales clerks in gift shops in Los Angeles' Little Tokyo district after entering with nonimmigrant visas as visitors. Because nonimmigrant visitors are not permitted to work without INS authorization, any who do so become deportable aliens.[27]

Refugees fleeing the turmoil of civil war or political repression in Afghanistan, Iran, Iraq, Lebanon, and other world trouble spots are often unwilling to wait the months or years necessary to qualify for an immigrant visa. Or, if they are able to qualify for admission as refugees, they must wait longer than they are prepared to for parole into the United States under the annual refugee quota. Those who come from countries with long waiting lists for immigrant visas may have no chance of ever entering the United States unless they have close relatives already living here.[28] Some of those for whom the likelihood of entry is slim or who face a long wait are caught trying to pass through airport inspections with fraudulent visas or picked up at work on the basis of a tip.

Because demand for entry into the United States far exceeds the supply of visa slots, it is hardly surprising that aliens should seek to circumvent the law. A middle-class Afghani family that has fled to Pakistan may sell everything they own to raise enough money to pay for airfare and fraudulent papers to get an elder son into the United States. The family hopes that the son will manage to stay on and in time bring other family members over.

Aliens who have left desperate conditions in their homelands will understandably resort to desperate efforts to remain in this country when INS officers finally catch them. A good example is the case of a man who had brought his two sons by air from Germany to the United States. Although they claimed later that they were fleeing their repressive Middle Eastern homeland, they did not request asylum at the time they arrived in New York. They only had transit without visa (TRWOV) status to travel on to Mexico as tourists. When an examination of their luggage revealed that they had contacts in New York but nothing to indicate they were going on to Mexico, the inspectors directed the airline to return them to Frankfurt. Before the flight left, however, the father collapsed with an apparent heart attack. He was hospitalized, and his sons were released on humanitarian grounds. Later, INS officers learned from the hospital that the father, who had merely fainted, had been released. The INS was unable to locate the father or to obtain a full medical report. Nor could the officers locate the sons after their temporary parole had expired.

A month later, the INS caught up with the trio at their apartment as they were trying to leave by a back door. The father was not arrested because he had a doctor's note explaining that he suffered from hypertension and needed four months of bed rest. When his sons appeared for the exclusion hearing, they and their father applied for political asylum and requested release on parole. This was denied. They then entered a habeas corpus petition in the second circuit court of appeals arguing that their detention by the INS was the result of discrimination against their particular nationality group and hence constituted "abuse of discretion" by INS officials.[29]

Salvadorans, and others from Central and South America, are caught crossing the southern border after having paid $1,000 to $3,000 to be smuggled overland via Mexico City. During 1981 alone, 8,000 Haitians arrived in South Florida in groups of 5, 10, or even 30 or more after a passage of hundreds of miles in battered fishing boats. By 1982, the number of Haitians who managed to land had been sharply reduced to between 130 and 150 because of the U.S. Coast Guard's interdiction program along the Florida coastline. Unlike the border patrol's effort to stanch illegal entries on the southern land border, the U.S. Coast Guard's interdiction program is an effective deterrent.[30]

Although small in number, apprehensions along the Canadian border include a diverse mixture of nationality groups. Canada imposes significantly fewer entry restrictions on visitors compared with the United States, and as a result, illegal aliens wanting to enter the United States often travel legally to Canada first. Because there are fewer than 300 patrol agents permanently stationed on the northern border, the risk of detection is small. That may explain why the number of aliens from the Caribbean basin who are entering the United States via Canada has begun to increase.[31] In fiscal year 1983, there were only 3,600 border patrol apprehensions along the Canadian border, and of these, 3,300 were Canadian nationals. The fact that only 28 Chinese, 6 Africans, 7 Filipinos, and 8 Italians were apprehended among the remaining 300 other-than-Canadian nationals probably does not mean that few are entering but rather that very few are getting caught.[32]

Although most EWIs tend to be from the poorer Caribbean basin countries, many illegal aliens from overseas are from the middle classes of their societies. Many Filipinos apprehended by the INS are working as nurses, pharmacists, or bank clerks or in other white-collar jobs because they can earn in the United States three to four times what they could earn in the Philippines. Immigration officers have stumbled across illegal aliens earning $40,000 and more a year working as accountants, antique dealers, and real estate agents. Deportable Dutch, German, British, and Swedish aliens are encountered, along with deportable aliens from Ghana, Nigeria, Pakistan, Poland, and other countries too numerous to list.

Most deportable overseas aliens, who are referred to in INS jargon as other-than-Mexican (OTM) aliens, enter legally as students or visitors but subsequently violate the conditions of their visas by either working without authorization or overstaying.[33]

Visa aliens who have overstayed their visas or worked without authorization are called visa abusers and, when INS officers encounter them, they join the Mexican, Haitian, and other Central American EWIs as deportable aliens. (Both EWIs and visa abusers are referred to as administrative violators.) Visa abusers from overseas face considerably less risk of apprehension than Mexican and Central American EWIs. In 1983, visitors and students accounted for only 4 percent of INS apprehensions—45,000 out of a total of 1.2 million arrests. Both groups (EWIs and visa abusers) are viewed by INS officers as a less serious violator group than some other violator groups, such as aliens who enter with forged or fraudulently obtained travel documents, who become involved in the smuggling of aliens or drugs or in document counterfeiting, or who are caught committing other crimes.[34]

PUBLIC PERCEPTIONS OF THE PROBLEM

Although it is believed that Mexicans may account for only 50 to 70 percent of all deportable aliens living in the United States, they account for the overwhelming bulk of both interior as well as borderland apprehensions.[35] Mexican nationals accounted for 94 percent of all fiscal year 1983 apprehensions nationwide. This is because southern border apprehensions account for about 90 percent of all INS arrests and Mexicans constitute 98 percent (1983) of the deportable aliens picked up in the border area. Yet even in the interior, Mexicans accounted for 68 percent of aliens apprehended by plainclothes INS investigators in nonagricultural (urban) occupations in 1983. Eighty-five percent of deportable aliens turned over by institutions (prisons and jails) and 99 percent of all illegals found in agriculture were Mexicans.

As a result of this, public perceptions of the illegal alien problem are highly skewed; when Americans reflect on the illegal alien problem, most think of Mexicans. A single illegal Thai, Filipino, or Swede picked up by the INS while working in a white-collar job is simply not as newsworthy as INS round ups of 50 workers (most of whom are likely to be Mexican or Central American foreign nationals) at a construction site or in a meat-packing plant. And such mass arrests are especially newsworthy when they trigger civil lawsuits—usually based on complaints of constitutional seizures of citizens who happened to be working in the plant at the time.[36]

In addition, the difficulties that have plagued the border patrol from the early 1970s to the present have reinforced the perception that illegal immigration is a Mexican problem. Thus the public has watched on television or read in *U.S. News and World Report* about how a beleaguered U.S. Border Patrol tries with helicopters, all-terrain motorcycles, and 4-wheel-drive trucks to corral large groups of aliens being smuggled across by *polleros* (guides) and how the patrol is daily overwhelmed by the sheer numbers of EWI crossers from Brownsville, Texas, on the gulf coast to San Ysidro, California, on the Pacific.[37] Incidents of violence caused by borderland bandits who prey on illegal border crossers or by rock-throwing *cholos* (young hoodlums) trying to divert the patrol agents' attention have, along with narcotics smuggling and discoveries of injured or suffocated aliens locked in car trunks, spurred the media's interest, thereby increasing the visibility of the problems along the southern border.[38]

Although the southern border remains the major enforcement concern for the INS because of the heavy volume of Mexican entries, important enforcement problems also exist in the interior, as is discussed in later chapters.

SURVEY FINDINGS ON THE PUBLIC MOOD

When queried about immigration issues, Americans say they want the immigration laws strictly enforced; they also say they would support penalties for employers who hire illegal aliens. In a May 1982 poll conducted by the Merit survey, 84 percent of the public expressed concern about the number of illegal aliens in the country. In a 1977 Gallup poll, 72 percent of the public agreed that penalties should be imposed on businesses that hire illegal aliens, and when Gallup asked the same question again in October 1983, the percentage agreeing had risen to 79 percent.

The consensus for tougher immigration enforcement exists even among U.S. citizens of Hispanic descent. In a poll conducted jointly by Peter Hart Associates and Tarrance and Associates in the summer of 1983, Americans of Hispanic descent (predominantly Mexican Americans) favored tough restrictions on illegal immigration by a margin of 57 percent to 32 percent; 60 percent supported a new law that would make it illegal for employers to hire illegal aliens. (This finding suggests that Hispanic activists, who are known to oppose penalties for employers caught hiring illegal aliens on the ground that such a law might lead to discrimination against Mexican Americans, appear to be out of step with their fellow Hispanics.)

Indeed, the American public is not feeling very hospitable toward foreign nationals seeking to enter *legally*. In March 1981, the Roper survey found 66 percent wanting legal immigration cut back, compared with 4 percent who said more aliens should be allowed to enter. That same year, NBC's August survey found 65 percent of the public wanting fewer immigrants admitted, compared with only 5 percent wanting more.[39] And although the United States has traditionally been a haven for political refugees, surveys over the past several years show Americans wanting to roll up the welcoming mat even for the oppressed of the world. Of those polled by Gallup in August 1979, 57 percent said they opposed allowing the Indochinese boat people to enter; only 32 percent favored their being allowed in. In May 1980, both the Harris and Gallup surveys found that Americans opposed letting the Cuban boat-lift refugees in by roughly a two-to-one margin. However, it is doubtful that Americans resent the admission of all political refugees. The public's negative attitude to the Southeast Asian and Cuban refugees may be due to the very large numbers who entered during the mid to late 1970s.[40]

Some scholars have argued that the rebirth of restrictionist sentiment during the 1970s and 1980s is no different from earlier cycles of antialien nativist reactions to immigrants. Arguing that the current wave of nativist agitation is due to increased economic insecurity, along with U.S. reversals in the international political and economic arena, Wayne Cornelius views the renewal of restrictionism as part of a traditional response pattern.[41] In Cornelius's view, illegal aliens are convenient scapegoats for collective frustrations. Aliens are an ideal target because they are seen as a threat to the American way of life. According to Cornelius, politicians worry that aliens will maintain their private cultures, thereby jeopardizing the mainstream culture Americans seek to perpetuate. The public, according to Cornelius, also perceives a link between increased crime and the new wave of illegal immigration.

However, there are problems with this hypothesis. True, the public clearly wants tougher enforcement of immigration laws and is also more restrictionist with regard to admission of additional immigrants. But this hardly warrants the conclusion that the public is antialien in the manner of earlier nativist movements. Americans are restrictionist mainly in regard to the numbers coming here, and not because of the nationalities or ethnic makeup of those who come. In June 1982, a Field Institute survey conducted in California found that although three-quarters of California residents favored both efforts to deport illegal immigrants and a new law that would impose penalties on employers who hire illegals, fully 73 percent also favored a generous amnesty that would legalize the status of those who had been in the country at least five years. Fifty-eight percent felt that a guest-worker program that would allow aliens to enter and work for a specific period of time would be a good idea. And when asked whether foreign-born immigrants make just as good citizens as native-born citizens, 70 percent said immigrants make just as good or even better citizens. Although the attitudes of Californians may not be representative of the nation as a whole, such findings are hard to reconcile with Cornelius's hypothesis that antialien nativism is on the rise. The fact that Americans want fewer immigrants coming into the country does not, unlike earlier periods in our history, appear to be based on hostility toward aliens because of their divergent life styles or cultural values.[42]

Although Americans appear to be worried about the economic impact of immigration, even the evidence on this point is ambiguous. In a June 1983 *New York Times* survey, 47 percent of those interviewed believed that immigrants take jobs native-born Americans consider undesirable compared with only 42 percent who said that the jobs immigrants take would be acceptable to most Americans.[43] On the other hand, Gallup's October 1983 poll found 79 percent of the public wanting penalties imposed on employers caught hiring illegal aliens, which suggests that the public is concerned about the impact illegal aliens have on jobs.

In a survey conducted jointly by Lance Tarrance Associates and Peter Hart Research Associates in mid-1983, fully 82 percent of all black Americans and 58 percent of Hispanic Americans believed that illegal immigrants take jobs away from Americans. But at the same time, 48 percent of blacks and 51 percent of Hispanics also agreed that many of the low-wage jobs taken by illegal aliens would not be performed in their absence and that, if illegals did not take them, the economy would suffer. In the 1982 Field Institute survey of California residents, 46 percent of those polled said that illegals take away jobs from citizens. Still, 30 percent also said that illegals were willing to take jobs Americans would not take and cited this as a favorable effect of illegal immigration. More recently, in a June 1984 Gallup poll, 61 percent of those surveyed agreed that immigrants take jobs from U.S. workers, but 80 percent also agreed that many immigrants take jobs Americans don't want.

What the available evidence suggests is not that Americans are ambivalent about illegal immigration (they oppose it) but that they are not unambiguously convinced that its effects are necessarily all bad. When they do express concern, it is mainly because they fear job competition and pressure on wages. Still, quite a few also think illegals take many jobs Americans will no longer undertake for the wages paid. As regards crime and welfare dependency, these problems are mentioned by relatively small percentages of respondents in the few surveys that have asked Americans to list other problems they associate with illegal immigration.

Nor is it altogether clear that Americans consider illegal immigration a major domestic policy issue. In Gallup's June 1984 *Newsweek* survey, the percentage of respondents who rated illegal immigration a "very important problem" (55 percent) was substantially lower than the percentages who thought unemployment (84 percent), inflation (73 percent), and the threat of nuclear war (70 percent) were important problems. Illegal immigration had roughly the same priority for the public as protecting the environment.

Finally, Americans appear to make a crucial distinction between those aliens who are still abroad and have few equities in American society and those aliens who have managed to come in, hang on, and build equities in the form of stable careers, home ownership, and the like. Americans seem to be ambivalent about deporting aliens who have settled into the society.[44] In the October 1983 Gallup survey, although 52 percent of the public opposed granting amnesty to illegal aliens who had lived in the United States for at least seven years, fully 41 percent favored such an amnesty. The findings of a February 1984 poll conducted by Kane, Parsons, and Associates for the U.S. Committee for Refugees lend additional support to this interpretation. Although 72 percent agreed with the general statement that too many foreigners were coming to the United States to live, when respondents were asked whether specific individuals (such as "a man from England," or "a man from Taiwan") ought to be admitted to the United States, large majorities said they favored admission.[45] In short, Americans have an easier time taking a restrictionist attitude toward anonymous and unknown aliens than they do toward specific individuals whose problems or circumstances they are informed about.

HOW THE PUBLIC RESPONDS TO ILLEGAL ALIENS

Many of the tips on illegal aliens received by the INS are sent in by individuals of the same ethnic or nationality group as the individual reported. Typical of the kind of tip received by investigators working in INS district offices is the following portion of an anonymous letter: "This people [names listed] gave me hard time. And I know they not legal in this country. That's why I'm sending this note to you. I don't know they personal address but I know where they work. So please do something about it."

Occasionally citizens will report illegal aliens to the INS, citing the need to protect jobs for Americans. For example, plant security guards who have observed illegals working at their firm may phone or write letters to the district office. However, many officers believe that personal grudges and grievances account for most tips, as when illegal aliens have gotten too far behind in their rent and are unwilling or unable to pay. Or, they may have overstayed their tourist visas and/or overstayed their welcome with relatives in the United States, who report them anonymously. Sometimes, citizens will call the INS to report that illegals are employed where they work, not when they first learn of the fact but only after they themselves have been fired or laid off.

Considering the nature of most tips, it appears that active public support for immigration enforcement, as distinct from the passive support registered by the polls, arises not from nativistic hostility based on cultural or ethnic differences as much as from the personal frictions that arise in the course of day-to-day social exchange, with the INS serving as a convenient vehicle for punishing an alien who has rubbed somebody the wrong way.

Although it is true that some citizens do occasionally complain to the INS or their legislators about illegal aliens, what bears noting is the fact that when aliens and their families are threatened with deportation, it is often *citizens* who will mobilize on their behalf. In their eyes, the aliens threatened with removal are good neighbors, reliable tenants, friendly fellow workers, or trustworthy friends. Funds may be raised for these aliens' legal expenses, and prayer vigils held during the time their families are in detention. Petitions on their behalf may be circulated and delivered to politicians in the hope that they will agree to sponsor private bills that will delay deportation until the aliens are able to qualify for relief under one or another of the INA statutory provisions.[46] That congressional bills are often a delaying tactic is indicated by the fact that less than 10 percent are ever finally approved. The more cynical among INS officers believe that they are often introduced as a favor to attorneys or campaign contributors to whom the legislator is indebted.

In sum, the public's attitude can be characterized as ambivalent when it comes to offering active support for enforcement efforts. Many who will tell a pollster that illegal aliens have no right to work in this country are certain to want to make an exception for the maid who works for their next-door neighbor or the cook at their favorite Chinese restaurant.[47] Many Americans do not object to the fact that their fellow workers are illegal until they themselves are fired or laid off. Indeed, some citizens will even agree to "marry" an alien fraudulently so that the alien can remain in the United States as a lawful permanent resident.

If nativism were truly on the rise, one would not only expect to encounter more vocal public concern but also expect to find organizations actively working to assist the INS in ferreting out illegal aliens. To the contrary, although such traditional hate groups as the Ku Klux Klan have been trying to stir up public animosity toward both legal and illegal aliens, there is little public support for such demagogic appeals. Given the severity of our nation's economic difficulties during the past decade, what needs to be explained is the absence of the kind of antialien hostility that was a prevalent feature of American life in earlier periods of our history.

THE SOCIAL AND ECONOMIC IMPACT
OF ILLEGAL IMMIGRATION

Although the polls show that many Americans are concerned about job competition from illegals, there is little consensus among scholars who have studied the problem. Some scholars, among them Julian Simon, argue that illegal as well as legal aliens make a substantial net positive contribution to our society because they pay more in taxes than they receive in welfare and other public benefits.[48] Although some economists agree with this view, the data that would definitively answer the question are not available. For example, it is hard to know the percentage of illegal aliens taking public welfare because thorough screening of welfare applicants is limited to a small number of state and county welfare agencies that have sought INS assistance. Moreover, one knows about only the welfare applicants who are ferreted out as illegal aliens.

Although many illegal aliens take jobs Americans will not do for the wages paid, especially in agriculture where they have become indispensable in some states, they can also be found in high-paying white- and blue-collar jobs that American citizens would take. Thus INS officers encounter illegal aliens earning $3.50 an hour picking lettuce or busing dishes, as well as illegals earning $7 to $14 an hour in landscaping, construction, welding, and drywall plastering, to cite just a few examples. Illegal aliens are also encountered in some unionized light industries, although they are not often encountered in high-wage industries (such as steel or auto manufacturing) that have strong unions.

That illegals are primarily concentrated in low-wage jobs is suggested by findings of researchers who have interviewed both apprehended and unapprehended illegal aliens.[49] In the spring of 1982, when the INS carried out its Project Jobs raids on businesses in nine major cities, the INS task force sought to target higher-wage employers. Yet the average earnings of the approximately 5,500 illegal aliens apprehended during these raids was only $4.80 per hour.[50]

The controversy among scholars over the extent to which illegals displace American workers arises partly because those who have studied the problem may not be looking at the same industries. Although Wayne Cornelius and his colleagues acknowledge that Mexican nationals may have driven American workers out of some industries, they claim that most undocumented workers are concentrated in low-skilled jobs that are not attractive even to low-income Americans.[51] However, their studies have focused mainly on Mexicans in the California service and garment industries. Donald Huddle argues that seven Americans are displaced for every ten employed illegal aliens.[52] Huddle's figure was arrived at on the basis of interviews conducted with unemployed Americans who said they would take the construction, landscaping, manufacturing, and service jobs liberated by the INS's 1982 raids in Houston.

The evidence that might settle this question is unlikely to be forthcoming because the effects of illegal immigrants on the U.S. economy are too complex to sort out in aggregate macroeconomic analysis. Hence, besides the issue of the extent to which American workers are displaced, little is known about the net aggregate economic impact of illegal immigration. One must also try to estimate and net out the welfare costs to taxpayers for displaced American workers, along with the income gains to consumers from the lower costs of production.[53]

Some argue there are productivity gains from using cheaper, and often more dependable, illegal workers. But other scholars argue that reliance on cheap labor may retard technological innovation in an industry. Philip Martin, agricultural economist, has argued that the availability of low-wage illegal aliens in agriculture will damage the competitive position of American growers over the long run as less developed nations catch up with the United States.[54]

Other interest groups, including lobbyists such as the Federation for American Immigration Reform and Zero Population Growth, worry that illegals will compete for scarce resources and thereby undermine efforts to conserve and protect the environment. But it is difficult to say what the optimal population of a country is. Most environmental problems arise not because of high population densities per se but because of rising levels of per capita wealth combined with inadequate controls over the disposal of waste. Moreover, population densities can reach very high levels without serious economic consequences in countries with highly skilled populations and high value-added productivity.

The Federation for American Immigration Reform is also concerned about the tax burden illegals pose and asserts that the percentage of illegal aliens taking unauthorized welfare and unemployment benefits is greater than is commonly believed. When state and county welfare agencies in California and Illinois have asked INS assistance in screening illegal aliens from welfare applicants, quite a few illegal aliens have been uncovered. Between 1981 and 1984 in California alone, 78,640 out of 107,415 aliens referred to the INS were found to be ineligible, resulting in an estimated savings to taxpayers of between 235 and 483 million dollars.[55] However, without knowing the base population of illegal aliens in these jurisdictions, one cannot know how their rate of discovered welfare use compares with that of citizens or lawful aliens of similar socioeconomic background. If it is true, as some INS officers claim, that Los Angeles has upward of a million illegal aliens, then the number on the welfare rolls is surely modest.

On the other hand, there is growing evidence that, as urbanized illegal aliens become permanent settlers, they are socialized to accept public assistance. In certain cities, such as Los Angeles, the evidence suggests that immigrants as a whole (legal and illegal aliens) are paying less in taxes than they are receiving in public benefits.[56]

Besides the prospect that illegal aliens may find their way onto the welfare rolls and thus place new burdens on the public treasury, there is concern that illegals from less developed countries will engage in crime or other law violations. Some violations are almost unavoidable for the illegal alien. For example, INS officers report that many illegal aliens drive without auto insurance or auto registration, which may explain why some simply abandon their vehicles after being involved in accidents.

Although close to 30,000 illegal aliens were turned over to the INS from prisons and jails in fiscal year 1983, turnovers represented a minuscule 2 percent of all apprehended aliens—hardly a statistic to occasion alarm. But again, nobody can say how many illegal aliens are actually involved in crime. Some pass through the courts and out of the prisons before the INS can interview and apprehend them upon their release; others hide their illegal immigration status from local law officers and thereby avoid deportation. Whether illegals have a higher or lower incidence of arrest or incarceration (let alone rates of crime) compared with the rest of the population cannot be known from currently available data.[57]

Offsetting the organized restrictionist groups (which are few) are the many groups that benefit economically from illegal immigration. Ranchers, landscaping and construction contractors, garment manufacturers, restaurant owners, and many others benefit because illegal aliens are not just cheap labor but are very reliable workers as well. Also, even when they receive the same pay as Americans for comparable work, the employer may be saving on the cost of workers' compensation or other fringe benefits and, in some cases, even on federal and state taxes.[58]

THE ISSUE OF EXPLOITATION

Today, unlike earlier periods, the legal and social handicaps aliens experience because of their illegal status has clearly emerged as an important issue in the policy debate. Thus wetbacks have become undocumented workers who are victimized when smugglers abandon them in desert wasteland without food or water, or when they are injured or killed because the vehicle they were being transported in ran off the highway. Also, when coming up by boat from South American countries, women are occasionally sexually abused in transit by male passengers or crew members.[59] The failure of smuggled aliens to pay smuggling fees or meet other extortion demands in exchange for the release of family members held as "collateral" has also led to violence and deaths.[60]

Still, once arrived here, many aliens who have been victimized will re-fuse to call on local peace officers for assistance out of fear of being sent home. The same fear of being turned in to the INS also explains the ease with which supervisors can extort kickbacks from illegals or require the per-formance of illicit services. In one case involving a Nevada casino, employees who were lawful resident aliens were requiring illegal aliens under their supervision to help pilfer liquor and silverware in exchange for keeping quiet about their illegal status.[61] Nor, it is believed, will aliens turn in their employ-ers when working conditions or pay are below the required federal or state standards. Female illegals have sometimes been pressured by supervisors to provide sexual favors in exchange for a job or the supervisor's agreement to keep their illegal status a secret.

Local law officers worry that illegal aliens will fail to report crimes or to cooperate as witnesses because of their fear that contact with any governmen-tal authority will lead to deportation. If true, this could handicap police efforts to deal with serious crimes. As a result of this attitude, for example, relations between the INS and the police departments of Los Angeles and the nearby community of Santa Ana (two cities having large illegal populations) have been severely strained in recent years, and Santa Ana's police chief, Raymond Davis, has publicly announced that his department will no longer cooperate when the INS comes out to apprehend deportable aliens.[62]

Chief Davis's views are not universally shared, especially by police offi-cials in towns closer to the border, where the border patrol is more apt to be viewed as necessary to deter borderland crime. For example, in Nogales, an Arizona border town, the enforcement functions of the border patrol and the local police overlap to a much greater extent than would be found in a larger city in the interior. Patrol agents will occasionally assist in chasing down a shoplifter or will break up a bar fight if they get there before local law officers arrive. Local police will alert the patrol when they spot a suspected border crosser and will sometimes trail or even detain the individual until patrol agents can come by to check the suspect's status.

In the interior cities, by contrast, illegal aliens are much more apt to have settled in. Often they have relatives who are citizens or lawful residents. Or they have developed other ties to their neighborhoods. As a result, INS officers are beginning to meet resistance from elected political authorities who find it expedient to side with the aliens because of the growing clout that ethnic communities have acquired. Although the INS usually receives assistance from local police when it requests help with crowd control during a raid on a business, it sometimes gets the cold shoulder when it offers to assist state license bureaus and welfare agencies in identifying applicants who may be illegal aliens. Local officials worry that, if they assist the INS, there will be political reprisals from Hispanic and other ethnic voting blocs.

The extent to which illegal aliens are exploited economically remains controversial. Some of the studies suggest that they receive less pay for the same work and are less apt to receive fringe and other benefits.[63] Other research suggests that illegals receive the going wage, although they may be required to work longer hours and may not be receiving the fringe benefits that citizens would expect. Not surprisingly, illegals themselves appear to take a more favorable view of their economic situation. Based on their interviews with 59 Mexicans who had worked illegally in the United States, Julius Rivera and Paul W. Goodman found most claiming they were treated better by American employers than by Mexican employers.[64] By and large, they considered American employers "considerate" and "fair." And in their study of undocumented Mexican women in Los Angeles in 1981 and 1982, Rita Simon and Margo de Ley found a high percentage who rated their employers and conditions of work favorably.[65]

In any case, the victimization argument is complicated by the fact that illegal immigration, like drug-taking, prostitution, and other *mala prohibita* offenses, is a consensual undertaking. Although aliens undoubtedly run risks in coming to the United States, these are risks the alien has decided to run. When a Salvadoran pays as much as $1,500 to $3,000 to a smuggling ring to get to a job in the United States, one must assume that both the monetary cost and other risks were considered and determined to be acceptable. Mexicans who pay $250 to $800 to be smuggled from border towns to Denver, Chicago, Los Angeles, New York, and other cities may not relish having to ride cooped up in the back of a van but apparently consider the cost and discomfort as part of the tariff they must pay to earn six to eight times what they can earn in Mexico—if they can find work in Mexico at all.

In searching for remedies to bring illegal immigration under control, policy makers have developed a novel, if somewhat paradoxical, argument. Illegal immigration, some claim, threatens democratic institutions because illegal aliens refuse to avail themselves of police and other legal protections, thereby fostering disrespect for the law. The Hesburgh Select Commission on Immigration and Refugee Policy (SCIRP), established by Congress in 1978 to study and report on immigration issues, argued in its 1981 report to Congress that illegal aliens not only depressed wages and working conditions for domestic workers but were also a "fugitive underground class" fearful of seeking help from government. Their vulnerability to exploitation, the SCIRP commissioners argued, created an unhealthy condition for society because it bred disrespect for the nation's laws.[66]

However, as long as such wide differentials in wages and job opportunities exist between the United States and other countries, the exploitation of aliens will continue—as long as illegals are able to enter in substantial numbers. Whether border controls can be tightened sufficiently or other enforcement measures employed to deter illegal entry is an important question addressed in later chapters.

THE POLICY DEBATE: PAST AND PRESENT

In the past, restrictionist sentiment was mobilized primarily for the purpose of limiting legal immigration. Although economic anxieties played a role, the nativist restrictionism of 60 to 100 years ago arose mainly from the cultural, religious, and political threat that native-born Americans believed certain nationalities and classes of aliens posed.

As a result, during most of the past century, the controversy centered primarily on legal immigration. The main axis of policy debate was the tension between the discriminatory application of nationality criteria (which masked unstated religious and racial bias) on the one hand and American egalitarian ethos on the other. Spurred in part by the more egalitarian thrust in federal policy during the Great Depression, along with the public's awareness of the brutal consequences of Nazi racial policies during the 1940s, public attitudes toward immigration began to undergo a gradual liberalization such that by 1965 new legislation was passed to ensure more equal treatment of aliens regardless of their country of origin.[67]

At the same time, the liberal thrust of domestic policy was also beginning to make itself felt in procedural areas of the law, especially in regard to the rights all aliens should enjoy under administrative proceedings. Because the federal courts had traditionally been deferential to Congress and the executive branch on immigration matters, most of the liberalization of alien due process and appeals rights occurred first within the framework of congressional legislation and executive branch policies.

By degrees, due process protections for aliens undergoing hearings were expanded through various amendments to the statute along with changes in agency policy. The passage of the Administrative Procedures Act (APA) in 1946 provided much of the stimulus for these innovations despite Congress's initial efforts to insulate immigration administration from the APA's provisions, especially the requirement that the INS's adjudicatory function be separated from its prosecutorial role.[68] However, when Congress revised the immigration statute in 1952, the INS was instructed to provide special inquiry officers, who had a better understanding of immigration law, to oversee deportation and exclusion proceedings. Officers who had had investigative or prosecutorial duties in regard to a given case could not also sit as hearing officers in the case. A Board of Immigration Appeals was also established to handle appeals from the immigration courts as a further guarantee against erroneous and arbitrary decisions.

This expansion of aliens' administrative due process rights, although it began with statutory amendments, eventually received a powerful assist from the federal judiciary during the 1970s.[69] The traditional, or classical view, of immigration law still characterizes most Supreme Court decisions in this field; however, some lower federal courts are much less deferential to the political branches of government today. Although it is usually not within the power of the courts to grant the substantive benefits sought by alien plaintiffs (such as adjustment of status to lawful permanent resident, suspension of deportation relief, or political asylum), civil lawsuits can still achieve a de facto liberalization of immigration policy because of the impact they have on INS resource allocations.[70] In particular, the "leveraged judicializing" of immigration policy through injunctions brought in class action suits—especially in districts and circuits where INS caseloads are heavy, as they are in the ninth circuit (which includes California and Arizona)—can effectively nullify expeditious enforcement.

Moreover, Congress's unique plenary power in regard to aliens, including the power to exclude aliens and set the terms for their entry into and residence in the United States, has begun to be questioned by some legal scholars. Critics argue that aliens who have managed to settle into our society, whether they came legally or illegally, acquire equities as a result of their economic contributions and the social ties they establish. In the words of the authors of a 1983 *Harvard Law Review* article, their status is "functionally close to that of the citizen."[71]

As is discussed in Chapter 8, it would be premature to assume that continuing judicial liberalization of the law is inevitable, especially in view of recent Supreme Court rulings that appear to have stanched the liberalizing trends of the 1970s. In addition, the INS has begun to stiffen its legal defenses against civil lawsuits that seek to weaken enforcement. For example, INS attorneys who had previously handled naturalization adjudications are being shifted to the general counsel's office to assist with litigation. One obvious result is that the INS can appeal more adverse rulings to the appellate courts rather than having to settle out of court on unfavorable terms. The newly created Office of Immigration Litigation in the Justice Department will also shore up the INS's defenses in civil litigation at the circuit and Supreme Court levels. Finally, the loan of INS attorneys to federal prosecutors as special assistant district attorneys will mean that more criminal actions against INA violators, which had previously been declined, will now be accepted for prosecution.

Thus the trends of the 1970s, which saw the INS giving up ground on the legal front because of weak support from its parent agency, the Department of Justice, are in the process of being reversed by the more enforcement-minded Reagan administration.

However, one trend is very clear. The mass deportations and hearings that were prevalent in the past are very unlikely to be resorted to again. Although SCIRP did not rule out deportation as an enforcement tool for selective use, it did not mince words in stating its aversion to mass deportation as a solution to illegal immigration—mainly because of the threat it believed such a draconian measure would pose to civil liberties. Also, a humanitarian concern to avoid uprooting the many illegal aliens who have settled into our society was an important consideration.

The control measures recommended by SCIRP in its 1981 report emphasized instead the deterrence of future illegal entry through a strengthened border patrol, along with new legislation that would prohibit employers from hiring illegal aliens.[72] This was to be coupled with a generous amnesty for those illegals who could establish that they had lived in the United States before a certain date.

The Hesburgh Select Commission on Immigration and Refugee Policy's two central policy innovations—amnesty and employer sanctions—came to be incorporated in the Simpson-Mazzoli Immigration Reform and Control Act in the early 1980s, the first major attempt to overhaul the immigration statute in 30 years. As will be seen in Chapter 8, the future of Simpson-Mazzoli, which both the 97th and 98th Congresses failed to pass, is still uncertain.

What is certain is that immigration control is breaking down in the interior as well as along the borders. Although Immigration and Naturalization Service apprehensions in urban areas account for only 10 percent of all arrests, they cause intense controversy because so many urbanized illegals have become permanent or quasi-permanent settlers. By contrast, southern border apprehensions provoke little protest, mainly because aliens caught at the border have few, if any, equities and because the defense of borders is more clearly linked to perceptions of sovereignty. However, as the illegal population becomes increasingly urbanized, resistance to the INS's enforcement efforts will increase.[73]

During the period of my field work, anti-INS activists were distributing handouts in factories urging the work force to refuse to talk to INS officers. Allegations of brutality by INS officers against illegal aliens have become commonplace. Even when these charges turn out to be without foundation, they may be prematurely disseminated by journalists and other critics eager to report allegations of government wrongdoing.

THE NEGLECTED ISSUE
OF IMMIGRATION RESEARCH

Regardless of whether illegal immigration is good or bad for American society, the INS's ability to enforce the law is an important issue in its own right. First, not all aliens who come to the United States are individuals we want in our midst. Some are here for the purpose of crime, terrorism, and espionage. Some engage in entitlement fraud by applying for government student loans or other welfare services intended for citizens and lawful residents. Although the rate of unauthorized welfare usage by illegal aliens is probably moderate at present, there are no guarantees that it might not accelerate, especially under an activist judicial regime that has too often extended individual rights to the new property of the welfare state without due regard for the controls required to prevent fraud and abuse.[74]

In the event the political situation in Central America deteriorates and more Marxist *commandantes* come to power, a tolerable level of illegal immigration might become intolerable and create severe dislocations in certain localities. If Mexico were also to become politically destabilized, serious problems would be presented because of Mexico's proximity and much larger population.

Finally, it should be kept firmly in mind that, even if scholars should eventually achieve consensus on the economic impact of illegal immigration, few voters are scholars. If localized publics come to perceive illegal aliens as having deleterious consequences and develop organized lobbies in response, they might carry the day in Congress. The result might be an immigration statute that is not only much more restrictive but also more punishing toward legal immigrants, including refugees.

As noted, most of the support for tougher enforcement is passive. Those who support a more restrictionist policy are neither well organized nor as active in their lobbying as the more numerous civil rights and other proalien activist groups that seek to protect illegal aliens from INS enforcement. As any student of American government knows, what counts in the political arena is organized political action. Organized lobbies, even though representing only a minority view, are often able to prevail in the legislative arena, regardless of what pollsters tell us a majority of the public wants done. What Americans must decide is how strongly they care about illegal immigration and whether they care enough to support stronger enforcement through active lobbying.

Even if the public does decide that tougher enforcement should be a congressional priority, how can the law be more effectively enforced? Will Congress authorize the funding required? Can employers effectively screen illegal aliens from the work force in the event that Simpson-Mazzoli or a similar bill containing employer sanctions were to be passed? What other approaches might be tried to regulate illegal immigration beyond the civil and criminal actions currently available to the INS?

Although policy research may not be able to change the public's mood by providing data that would validate either a restrictionist or antirestrictionist attitude toward the problem, such research can clarify the realistic policy options available to legislators once the system of immigration enforcement is better understood. Until recently, INS operations were a black box. Many legislators were aware of the agency's output in the form of statistics on arrests, deportations, prosecutions, and the like, but very few outsiders knew what was happening inside the agency or how the statistics were produced. Hopefully, by illuminating some of the problems the INS confronts in trying to administer the present law, the following chapters will allow for a more realistic assessment of the available policy options.

TWO

BENEFICIARIES
AND VIOLATORS

 The INS has a dual obligation in administering the 1952 INA and other statutes pertaining to alienage. On the one hand, they are responsible for providing statutorily eligible aliens with benefits and relief under the INA (which some officers refer to as the agency's service role), and on the other, they must enforce the civil and criminal provisions of the act against alien and citizen violators.[1]

Judging solely on the basis of the agency's budgetary allocations, it would appear that the INS's commitment to its enforcement function is stronger than to its service role, a complaint often made by the agency's critics. In fiscal year 1983, enforcement functions accounted for about 60 percent of the INS's $492 million budget. By contrast, the service function (citizenship and benefits adjudications) accounted for only about 9 percent. Most of the remainder went for administrative and other overhead activities.

However, budgetary allocations can easily convey a misleading impression. Thus service functions are often performed by officers who are counted in the enforcement budget. In 1983, these included approximately 1,400 inspectors, 1,000 detention and deportation officers, 2,800 border patrol agents, 300 antismuggling investigators, and 900 criminal investigators.[2] For example, POE inspectors, who come under the adjudications branch, seek not only to deter unauthorized alien entrants but also to facilitate entries by citizens and authorized aliens. Investigations branch officers may be detailed to help inspectors during peak hours at airports or to help examiners clear up adjudications backlogs. Investigators may also assist aliens who are applying for benefits simply because the information they gather may establish an alien's benefit eligibility. (Of course, their investigations can also result in adverse information sufficient to deny relief or benefits to the alien.)

When border patrol agents or plainclothes investigators apprehend illegal aliens in field operations, they sometimes turn up aliens who did not know they qualified for benefits under the law and learn about possible eligibility during the course of their interrogation. So, for example, a border patrol agent might encounter an individual of Hispanic origin who the agent initially assumed had entered from Mexico without inspection. But if the individual claims to have been born with the aid of a midwife in Texas, the officer would be obliged to explain to the individual how to obtain a citizenship card—assuming the officer credited the person's story.

Budgetary allocations are a misleading measure of INS priorities. Most benefit requests are quickly adjudicated and therefore cost little to process. By contrast, enforcement actions impose much heavier costs on a per-case basis, especially when they involve overseas deportable aliens who must be located, apprehended, processed for deportation, and in some cases, returned to their homelands at government expense.

THE SERVICE FUNCTION

The INS provides a wide assortment of services to aliens. These range from such simple clerical operations as helping an alien file a benefit application to the adjudication of more than 30 different kinds of benefit requests. Benefit adjudications include the issuance of travel documents and re-entry permits to authorized aliens and the replacement of lost or stolen alien registration receipts (the I-551 green cards) along with such important immigration benefits as the grant of lawful permanent residence (immigrant visas) and naturalization (U.S. citizenship).

Although the important benefit applications do not always require elaborate investigation, some will require time-consuming inquiries, especially if questions arise about the validity of the documentation the alien has submitted or the individual's statutory eligibility.[3]

When an alien's eligibility for a benefit is clear, the request can often be adjudicated on the basis of the submitted application and supporting documents alone. In such cut-and-dried cases, the district office where the application was submitted may turn over adjudication to INS inspectors at the POEs, where they will be processed during standby (nonpeak) hours when inspectors have free time. Most other cases are adjudicated by approximately 1,300 examiners located in 34 district offices or by special teams at one of the four Regional Adjudications Centers. An innovation of the current commissioner, Alan C. Nelson, these centers were implemented to clear up heavy backlogs. They were also intended to achieve more consistency in the adjudication of the more complicated visa applications.

This centralization of certain visa adjudications may have helped to reduce the considerable variation between the districts and regions that resulted because of differences in the way examiners interpreted legal rulings and agency policy. Not surprisingly, benefit applicants and their attorneys often complained that determinations were unfair or unreasonably delayed. One consequence was that applicants would shop around and then make application in a district whose examiners were known to render more generous interpretations of agency regulations.[4]

If one excludes POE inspections, which numerically account for most of the agency's contacts with the public, adjudications account for most of what the INS does in its service role. In fiscal year 1982, the INS received 2 million requests. These included 655,000 petitions for lawful permanent residence, 435,000 requests for extensions of temporary stay, and 220,000 requests for I-186 border-crossing cards. In addition, there were 203,000 applications for replacement of I-551 immigrant visa receipts (green cards) and 185,000 requests for Section 245 adjustment of status, among tens of thousands of other requests.[5] Of the total benefit requests, approximately 1.3 million were adjudicated by examiners and another 688,000 were completed by inspectors on standby at the POEs. (Some of the completed requests were pending receipts from earlier fiscal years; some received in 1982 would remain pending at year's end to be adjudicated in 1983 or later.)

Additionally, there were 360,000 naturalization applications in fiscal year 1982; more than 183,000 aliens were naturalized by the naturalization section of the adjudications branch that year. Naturalization applications have been increasing, due in part to the heavy surge in immigrant and refugee admissions during the mid to late 1970s. Heavy backlogs continue to exist, especially in districts, such as Los Angeles, that have become home to disproportionately large numbers of refugees and other immigrants. By September 1983, the servicewide backlog of pending naturalization receipts had grown to an average of nine months. By the spring of 1984, clearing both the naturalization and political asylum backlogs had become the INS's main service priority.

Visa adjudication backlogs (such as petitions for lawful residence and adjustment of status) have also been building up in certain districts. However, Commissioner Nelson has sought to streamline managerial procedures to reduce backlogs and the resultant complaints of poor service. Commissioner Nelson has continued with innovations begun in the mid-1970s—in particular, with the overhaul and streamlining of automated data processing systems. Indeed, overall productivity in adjudications has increased substantially from 1.23 benefit requests completed per productive officer hour in 1977 to 2.0 per hour in 1982. According to the INS, this 62 percent rise in productivity over the five-year span is due to the gradual introduction of improved managerial controls and new data processing technologies.[6]

Typical of the routine, and usually easily adjudicated, benefit requests are those involving minor adjustments in a nonimmigrant alien's status, such as a change from a B-1 or B-2 visitor visa to an F-1 student visa or, in the case of students who have run into financial difficulty, a request for permission to work. (As part of the effort to expedite its adjudications caseloads, the INS recently decided it would no longer require aliens with student visas to petition for a change in school or course of study.)

Some benefit requests require more careful scrutiny, especially when a nonroutine investigation of the applicant's background (a character check) is required or when there are questions relating to eligibility.

In the case of petitions for permanent resident status, many can be quickly and routinely adjudicated, but not all. For example, an immigrant visa petition for a dependent child might not only require that the examiner check the administrative regulations to determine whether the child qualifies under the statute but also research the marriage and family law of the petitioner's homeland to be certain that the child can qualify as a dependent under American law.[7] In addition to deciding whether the law applies (whether the child is eligible), the examiner may also have to decide whether the child is in fact related to the petitioner as claimed. (Some children are known to be fraudulently immigrated by individuals who are not their parents.)

In the main, the INS has been searching for ways to rationalize both its adjudications and its enforcement activities by, among other things, reducing the amount of unproductive monitoring and investigation of alien benefit claims. Thus background character investigations are no longer routinely carried out unless there are good indications that an alien applying for lawful residence has been involved in immoral or criminal activity, or an immigration judge specifically requests such a check. Also, until recently, aliens entering as visitors with nonimmigrant visas had to petition for extensions beyond the period of stay they had individually requested at the time of application. Now, all visitors are routinely granted six-month visas, which has reduced the volume of extension requests examiners must review.

INSIDE THE DISTRICT OFFICE

On any working day, the INS district office in a major city is a busy place. In places like Los Angeles and Miami, lines will sometimes form in the lobby of the federal building and even extend outside. In the corridors outside the

INS's office suites, aliens and petitioning citizens will be waiting to talk to an INS contact representative or examiner.

Lawful residents who have lost their green cards come in to apply for replacement cards. Because of the inconvenience of having to wait in line to be photographed and fingerprinted, along with the fact that it may take up to six months for a new card to be issued, many lawful permanent residents do not carry their cards on their persons—in order to reduce the risk of losing them. This creates problems when enforcement officers conduct alienage and deportability checks on farms and businesses. They encounter and question many aliens who claim to be immigrant visa holders but who are not carrying their cards.

Lawful residents who have resided in the United States for the statutorily required period appear at district offices to apply for naturalization. Once naturalized, they return later to put in petitions for immigrant visas for relatives still abroad.[8] The fact that our immigration law has no numerical limitation on visas for aliens who are the immediate relatives (spouses, unmarried children, and parents) of U.S. citizens has created an added incentive, beyond a patriotic love for our country, for aliens to naturalize themselves.

Apprehended aliens from overseas or more distant Latin American countries appear at the detention and deportation (D&D) section after having been ordered to depart the United States. If they have good moral character and have not been deported previously, they are usually allowed to depart voluntarily, thus avoiding an official record of deportation. In the case of many overseas aliens, they present a nonrefundable airline ticket and pick up their travel documents. At the airport, they turn in their I-94 arrival/departure form to the commercial carrier, which in turn will forward it on to the central office. In theory, the district office should eventually receive notification of their departure.

All aliens with nonimmigrant visas are required to turn in their I-94 receipts to the airlines at the time they leave. Until recently, the INS had difficulty tracking the departures of the 10 to 12 million visitors who entered the United States each year. This was primarily because all I-94 arrival/departure receipts were hand processed.[9] Since January 1983, use of the automated Non-Immigrant Information System has reduced the time required to post I-94 receipts from several months or longer to a current average of thirteen days.[10]

As regards alien violators allowed to depart voluntarily, D&D officers often had difficulty determining whether aliens who had been issued I-210 letters instructing them to leave the country had in fact left within the 30 days allowed. In theory, the D&D officer in charge of docket control would notify the investigations branch if a violator's I-94 departure receipt failed to come back from the central office within a reasonable period of time. However, many of these cases were never actively pursued by investigations because they had a lower priority than other case investigations. (There were reasons for this. For example, the alien could have actually departed but the I-94 receipt may not have been collected by the carrier, or it may have become lost—a not infrequent occurrence. In such cases, investigators find themselves searching for an individual who is no longer in the United States.)

When citizens appear at a district office, it is usually for the purpose of submitting a petition for relatives they wish to have immigrate as lawful permanent residents. Immigrant visa petitions usually receive close scrutiny because of the substantial benefits they confer on aliens. Immigrants are entitled to most of the welfare benefits citizens enjoy, and they can remain and work in the country indefinitely. Because there is a powerful incentive for fraud, these benefit applications are scrutinized with more care.

For example, when a citizen marries an alien and submits a petition to immigrate his or her spouse, the couple will be interviewed by an examiner in the unit that handles I-130 immediate relative visa petitions. Both the citizen and alien must affirm that they can legally marry and must bring with them documents showing that they are lawfully wed to one another. If there was a previous marriage, they must present evidence of a legally valid divorce, an annulment, or the death of the former spouse. If the couple is very dissimilar in age or cultural background, if they appear unable to communicate because of language differences, or if they are represented by an attorney suspected of involvement in sham marriages, they will likely be called in for a lengthier second interview. The examiner who still has doubts after the second interview may ask a supervisor to request an investigation from the investigations section. The request will be in the form of a "predication" that specifies what it is the investigators should check out.

Most I-130 spousal petitions involve bona fide marriages: that is, marriages that were not entered into primarily for the purpose of obtaining immigration benefits. However, examiners must be alert for tip-offs of fraud because many aliens do seek to arrange "marriages of convenience" with citizens. (The citizen is sometimes not aware of being used for this purpose.) Because there is no numerical limitation on visas for immediate relatives of citizens, marriage to a citizen is, to quote the officers, the "brass ring" for an alien determined to remain in the United States. How many marriages are contrived for the purpose of obtaining immigration benefits is not known and is probably unknowable. Marriages arranged by third-party intermediaries for money can be shown to be fraudulent, but in the case of many marriages arranged by just the husband and wife (one-on-one cases), it is much harder to prove that the immigration benefit was the sole, or even the primary, motivation behind the marriage. This is discussed further in Chapter 7.

ADJUDICATIONS AT THE
DISTRICT DIRECTOR'S DISCRETION

Most immigration benefits are granted solely at the discretion of the INS district director, although typically this authority is delegated to subordinates in the adjudications or D&D branches. In the case of most requests involving nonimmigrant visas, the sole avenue of appeal of the alien whose request is denied by the district director is usually to the INS commissioner.

As is discussed later, in the case of aliens ordered to appear for deportation hearings, there are a few benefit requests that can be adjudicated at the time of a deportation hearing both by a district director and, in the event the director denied the request, by an immigration judge. Among these are political asylum and Section 245 adjustment-of-status requests. (In a Section 245 request, an eligible alien seeks to adjust to lawful residence in the United States rather than having to return home to apply at a U.S. consulate.) Should the immigration judge deny such requests at the time of the deportation hearing, the alien can pursue an appeal to the Board of Immigration Appeals, which is the appellate review body for appeals from the immigration courts. (The government can also appeal decisions by the immigration courts to the Board of Immigration Appeals.)

However, most benefit requests are not reviewable by the immigration judges. For example, a deportable alien might apply to the district director for deferred action, which is wholly at the discretion of the INS to grant. Usually the ground is personal hardship. For example, the alien may be ill and undergoing medical treatment or may be the sole support of an ill or very elderly parent living in the United States. If deferred action were granted, this individual would be allowed to remain in the United States, perhaps indefinitely. Although there are agency regulations that specify the criteria to be used in deciding whether to grant deferred action, aliens cannot appeal denials in the immigration courts. (However, an alien who believed that agency guidelines had not been followed or that the district director had abused his or her discretion, might have recourse to appeal to the federal district court.)

The district director can also grant extensions of time beyond the 30 days deportable aliens offered voluntary departure are given to leave. Often the alien needs additional time to put business or other personal affairs in order. Usually the D&D section will honor the extension request unless it appears that the alien is just procrastinating. In the case of aliens whose immigrant visas will become available within 60 days, extensions of voluntary departure are automatic.

Section 212(c) waivers of excludability are also granted, at the discretion of the district director, to a lawful permanent resident (immigrant visa holder)

who becomes deportable as a result of criminal offenses or other conduct that
would make that alien inadmissible, but only if the alien meets certain statutory requirements. The alien must provide proof of rehabilitation and must
show that severe hardship would result to a U.S. citizen spouse, child, or parent if that alien were deported.[11] Originally the 212(c) waiver applied only to
resident aliens who had gone abroad and had been denied re-entry. But it
came to be extended to lawful residents in the United States as a result of a
court decision that held that immigrants already in the United States should
enjoy the same protection under the law as aliens seeking to re-enter. In consequence, many immigrant visa holders who become excludable as a result of
criminal convictions routinely request the 212(c) waiver. By doing so, they
gain additional time, even if their requests are almost certain to be denied. In
the view of many INS officers, these appeals simply add to the caseloads of
the investigations branch and the immigration courts.

Granting work authorization to aliens with student visas is also at the district director's discretion. To qualify, students must demonstrate that unforeseen circumstances have arisen since their arrival. Aliens who receive visas to
study in the United States are expected to be able to support themselves without having to work. The examiner will want to know why a parent or guard-
ian is no longer able to support students who request work authorization.
Such students may claim that a father or other source of financial support has
died or that their family has suffered serious business reverses. If true, such a
stroke of bad fortune would be considered unforeseen and these students' requests would be approved. But students who say they need to buy cars because they did not know that mass transit was poor in the city where they are
attending school or that they must rent an apartment because the college dor-
mitory is uncongenial are likely to find the examiner unsympathetic.

Examiners who are suspicious of a student's claim that a parent has died
(which would be a valid ground) might want to see a death certificate or other
documentary evidence. However, most examiners will make their determinations based on what is written in a student's request along with the verification turned in by the student's foreign advisor at school. (Currently, most student work authorization requests are sent to inspectors for adjudication.)

Many students simply decide to work without INS authorization, which
is illegal. Some made fraudulent representations about their parents' ability
to support them in the United States at the time they applied for their student visas. They may then compound the earlier fraud by falsely claiming
that a parent has died, apparently a common ruse used by students from certain West African states.[12] A bogus death certificate may be signed and sent
via their embassy or consulate in this country. Because of the rampant official
corruption in many less developed countries, official documents (such as
birth or death certificates and police records) have the potential of having

been fraudulently obtained, even when they appear valid on their face. Fraud is a more serious problem in those countries where, despite efforts by U.S. consular officials to tighten screening of nonimmigrant visa applications, the wait for immigrant visas can stretch to five, ten, or even more years.

Examiners must set priorities. Because denials have to be justified in writing and may have to be justified a second or third time if the alien follows up a first request with a second or even third, the easier course of action is to grant rather than to deny. If the alien continues to file requests, eventually the file may come to an examiner who will decide to approve it. (Or the alien may decide to move to a district that has a reputation for greater leniency.) As one officer explained the problem:

> A student can file a request for work permission every day. We could deny everyone. He can file a motion to reopen and a motion to reconsider for $50. A lot of legal work can go into writing up the denials. We can keep a handle on it in a small office, but in Los Angeles if the guy keeps filing, he'll probably get through. He may get a different examiner who will finally approve. Persistence and perseverance are the things the alien banks on in getting through.

From the perspective of examiners, those requests that entail significantly greater benefits for the alien, especially permanent residence, must take priority over the scrutiny of lesser requests.

COPING WITH COMPLEXITY

Because of the many different visa classifications and varieties of benefits and relief (each with its own bundle of statutory eligibility standards), adjudicating INA benefit and relief requests is no simple matter, especially when one considers the barnacled layers of case law that have grown up around the statute over the years.

For all benefits, there are requirements that an alien *must* meet (statutory eligibility). At a minimum, the standards for admissibility must be met. In some cases, an alien who is admissible will in all likelihood receive the benefit. For example, permanent residence is almost automatic if an alien has married a U.S. citizen. (Even an alien who is statutorily excludable may receive the benefit because there are waivers for inadmissibility.) The district director might, however, refuse the alien's petition to adjust his or her status to lawful permanent resident in the United States, which means the alien would have to return home to get the visa. The director is more apt to do this if there are indications of prior bad faith dealings with the government in the alien's file. (In the case of an alien who entered without inspection, or who was caught working without authorization, the district director has no discretion. The alien would have to return home and apply to the U.S. consulate in person in order to get a visa.)

In other cases, the discretionary component will loom much larger. The discretionary factors *allow* (but do not necessarily require) the district director or immigration judge to deny a benefit or relief request. An alien's favorable equities will normally be weighed and balanced against any adverse information in that person's file. By contrast, an alien's failure to meet any of the statutory requirements will usually make a denial mandatory, except in those cases where waivers are allowed by statute.

Consider the case of a lawful permanent resident who has committed an offense which makes him deportable. He requests a 212(c) waiver and is able to establish that a relative, who is a citizen, would suffer extraordinary hardship were he to be deported—the statutory requirement. Perhaps he has an elderly parent dependent on him for financial support. However, if he committed a serious felony, the waiver request may still be denied at the district director's discretion. If he was convicted for drug smuggling (other than possession of a small amount of marijuana), he would be statutorily ineligible for a waiver. Nonetheless, lawful residents convicted of drug dealing will often apply for the waiver simply to achieve delay.

By the same token, when an alien gives false and misleading information in the course of applying for a visa to enter the United States, how seriously this is taken can depend on other aspects of the case. Minor misrepresentations are apt to be disregarded for an alien who has married a citizen and has a petition for lawful residence pending. For example, when she applied for her nonimmigrant visa, she may have lied when she told the consular official she had a bank account that didn't exist (or was borrowed from a relative) or when she said she had no close relatives living in the United States. (Having relatives in the United States is assumed to increase the risk of visa violation.) Such misrepresentation is apt to be waived if she has married a citizen. (INS officers might, however, look somewhat more closely at the I-130 petition to check the authenticity of the marriage because, when fraud is uncovered in a nonimmigrant visa application, the chances are greater it may surface in an immigrant visa petition as well.)

Now consider the case of an alien who becomes a naturalized citizen but who failed to disclose past activity as a Nazi concentration camp guard. If such facts about the past come to light, and it is determined that misrepresentations were made in the course of an earlier visa application, this is certain to lead to denaturalization proceedings despite the substantial cost to the Department of Justice for litigation.

Because of this large discretionary component, aliens who are similarly situated with respect to their immigration equities may nonetheless receive different outcomes. Examiners may differ in the importance they accord to various adverse considerations, such as prior immigration offenses. Because of the many potential factors adjudicators can take into account and the difficulty in applying a uniform measuring rod to the variable factual circumstances of so many individual cases, variability in adjudicatory outcomes is unavoidable.

The law's complexity poses inherent dilemmas that work against completely equitable adjudication. Consider requests for Section 244 suspension of deportation relief. This relief is available only to aliens undergoing deportation proceedings. To be eligible for suspension relief, aliens must meet three statutory requirements: (1) seven years continuous residence, (2) good moral character, and (3) evidence that extreme hardship would occur to themselves or family members if ordered to leave. Most aliens meet the first two requirements without difficulty. It is the third requirement that is the major barrier to a favorable outcome for the alien. The equity issue arises because of the difficulty of assessing the multiple aspects of an alien family's hardship in a way that would ensure uniformly consistent determinations across all cases. At the poles of the distribution of cases this may not be a problem. An affluent alien from Bombay, who has skills, capital, and connections, presumably will not experience as much hardship if forced to return to India as an unskilled older alien who might face destitution. The agency knows in general terms the kinds of hardship factors that Congress wants taken into account. The problem is finding a consistent and uniform measure of hardship that can serve as a reliable standard across a wide range of individual cases. How, for example, can the medical problem of alien A and the quality of medical care in A's homeland be competently compared with the medical problem of alien B and the ability of physicians in B's country to deal with that problem?

Given the limited time available for hearings, rough rules of thumb may come into play. An immigration judge may decide to deny Section 244 suspension relief to a Nigerian for the reason that the judge knows Nigeria is among the wealthier countries of Africa. Because Nigeria is relatively wealthier, the judge reasons, Nigerians and their families should, in theory, be able to get adequate medical care—at any rate by comparison with an applicant from a less developed African state. Such rough judgments probably account for a large number of Section 244 dispositions. (On appeal, the Board of Immigration Appeals may scrutinize the family's hardship claim in more detail, or a federal court may remand the case to the immigration court for further scrutiny after a finding that the immigration court had abused its discretion.)

The dilemma that faces the 55 immigration judges is not very different from the problem that arises in other administrative law contexts. In his study of the adjudication of Social Security disability claims, Jerry Mashaw noted that disability examiners faced an inherent difficulty in applying the general language of the statute to the highly varying and particularized factual circumstances of individual claimants' cases. As Mashaw states, "The line that Congress drew through the ability-disability continuum when establishing its eligibility standard cannot be precisely located. This imprecision obviously limits the degree to which one can say with confidence that any particular decision is or is not a correct application of the statute."[13]

Immigration and Nationality Act adjudications differ from other public law contexts in one crucial respect. Although unfavorable adjudications may lead to litigation in the federal courts, the alien's sole recourse is usually to establish that a district director or an immigration judge exercised discretion in an arbitrary or capricious manner in violation of the provisions of the Administrative Procedures Act. This, however, is not worth very much to the plaintiff because the immigration courts can arrive at the same determination after reviewing the case again. The federal courts can tell the immigration judge to take another look, but they cannot, as a rule, dictate that the substantive relief being sought be granted. Because Congress gives the attorney general such wide discretionary latitude in immigration cases, alien plaintiffs have many fewer grounds for appeal.[14]

On the other hand, the absence of uniform adjudication under the INA can fuel continuing litigation by plaintiffs who will claim that determinations by district directors or immigration judges are at variance with congressional intent. The problem is that because individual cases will always differ in some particulars, it is hard to know the extent to which adjudicatory outcomes arise because of the different factual circumstances presented by a given case, as distinct from differences in the way individual officers or immigration judges interpret the statute or agency regulations.

Previous research indicates that variable interpretations of agency policy guidelines by INS officers do occur. In his study of Section 245 adjustment of status adjudications in the New York district office in the late 1960s, Abraham Sofaer found that examiners sometimes applied different standards for the discretionary component in Section 245 determinations. Sometimes the alien's perceived desirability as a U.S. resident was considered an immigration equity by the examiner. The usual discretionary ground for denial in cases where the alien had met the statutory eligibility standards was evidence of bad faith dealing with the government (misrepresentations in the course of a visa application, for example). However, some adjudicators apparently used the discretionary grounds for denial as a convenient device to deny the benefit in cases where the alien appeared to be undesirable but there was insufficient evidence to establish that the alien was statutorily inadmissible. In addition, there were marked inconsistencies between regions in the percentage rate of denials of 245 requests.[15] In his study of Social Security disability insurance adjudications, Mashaw also noted considerable disparity between the states in the percentage rates of denial.[16]

Whether inconsistencies in benefit and relief determinations among examiners within the same district office, or among the 34 district offices, have lessened as a result of recent efforts to centralize and streamline adjudications is not known. Yet the issue remains an important one for the INS. Even though the INS is empowered with substantially more discretion in its benefit determinations than many other public agencies, the legitimacy of its authority depends crucially on the public's perception that the statute is being administered as fairly as possible.

Efforts to elevate equitableness to a paramount norm of administrative behavior could require such rigorous standards of scrutiny that agency resources would be exhausted in the process. The most probable impact of such a demanding norm would be erosion of the standards for screening out ineligible benefit applicants. The reason is clear. It is always less costly and troublesome to grant benefits to aliens than to deny them. And as is noted in Chapter 8, few if any costs are directly internalized by the INS as a result of gearing both official and unofficial policy in the direction of greater leniency when the facts are murky or the resource costs of digging into the matter, or fighting it out in the courts, are judged to be heavy. What is not known (and is perhaps unknowable) is the extent to which leniency has increased over time. Other things being equal, are more borderline cases decided in favor of the alien today than ten or twenty years ago? Some officials believe so, but there is no evidence that would settle this point.

ENFORCEMENT AGAINST VIOLATORS

At any major district office, while alien benefit applicants stand waiting in INS office suites to talk to examiners or contact representatives, other aliens are being brought into the investigations or the D&D sections for processing as violators. Among them will be aliens apprehended in the course of area control surveys, aliens and citizens arrested for criminal INA violations, and aliens who absconded after being ordered to depart and who have been picked up on deportation warrants.

Most aliens who are found to be deportable after a deportation hearing are issued an alternate (double-barreled) order that allows them to depart voluntarily within 30 days. Should they leave after the 30-day period without having obtained an extension, they become "self-deports." If they fail to leave before the 30-day period expires, the deportation order becomes automatic. Aliens not given the option of voluntary departure at the time of their hearing are notified by letter when to return to the D&D section with their "bag and baggage" for escort to the airport. This I-166 letter instructing aliens to surrender with their luggage is often referred to as the "run letter" by officers because aliens who receive it know they have 72 hours in which to abscond. (Those judged as posing a threat to the public or as being likely to abscond may be detained until their departure.) Both those who have had hearings and failed to depart voluntarily and those ordered deported but who failed to return to the office with their baggage become abscondees. When located, they can be apprehended on the original warrant of deportation and are escorted directly to the airport after the D&D section arranges their travel documents.

Other aliens, who have finished serving time in county, state, or federal prisons, are picked up at the time of their release from jail and processed by the investigators. Often the officers will drop by a jail or prison to pick up one or several of these "turnovers" while en route back from other official business. (The INS is billed by local and state prison authorities for any additional time aliens are kept beyond their release date if they are being held on a service detainer.)

Immigration and Nationality Act violators suspected of producing or vending counterfeit immigration documents, operating alien smuggling rings, or participating in other fraudulent immigration schemes, and who are usually lawful residents or U.S. citizens, are picked up at their residences or places of work with arrest warrants. As is discussed in Chapters 6 and 7, such individuals, along with illegal aliens involved in crime or entitlement fraud, are considered serious violators. They are investigated by the antismuggling; fraud; and criminal, immoral, narcotics, and subversive (CINS) units.

Aliens referred to as administrative violators (EWIs and visa abusers) are generally not arrested at their places of residence unless perhaps they are "reportable cases" (requested by the regional or the central office, usually as a result of a congressional inquiry). Occasionally, an administrative violator who has no place of work might be picked up at a residence. However, residential pickups require advance approval by the regional office because the INS is highly sensitive to the legal and political problems that can arise when officers search for aliens at residences.

Sometimes a criminal investigator (CI) will be called to take into custody an alien who has been caught committing immigration fraud. After being questioned by the examiners, the alien's citizen "spouse" admits that the marriage was fraudulent and agrees to withdraw the I-130 visa petition. Usually no action will be taken against the citizen. Although criminal prosecution is open to the agency, it is infrequently pursued. The reason relates partly to the evidence problems investigators face in establishing fraud from inception, which is a key element for making such a case. But the main reason is that federal prosecutors view most one-on-one marriage shams as less serious violations. Indeed, federal prosecutors are reluctant to prosecute all but the most serious or aggravated I-130 marriage fraud cases, as is discussed in Chapter 7.

However, INS officers view an alien who attempts a sham marriage as a determined and serious violator. In consequence, the likelihood that the INS will decide to order such an alien deported without the option of voluntary departure is much higher than would be the case for most administrative violators. The investigators may decide to look into these aliens' backgrounds more closely to develop as much adverse information to put in their files as they can. Among other things, this will bolster the grounds for a denial should they seek other avenues of relief during a deportation hearing. For example, the CIs may check to see whether these aliens obtained their nonimmigrant visas fraudulently or whether they have sought to immigrate themselves fraudulently in another district office (some aliens are known to have had fraudulent marriage petitions pending in more than one district office).

Deportable aliens who voluntarily turn themselves in (called walk-ins) are tallied as apprehensions. Some are administrative violators who request transportation home. (If they agree to voluntary departure, they are usually required to pay. In other cases, the INS will insist that they be officially deported because of the cost to the government for their travel. Aliens who are returned voluntarily at government expense will be required to reimburse the government should they apply to re-enter the United States in the future.)

Also, some aliens who have been living underground for years decide to turn themselves in because they believe they have the required equities for suspension of deportation or other relief.

Crew members whose ships remain in port more than 29 days become technical violators; even though they have not willfully circumvented the law, they are still counted as apprehensions. Also, some aliens are written up as apprehended aliens when they walk in to request visa extensions because the officer found that they had overstayed, a fact the alien may have been unaware of. Because their violations were not willful, their cases resemble those of the technical violator.

Most walk-ins are not considered quality apprehensions, especially in the case of aliens who have themselves chosen to return home. Moreover, a walk-in who has sent savings ahead to relatives (or locked it away in a bank account) and claims to be unable to pay the return fare is viewed as defrauding the taxpayers, which is another reason these are considered "garbage arrests."

However, the vast majority of INA violators are involuntary apprehendees. Picked up by investigations branch officers, who are stationed mainly in the cities, or by patrol agents in the course of alienage and deportability checks, they usually have no wish to be returned home. However, it sometimes happens that Mexican EWIs are delighted to be discovered when INS agents are checking jails—if they believe they will beat a local police charge and get back into the country sooner than they can expect to be released from jail. Officers claim that some lawful residents and even citizens of Mexican descent make false claims of being illegally in the United States for the purpose of beating local police charges. They assume overburdened local police and prosecutors will turn them over to the border patrol, and sometimes they do.

DEPORTATION PROCEEDINGS

As of 1983, there were fewer than 60 immigration judges to preside over deportation and exclusion hearings. (Aliens who have entered the United States, legally or illegally, and who have been issued orders to show cause [as to why they should not be deported] are processed in deportation hearings. Aliens who are stopped at POEs, or who otherwise present themselves for inspection without having made either a legal or illegal entry, are held for exclusion hearings if they have been denied admission and wish to appeal.) Most aliens in deportation proceedings have decided they want a hearing after having been first offered voluntary return by the INS in exchange for waiving their right to a hearing. Some, however, are not offered voluntary departure and must appear for hearings.[17]

In the case of an alien who is under proceedings, the immigration judge (also called a special inquiry officer) must establish that the individual is both an alien and deportable. As a practical matter, an individual's foreign birth (alienage) is rarely at issue because almost all aliens concede their alienage by the time of their hearings, and in many cases, they did so at the time they were apprehended. Nor is deportability usually at issue because most aliens also concede the violations for which they are charged. (It is incumbent on any alien who admits to alienage to establish that entry into and residence in the United States have been authorized.)

In some cases, an alien will request a hearing simply to gain time. In other cases, the alien asks for a hearing in the hope of obtaining one or another major form of discretionary relief available under the INA (suspension of deportation, for example). However, minor forms of relief are also petitioned for. The alien may ask the immigration judge to reduce the bond set by the district director (bond redetermination) or may make a pro forma request for voluntary departure after all appeals have been exhausted or the fight has been given up for whatever reason.

Typically, aliens who request hearings usually either have substantial equities as a result of their stay in the United States or have invested a considerable sum of money to enter illegally and will be severely inconvenienced if forced to leave. If they have settled in, they may have good jobs or businesses, homes, and perhaps relatives who are citizens or immigrants. (Technically, the only equities relevant for immigration purposes are those that establish an alien's eligibility for a benefit, such as a citizen spouse or suspension eligibility because of seven years continuous residence and a showing of extreme hardship.) However, many officers use the term equity in a broader sense, to refer to the social and economic ties, job experience, and the like, that have been acquired by an alien and that may enhance the possibility of eventually qualifying for relief under the statute. Immigration and Naturalization Service officers claim that even time is an equity because, with added time, an alien may acquire the other statutorily relevant equities.

Equity in the sense of an alien's cost of entering and staying illegally comes into play in arrest encounters as well. Immigration and Naturalization Service officers claim that aliens from more distant countries are much more apt to resist arrest by running and fighting than Mexicans because Mexicans will incur only a week or two of lost time if returned to Mexico.

Overseas aliens who have made a heavy investment to enter the United States, or who have acquired good jobs, can gain time just by initiating requests for suspension of deportation relief or political asylum. They have considerably more incentive to fight their removal than, say, the Mexican EWI who accepts I-274 voluntary return under safeguard. (Mexicans know they can re-enter with relative ease. But according to INS officers, Mexicans also accept voluntary return because they do not want to acquire official servicewide files that contain their fingerprints and photographs.)

Less sophisticated aliens from overseas may also accept voluntary departure and forego hearings because they are unaware that they can so easily gain additional time and would most likely be granted voluntary departure even after being found deportable in a hearing. Some aliens apparently still believe that a deportation hearing will result in deportation. In other cases, aliens agree to leave because they are ready to return home, and apprehension has helped them make up their minds to do what they would have done in a few weeks or months anyway.

There are also aliens involved in criminal activities who accept voluntary return to avoid the possibility that their criminal backgrounds might be investigated. An alien known to be involved in crime (or to have previous criminal convictions) is statutorily ineligible for voluntary return. If such a record were known to the arresting officer, the alien would have to be processed for deportation.

When an alien is required to appear for a hearing (is not given the option of voluntary return by INS officers), this is usually for one of two reasons: (1) the INS has evidence that the alien is involved in crime or has been previously deported, which would make that individual statutorily ineligible for voluntary departure, or (2) at the time of apprehension, the alien, although eligible for voluntary return, "flunked the attitude test." Either the alien behaved abusively toward the arresting officer or was recognized as a repeat border crosser who had been previously granted voluntary return.[18] It should be noted that both I-210 voluntary departure (used for some Mexicans but mainly for overseas aliens) and I-274 return under safeguard (used for most Mexicans and some Central Americans) are granted solely at the discretion of the INS. They are not a right to which an alien, even a statutorily eligible alien, is entitled.

Even so, many aliens written up for hearings because of aggressive behavior toward agents or flagrant surreptitious crossings will still be granted voluntary departure by the immigration judge because of the need to reduce both the caseload pressures on the immigration court and appeals to the Board of Immigration Appeals. (Aliens involved in serious crimes or known to have criminal records would not likely be granted voluntary return.) In such cases, a field officer's decision to "dep proc" the alien (begin deportation processing) for a hearing means that the alien will spend between five and ten days in detention before being returned to Mexico. Officers believe that this threat of detention facilitates their control over aliens apprehended in field operations. Temporary detention, they reason, will cost these aliens whatever income might have been earned at their U.S. jobs.

When aliens are served with an order to show cause, a warrant of arrest may or may not be issued along with it. An alien who lacks a stable residence, community and family ties, or a regular job can be judged more likely to abscond, and this would justify issuing an arrest warrant. Aliens who resist their arrest or who are found hiding at the time they are encountered are more likely to have a warrant of arrest attached to their order to show cause and may be required to post a higher than average bond. Although the decision is motivated partly by the officers' need to achieve social control over troublemakers in the field, resistance is considered a valid basis for believing the alien might abscond.

The alien who cannot post the service bond set by the assistant district director of investigations can be held in detention until time for a hearing. However, because service detention space is limited and local jail space (when available) is expensive, some aliens are released on their own recognizance (OR) pending their hearing, even though they might not have sufficient community ties to warrant release on recognizance.

Although most violators ordered to hearings are illegal aliens in the sense understood by the public—that is, individuals who have abused the terms of their nonimmigrant visas and have chosen not to depart voluntarily or who have entered with fraudulent documents or without inspection—some lawful permanent residents are served with orders to show cause because they have been convicted of crimes that subject them to expulsion proceedings. Unlike citizens, their permanent residence can be revoked because of crimes or other conduct that make them inadmissible to the United States.

LIMITS OF THE CIVIL SANCTION

Although approximately 1.2 million aliens were apprehended by the INS in fiscal year 1983, approximately 95 percent returned to their homelands voluntarily. Most of these were Mexicans returned under service escort. However, a substantial number of overseas visa aliens also returned voluntarily, either before issuance of an order to show cause or after having been found deportable in a hearing and granted voluntary departure. Only 17,000 aliens, or less than 2 percent of all apprehendees, were officially deported in 1983.[19] Indeed, during the past two decades, the percentage of aliens who are formally deported has been a declining percentage of all aliens ordered to return home. It was 12 percent in 1961, had dropped to 5 percent by 1971, and fallen to less than 2 percent by 1982. The reason may be partly owing to the substantial increase in the percentage of Mexicans among all aliens annually apprehended from the mid-1960s to the present. Mexicans accounted for 94 percent of all INS apprehensions in 1983. More than 95 percent of Mexican arrestees agreed to voluntary return that year.[20]

The decline in formal deportations in recent years may also be partly attributable to the increasing caseload pressures on the immigration courts. This trend is partly due to the swelling number of illegal aliens from Central America, many of whom routinely put in asylum applications under the Refugee Act of 1980. (There were 170,000 pending political asylum claims in 1984 compared with 440 in 1970. Although most of these claims were pending before district directors, many will be raised again when the applicants are ordered to appear for deportation hearings.) In fiscal year 1983, the country's 55 immigration judges had more than 120,000 case receipts, of which deportation cases were 75 percent; exclusion cases, 6 percent; bond redetermination hearings, 17 percent; and motions to reopen, 2 percent. Decisions were rendered in more than 80,000 of these cases.[21]

Another factor contributing to caseload pressures is the growing sophistication of the alien community, combined with an increase in the number of immigration attorneys available to assist them with appeals. To reduce clogging the appeals pipeline further, the INS is constrained to be as liberal as possible in granting the discretionary option of voluntary departure. Although to be eligible for voluntary departure, a deportable alien must show good moral character and be ready, able, and willing to leave, in practice this usually requires only that the alien has no criminal (police) record or convictions. Paradoxically, behavior, such as visa fraud or other misrepresentations, that might be used to justify a benefit denial on the moral-character grounds will often be waived for an alien who agrees to accept voluntary departure. Some officers claim that pressures on the immigration courts and other resources may mean that occasionally even aliens who are strongly suspected of having minor criminal records are granted voluntary return. Even though officers may suspect an alien has a minor record, they may not inquire closely. It requires more time to process an alien for deportation, and official deportation is no guarantee against re-entry. Even if aliens are caught re-entering after deportation, the chances are good that they will not be tried for the 18 U.S.C. 1326 felony of re-entering after having been deported.

Moreover, hundreds of thousands of Mexican EWIs are returned under safeguard annually. Clearly, INS officers would not normally have the time to establish whether every one of them had a criminal record. Among other things, FBI fingerprint checks, which were routine twenty years ago, are no longer carried out. In consequence, it is probable that quite a few statutorily ineligible aliens are mistakenly granted voluntary return. (Officers may carry out a more thorough background check if they have reason to believe that the individual is a serious INA violator or involved in serious crime, such as drug smuggling or crimes against persons and property.)

Although discretionary voluntary return was written into the law in 1940, partly for humanitarian reasons, the system could not function today without it. Among other things, when the alien agrees to voluntary departure before having a hearing, the government is spared the cost of a hearing and (in many cases) of the alien's detention.

Some INS officers believe the discretionary grant of voluntary departure at almost all stages of litigation (even after a full panoply of appeals to the Board of Immigration Appeals) creates incentives for aliens to make the fullest possible use of the immigration courts. (In sharp contrast, criminal proceedings function quite differently. When a defendant charged with a criminal offense insists on a jury trial after being offered the opportunity to plead guilty to a lesser charge for a reduced sentence, there is a strong likelihood that, should the jury find that defendant guilty, the sentence will be much more severe.[22] In criminal proceedings, the offer of a lighter sentence must be extended by the prosecutor to reduce the caseload pressure.) Aside from attorney fees, the use of the appeals system is essentially costless to the alien.

Indeed, such a system is ideally suited for the alien whose eligibility for relief is, at best, marginal but who wants to buy time with the assistance of either paid counsel or a legal aid organization working on a *pro bono* basis. Because of crowded calendars and the fact that the immigration judges must usually give priority to aliens being detained at government expense, aliens under proceedings can usually obtain a few months' time simply by having their attorneys request postponements and continuances, even before the full hearing, at which time other motions can be introduced. When requests for relief have been denied, the alien's attorney can introduce motions to reopen or to reconsider. Such dilatory tactics can sometimes stretch the day of reckoning out a full year or two. In 1983, an alien requesting political asylum could gain as much as eighteen months because of the time required to obtain a recommendation from the Department of State's Bureau of Human Rights and Humanitarian Affairs.[23]

The liberalization of political asylum policy, which occurred with passage of the Refugee Act of 1980, has not only added heavily to the immigration courts' workload but also created powerful incentives for frivolous claims.[24] Illustrative of the abusive loophole asylum has become is the case of the Philippines national I heard about who appeared before the immigration judge of a western district court. He told the judge that if he were returned home, the Marcos government might persecute him. When the judge asked why, he said that when he was a cab driver in Manila he had made disparaging remarks about President Marcos to a passenger. Although, as the Aquino case proves, some Filipinos involved in their nation's political affairs doubtless do run risks of persecution because of their activities, it is hardly credible to believe that cab drivers who make occasional disparaging remarks run serious risks of persecution.

Although the fact that a high percentage of asylum claims are finally denied by the INS—after the State Department's Bureau of Human Rights and Humanitarian Affairs has rendered an advisory opinion—many civil rights activists and immigration attorneys dispute the reliability of the State Department's foreign policy judgments. On the other hand, the behavior of many asylum claimants strongly points to abusive use of the 1980 Refugee Act's provisions. Many Salvadorans, for example, who enter the United States illegally are known to travel back to El Salvador; some return home even while they have asylum claims pending. Many do not put in asylum claims until after they have been apprehended. Many candidly admit to INS officers that they came to the United States for economic reasons; they may, of course, change their story after being coached by relatives, friends, or attorneys.

As an example, while I visited an INS suboffice in the West, a Salvadoran of about 20 to 25 years of age showed up with his baggage. An officer explained that the man had applied for asylum a month or so earlier but apparently had been unable to find work. So he had come back to the office to request deportation back to El Salvador. But because there was still paperwork to get in order, he had arrived two days too soon. The officer told him to return with his luggage later in the week. Then, turning to me, the officer said, "We send them back when *we* are ready to send them, not when they are [ready to leave]. What they have to realize is that deportation is a privilege, not a right."

Besides illustrating the ease with which the asylum provision can be abused, this case also illuminates the welfare function the INS provides for aliens who have run out of luck in their search for work and who decide they want to go back home.

BENEFICIARY OR VIOLATOR?
THE DUALITY OF INS ENFORCEMENT

Although the INS's operational environment differs from that of other Department of Justice agencies in significant ways—especially when compared, for example, with the FBI or the Drug Enforcement Administration (DEA)—the most important difference is the dual orientation that INS officers must adopt toward many INA violators.

For example, whenever aliens apply for lawful permanent residence, suspension of deportation relief, or naturalization, there is a routine check of FBI and other police records to ensure that they are not involved in narcotics, immoral, or other criminal activities that might make them statutorily inadmissible and hence ineligible for a benefit.[25] In addition to previous actions or current behavior that might make them inadmissible, the validity of their benefit claims may also have to be checked, which may trigger case investigations for the investigators. If fraud or misrepresentations are indicated, the involved alien may not only be ineligible for the benefit but also be subject to expulsion and/or criminal prosecution. Thus the INS deals with "subjects" (also called respondents) who can be both objects of enforcement interest and potential beneficiaries.

By contrast, the FBI deals with individuals (or groups) who are either clients to whom the agency renders services, such as fingerprint and record checks, training courses, or security checks for federal employment, or deals with suspected violators who must be investigated, located, arrested, and charged with federal offenses.

Besides the fact that an alien initially perceived by the INS to be a violator may well turn out to be a beneficiary, there is a further irony that an INA violator may become eligible for benefits despite prior violations. Some INA violations which theoretically could lead to felony prosecution may be waived, not only for criminal prosecution but also for the purpose of granting immigration benefits.

This duality reaches down to the lowest levels of field enforcement policy in the agency. For example, although benefit requests may be formally adjudicated either by an examiner or an immigration judge after a violator has been apprehended, INS field officers will often carry out an abbreviated adjudicatory screening to assess whether an alien might qualify for a benefit, once that individual has been determined to be a deportable alien. This is done not only to ensure, for example, that a deportable alien whose citizen wife has just petitioned for his visa is not returned to the border by mistake but also to determine whether a warrantless arrest is really necessary.

Aliens who appear to have "something going for them" (a petition that will soon be in the works or equities that probably will make them eligible in the event they apply) hardly warrant apprehension—unless there are other aggravating factors or the officers have reason to distrust their stories. As one officer pointed out, if they were to arrest such individuals, then they might well be doing them a favor by moving them to act in getting a benefit petition into the mill.

The same duality of perspective applies to examiners. When they review an alien's benefit request, they must also consider the possibility that the applicant should be investigated for a possible violation of the law. Thus, INS examiners may flag an application they suspect might be fraudulent and send it down to investigations to be checked out.[26]

There is yet another anomaly of INS enforcement. Like the FBI and the DEA, the INS has traditionally sought out and apprehended individual violators. But the INS more closely resembles other regulatory agencies, such as the Occupational Safety and Health Administration and the Food and Drug Administration, in that the bulk of its enforcement actions against individuals are civil rather than criminal. Less than 2 percent of all INS apprehensions have resulted in prosecution in recent years.[27] Indeed, the blanket waiver of criminal prosecution for alien violators is so routinized at the time the I-213 Report of Deportable Alien form is written up that the prosecutable (criminal) aspects of the violation are unlikely even to come up for discussion during the questioning. And as noted earlier, the violations of many INA offenders are apt to be disregarded for the purpose of deciding whether the statutory good moral character requirement has been met in the case of an alien applying for relief. Ironically, although officers frequently complain that the American public fails to take immigration violations seriously (an attitude they attribute to what they call the Statue of Liberty syndrome), such routinized neglect of the criminal side of INA enforcement suggests that the Justice Department puts immigration violations at a steep discount in the scale of federal enforcement concern.

In sum, despite the ample criminal sanctions embroidered into the law, INS enforcement more closely approximates a regulatory than criminal-justice model of law enforcement. Although the discretionary grant of voluntary departure bears some resemblance to the plea bargaining that occurs in criminal courts (arising as it does from the need to reduce congested immigration court dockets—and, or so INS officers assert, partly from humanitarian considerations as well), the plea bargaining in criminal cases at least imposes some kind of sanction on an offender even if not the one that the penal code prescribes for the actual offense. By contrast, what INS civil enforcement seeks is simply a return to the status quo ante. The alien is asked to desist from violating the law, which is achieved in most cases when he or she consents to return home.[28]

THREE

APPREHENDING
EWI VIOLATORS IN TRANSIT

The principal mission of the U.S. Border Patrol, the uniformed enforcement branch of the INS, is the deterrence of uninspected entries across the nation's land borders.[1] In recent years, approximately 85 percent of the border patrol's 2,800 agents have been stationed along the Mexican border, which is of primary enforcement concern because of the large number of uninspected entries and smuggling operations occurring there. Indeed, southern border apprehensions accounted for 98 percent of all border patrol apprehensions in 1983.[2] A concentrated and visible presence at the immediate border (especially in urban areas, such as Chula Vista [California] and El Paso [Texas], which together accounted for 57 percent of all 1983 apprehensions) will—or so INS officials theorize—serve to deter those wanting to cross illegally. For this reason, patrol agents are heavily concentrated right along the border in what is called linewatch patrolling. Forty percent of all patrol officer hours are devoted to the linewatch function along the northern and southern borders. Outside of the cities, the desert is viewed as the most important barrier because of the natural hazards it poses.

With the use of technological gadgetry (such as seismic and electronic sensors) placed strategically in areas where the heaviest crossings occur along with helicopters, all-terrain cycles, horses, spotter aircraft, and vans, linewatch patrol agents seek not only to deter entry by their presence but also to interdict those making unauthorized entries before they are able to get into the interior.[3] A smaller complement of patrol agents is stationed inside the border to apprehend those who manage to circumvent the linewatch. Some of the illegal aliens who manage to evade the linewatch will be caught at fixed highway checkpoints, such as the San Clemente, California, checkpoint located on Interstate 5 between San Diego and Los Angeles. Patrol agents also check bus and train stations, watch for smuggling vehicles on the roads, and carry out farm and ranch checks in the interior.

Because of the high concentration of illegal aliens in California agriculture, smaller contingents of patrol agents are stationed on a permanent basis as far north as Fresno and Sacramento. From time to time, special details are sent elsewhere in the interior to carry out farm and ranch checks or to assist in urban interior enforcement.

This chapter focuses on those enforcement activities of the border patrol aimed primarily at interdicting aliens in transit to jobs in the U.S. interior. Some aspects of field operations are described in the context of the specific field encounters I observed during my time with the patrol agents.

It should be noted at the outset that patrol agents have the highest productivity of all INS enforcement officers in terms of the number of arrests made per field-officer man-hour. An average of approximately two officer hours is required per arrest in the most productive activities—linewatch and farm and ranch checks. The border patrol accounts for most of INS's nationwide apprehensions of administrative violators (EWIs and visa abusers)—88 percent in fiscal year 1983. Overwhelmingly, patrol agents deal in Mexican EWI offenders, most of whom are returned to the border under voluntary return.

In Chapter 4, the very different operational styles and objectives of the border patrol and the investigations branch are compared. Chapter 4 also includes a brief description of the border patrol's farm and ranch check operations. In Chapters 5, 6, and 7, the interior enforcement activities of the investigation branch are examined in depth.

ON THE LINE

In the old days, as agents refer to the relatively tranquil period of the early 1960s, before the trickle of illegal crossers became a torrent, stations like Calexico in central California or Nogales in Arizona might apprehend between 30 and 50 illegal aliens a month; compare this with the 4,000 and 1,500 respective monthly apprehensions that were being made during the peak agricultural season in 1983. Twenty years ago, in the Chula Vista sector, it was rare for the monthly catch of illegal aliens crossing from Tijuana to exceed a hundred. Now, between 30,000 and 50,000 are arrested in the peak spring and summer months. In the 1960s, agents had the time to "cut sign" (apply the old Indian art of tracking learned at the border patrol academy) on illegal desert crossers. (Ironically, today this method is sometimes used by the patrol to track reservation Indians, and other outdoors enthusiasts, who have become disoriented and lost in wilderness areas.)[4]

Those agents whose service extends as far back as the 1950s and early 1960s recall how an agent might spend one or two days tracking a single alien through the desert. Agents took pride in being there first, before somebody else made the arrest. Now, although cutting sign is still practiced in areas where the flow across the border is light (for example, in desert areas near El Centro, California, or in the Tucson sector), it has become a luxury in such urban areas as Chula Vista and El Paso. The reason is obvious: Illegal entries are far too numerous. (In April 1983, Chula Vista's 600 agents were apprehending 2,000 illegal aliens a day.)[5]

Despite the mobilization of patrol agents in vans, helicopters, and all-terrain cycles, many aliens elude apprehension simply because they vastly outnumber the agents on duty, who must also spend time writing up the I-213 arrest forms and returning those they apprehend back to Mexican customs. Also, the paved roads in urban areas hamper efforts to cut sign on illegal crossers. On dirt roads, too, where tracks can be spotted, prints of illegal aliens are apt to be intermingled with the foot traffic of citizen and lawful alien pedestrians. However, the agents sometimes use their tracking skill to detect fresh crossings in a river bed or along a trail.[6]

How many illegal entries are, in fact, deterred by agents on linewatch cannot be known. However, it is known that when special details of agents are added to a station on the line—as happened during 1983 when Mexico's worsening economic crisis led to an increase in apprehensions, and hence presumably in the total flow (detected and undetected crossings)—some of the pressure of illegal traffic moved along the border to less heavily patrolled segments. In March 1983, when an additional 100 patrol agents were assigned to Chula Vista to help stanch the increased influx, many illegals simply moved eastward, and in April, apprehensions rose 67 percent in El Centro and 126 percent at Yuma (Arizona).[7]

Although some agents claim the patrol catches between 25 and 35 percent of the illegals coming across, there is no valid way of determining the catch ratio. If it is as low as the agents suggest, an alien would appear to have a better than fifty-fifty chance on any given attempt. If the chances are that good, it is hard to understand why aliens would pay $30 to $50 for guides to lead them across. (It is possible that some aliens prefer to cross over with guides in groups because they fear being victimized by borderland bandits.) It may also be that the risk of apprehension has diminished because more professional smugglers are being used today, which the dramatic increase in border patrol apprehensions of smugglers, in fact, suggests. In 1983, more than 13,000 smugglers and 86,000 smuggled aliens were apprehended. Contrast that with the 3,800 smugglers and 20,000 smuggled aliens interdicted in 1971.[8]

Even if an alien's risk of apprehension by linewatch officers is substantially higher than the agents' estimate of 25 to 30 percent, this may not mean very much because the determined alien will always get through. The cost to the alien is the inconvenience of having to try more than one, two, or perhaps even three times. As the agents say, the odds favor the alien. (Aliens unlucky enough to be caught repeatedly over a short period of time may be set up for a deportation hearing, if they are visually identified as repeat crossers by the agents despite the use of aliases and the absence of documentation. Sometimes they are held overnight in barracks so the agents will not have to chase them down again that evening. Although the chances are low that an alien will be written up for a hearing, the fact that the risk does exist may explain why perhaps as many as 50 percent of border crossers decide to use guides and professional smugglers.)

That large numbers of aliens successfully elude the linewatch screen is common knowledge because of the known presence of large concentrations of illegals in the interior. That it is fairly easy to circumvent the linewatch is indicated by the fact that many Mexicans apprehended far into the interior do not bother to collect their pay or belongings before being returned to Mexico by the INS. As one youth who was picked up three times in El Paso before finally getting to his job in New Mexico put it, "Getting stopped is no big deal. You take the bus back, hang around Juarez near the railroad yard, talk to people, and find out about a better spot to cross."[9]

Although the linewatch screen cannot deter the determined illegal entrant, the fact that large numbers of aliens (40 to 50 percent by INS estimates) use smugglers would indicate that the border patrol's enforcement activities create an unofficial tariff for entry that would not exist in its absence. The growth of professional smuggling rings during the 1970s, following on the heels of the border patrol's increase in manpower and their technological upgrading, suggests that the risk of apprehension may have increased somewhat compared with that of the late 1960s and early 1970s.

Aliens who are unwilling to risk making an unaided effort to enter and are also unable or unwilling to pay a smuggler's fee could be said to have been deterred. But one cannot know their number. Because single males in the prime working ages are disproportionately apprehended, the border screen might be viewed as a sorting mechanism that selects those EWI aliens who enter with the expectation of working and who presumably are able to afford the costs of entry. Absent the screen, it is conceivable (though not certain) that a less productive group, including more women, children, and elderly persons might attempt surreptitious entries in larger numbers. (Of the 946,000

Mexican aliens listed as arrested in transit in 1983, less than 14 percent were females and children.) [10]

However, it is known that a much higher percentage of illegal Mexicans in the United States are females. [11] Small children and elderly relatives are also known to be living illegally in the United States. That they are less frequently arrested may be due to the fact that they cross back and forth less frequently, but it is also possible that more of them pass into the United States with inspection by using borrowed shoppers' cards or other fraudulent immigration papers. [12] Conceivably, females may run less risk of apprehension in the interior because they are more apt to be working at places that are less frequently raided. More work as private domestics or motel workers. Also, females are apparently more likely to keep to their neighborhoods. (Their arrest rate may also be lower because of unofficial INS policy decisions that seek to minimize female apprehensions. When this does occur, it is due to the added resource costs of processing and detaining females and children.) [13]

In monetary terms, if the alien has a package deal, which sometimes includes delivery to a guaranteed job in the interior, the smuggling cost can run from $200 to $800 for passage across by foot and vehicle transportation into the interior. Some smugglers charge half price for children, although children are apparently more likely to be smuggled through POEs posing as lawfully resident children of (usually) lawfully resident or citizen relatives who transport them into the country as a favor to parents already in the interior.

Aliens can get through at lower cost if all they want is a border guide. A *pollero* (literally chicken boy) charges $30 to $50 to guide aliens several hundred yards across the line, from which point they arrange their own travel by bus or cab. Some illegals arrange to have a friend who can cross legally pick them up on the U.S. side by car after they have crossed on foot. Others borrow I-186 shoppers' cards to cross through inspected auto or pedestrian lanes and hope that if the lines are backed up and the inspectors are too busy to do more than give the cards a cursory look, they will be waved through primary inspection. Some try to sneak through inspected vehicle lanes by hiding in luggage compartments, in tire wells, under the hood, in the toilet compartments of recreational vans, and so on.

A NOGALES ARREST:
THE DYNAMICS OF FIELD INTERROGATIONS

The following account, which is based on observations I made during a field trip to Nogales, Arizona, illustrates some of the dilemmas agents face when they seek to sort out the facts about the immigration statuses of the individuals they suspect may be deportable aliens.

The patrol agent I am riding with accelerates the green Volare sedan down the hill toward the commercial center of Nogales, Arizona, a small border town. We are driving along a parched gully that runs parallel to the Mexican border, which is a hundred or so yards to the south. In the Nogales border patrol station, it is policy to respond whenever a sensor is triggered.

Behind a cinderblock house visible just beyond the gully, there is a cyclone fence with a gap in it. Hidden in the mesquite a few yards away from that gap is an electronic sensor that alerts the border patrol station to any foot traffic in the area. Sometimes it is "good traffic," but occasionally the sensors are triggered by stray animals or kids riding dirt bikes.

Sometimes the holes in this fence are patched, but there are advantages to leaving most of them alone. If they are patched up, new gaps may be opened up elsewhere along the line, and new sensors will have to be installed at the new locations, which may not be readily accessible for the agents.

When sensors are triggered anywhere along the border, this information is transmitted electronically to an agent who monitors a central control panel in the station headquarters and who relays it on to the patrol sedans; the patrol unit nearest the sensor will usually respond.

Although the agents appreciate having seismic and electronic sensors as technological aids to their work, some are irritated by the fact that these hidden sentries now control their initiative in the field. Although often helpful, they can also be a nuisance, as when they are triggered not by illegal crossers but by animals or children. A technological spin-off from the Vietnam era, the sensors have routinized certain aspects of linewatch enforcement. When sensor 187 on the western edge of town goes off, for example, the agent knows exactly where to park and exactly how many minutes should elapse before heads pop up on the ridge a hundred or so yards from the parked patrol car. Also, the triggering of strings of sensors that fan out along the parched gully defiles indicates the direction a group is taking and their approximate number. The agents can wait until the illegals reach the most convenient place for apprehension.

Smugglers eventually catch on as their groups are apprehended with increasing frequency. Then they either search out new crossing points or try to locate and disable the sensors. When the border patrol becomes aware of a shift in smuggler crossing points, the agents adjust their tactics accordingly.

Illegal crossers are often allowed to load up in smuggler vehicles and move down the highway because it is easier to "take down" (arrest) a load on the highway. Aliens have nowhere to go in the desert, which is a dangerous place. A sudden summer downpour can turn a wash into a watery grave. Rattlesnakes are everywhere and can't be seen at night. Also, apprehending a load about to assemble in the town parking lots favored by smugglers can cause problems. If the aliens run, they may knock over shoppers. Apprehensions must be carefully orchestrated to ensure safety as well as productivity. The best apprehensions are those that go smoothly, with no injuries to the agents, the aliens, and any pedestrians in the area. In the view of most agents, the safety of aliens and other traffic takes precedence over arresting a load. For example, when a smuggler's load car is stopped on the highway, if the driver and the illegals pile out and make a run for it, the first thing the agent does is to make sure the car is under control and the ignition off. When the driver tries to outrun a pursuit sedan, the agent will turn on the red lights and pursue for a while. The hope is that the red lights will intimidate the driver into stopping, but if it becomes obvious that this will not happen and there is traffic in the area, the agent will usually abandon the chase. Catching a few more illegal aliens isn't worth risking human life in a highway crash.

As the agent I am riding with turns the sedan down the winding residential street leading to the center of town, he observes two men emerge from a gravel drive near the gap in the fence by the cinderblock house. As they begin walking down the street, it becomes clear to the agent that they are headed for the department store at the bottom of the hill. If they get to the store, they can lose themselves in the crowd and then re-emerge on the main street and continue walking to their rendezvous with the smuggler. Soon they would be on their way to Houston, Los Angeles, Denver, or wherever they have arranged to be taken.

Aliens in transit to jobs in the interior take priority over locals who live on the Mexican side. Many Nogales Mexicans cross the border to fill water barrels or, lacking the I-186 border-crossing cards more affluent Mexicans can obtain, cross through the holes to buy goods in U.S. stores. Others cross to visit relatives living legally on the U.S. side, often for a holiday visit. The agent either knows them by sight or can tell they are locals because they exhibit less apprehension when they sight a patrol agent. Illegals, according to the agents, always give themselves away—usually by their furtive behavior but sometimes by the kind of clothing they wear and their haircuts.

Although technically they are immigration violators, locals are usually not worth troubling over. Little is gained from apprehending Mexicans who intend to return to the Mexican side of town. Strict enforcement of the law against the locals would only irritate people who are not going to be prosecuted under the criminal provisions of the law or even processed for deportation unless they are suspected of coming over to shoplift or burglarize.

The agent I am riding with suspects that the two men are illegal aliens in transit. Having reached the bottom of the gully, the sedan sprints past the loading docks at the rear of the commercial buildings that front on Nogales's main thoroughfare. Then the agent turns the car up the narrow street on the south side of the gully to meet the two males. The agent is certain that they triggered the sensor. One of the men, who is wearing a goatee, Levis, and a white T-shirt, suddenly veers into a driveway, while his companion, a slender man dressed in chino pants, continues along the street toward the department store. He looks straight ahead as though nothing unusual is going on despite his companion's abrupt departure.

Patrol agents claim that U.S. citizens of Mexican descent can easily be distinguished from illegals. United States citizens are much more likely to give an agent a belligerent look than illegals, who will often pretend the agent doesn't exist. They appear to assume that if they don't look at the agent, the agent won't look at them.

The agent leaps out of the car and calls to the man in the T-shirt, who has been dead-ended at a carport. He orders him straightaway into the rear seat, then goes down the hill after the second man. He returns with the man wearing chinos a minute or two later. Resting his clipboard with the I-213 form on the steering column, the agent turns to the first man and asks, "*Donde nacio?*" As a general rule, agents at the border (and depending on the circumstances, occasionally in the interior) would avoid using a question such as "Are you a U.S. citizen?" or "What country are you a citizen of?" The reason is that doing so might create unnecessary complications. For one thing, it might encourage an illegal alien to try to evade apprehension with a false citizenship or lawful residence claim. Near the border, when the agent asks the individual "*donde nacio?*" there is a useful ambiguity. Individuals from Mexico are expected to tell the officer where in Mexico (which state or city) they are from. The agents assume that, if those they approach are U.S. citizens, they can be expected to say so. If they are lawful permanent residents (green-card holders) or are carrying valid I-186 cards, they can also be expected to show their cards or explain their status at the time they answer.

Deeper in the U.S. interior, an officer might first ask the question in English to determine if the individual understands English. The reason is that if the person appeared uncomprehending, when asked the first question in English, it would bolster the reasonable suspicion needed by the agent to continue the interrogation. The agent would then be justified in forcibly detaining the person while determining the individual's immigration status through additional questioning. Because of the potential legal hazard, agents do not lightly make decisions to detain.[14]

In this particular case, the first man to be ordered into the car gruffly replied in English that he was born in Los Angeles. The agent, immediately skeptical because of the way the individual had behaved when the car pulled up, asked the man a series of questions about his background. Where did he live in Los Angeles? Who are his parents and where were they born? What hospital was he born in? What part of Los Angeles did he grow up in? The man's evasive and uncertain replies prompted the officer to try several more questions. Did he graduate from high school? The man claimed he had. Did he graduate in math? He nodded that he had. Did he graduate in prom? Again, the suspected alien said he had.

The agent then informed him that prom is not taught in U.S. high schools. Impatiently putting aside his pen and the arrest form, the agent turned to the second man and asked him where he was born. The second man readily conceded both that he was Mexican and that he had entered illegally. (Later, the agent told me he had broken off his interrogation of the first individual and decided to question his companion in the hope that the second man would set an example, thus helping convince his companion it was useless to stonewall.)

The agent obtained the necessary information for the I-213 arrest form and then turned around in his seat toward the man in the T-shirt. With an impatient look he asked, "*Otra vez, donde nacio?*" (One more time, where were you born?) After a brief pause, the man told the agent he was born in Mexico City.

Within the span of about twenty minutes, the two men were apprehended, written up on the I-213 form, given the I-274 waiver to sign, and then returned to the border. (The I-274 informs aliens of their right to be represented by an attorney and have a hearing; in signing it, aliens waive their right to a hearing.) The agent realized that the men could walk a hundred yards back up the hill and try to enter again later. If he caught them a second time, he said, he would take them down to the station and dig into the problem in more detail because the one who spoke some English might have been a smuggling guide.

Had they been brought back to the station and identified as repeat violators by the agent's colleagues, the officer might have decided to write them up for a deportation hearing. Identifiable repeat border crossers will sometimes be written up for hearings (rather than granted voluntary return) to get across the important point that there are limits to the agents' patience with flagrant abuse of the law and that a grant of voluntary return is always at the officers' discretion.

Away from the border, the officer must give more thought to the grounds for approaching and questioning an individual. Although the same constitutional requirement (reasonable suspicion based on articulable facts of alienage) applies everywhere except at inspected POEs and certain checkpoints near the border, the officer is apt to encounter more ambiguity in the interior. In some cases, the officer will have prior knowledge of the individual's alienage based on an informant's tip or an alien's prior service record. When there is no prior information because the individual has no prior INS record (or is not recognized by officers as a person previously apprehended), the officer must be able to observe and articulate aspects of behavior and appearance that point to alienage. (In some jurisdictions, court decisions require that agents have articulable facts pointing to illegal alienage.) After approaching and beginning to talk with the individual, the agent's founded suspicion may ripen further as additional facts suggestive of illegal alienage come to light. This in turn would justify forcibly detaining the individual until it can be determined whether the individual is likely to be deportable, which would be based on how further questions are answered or on the alien's own admission.

For example, suspected illegal aliens may become flustered and nervous. Upon sighting a patrol agent, they may refuse to look the officer in the eye and glance around nervously. Their hands may start to shake. They may try to elude apprehension by claiming to be citizens or lawful residents. As the agent talks to them, inconsistencies in what they tell the agent begin to crop up. When the agent asks to see identification, their wallets contain a bogus green card in one name and a purchase receipt for an auto in a different name (probably the real one).

When dealing with Mexican EWIs, especially in the border areas, the agent will usually have at least two or more articulable facts pointing to *illegal* alienage (rather than just alienage) to go on even before beginning to talk to the individual. The officer notices clothing of Mexican manufacture or furtive behavior on the alien's part that might have been triggered by the officer's appearance on the scene.

As a matter of professional routine, agents try to single out and approach only those they think have a reasonable likelihood of being illegal. There is no statistical credit for spending time on persons who are not illegal; also, citizens and lawful residents may be irritated when stopped and questioned. Because there are always more than enough illegal aliens to go after, agents have every incentive to make productive apprehensions. Organizational incentives dovetail with the agents' professional pride in their ability to make accurate (even if only probabilistic) judgments of an individual's immigration status in advance of approaching and talking to the person.

Most agents are also mindful of the need for good public relations. Americans of Mexican descent who are approached and questioned may become annoyed. They are irritated, less because of the fact that the agent has taken up a half minute or so of their time than because of the fact that the agent mistook them for a *mojado* (wetback). Such individuals are apt to respond, "Do I look like a *mojado*?" or ask, "When are you guys going to realize who I am? How many times are you going to keep asking me about my status?" To spare embarrassment on both sides, agents will sometimes mask their purpose when they approach individuals they aren't sure about. They will ask in English if the suspected illegal happened to see two men pass by and then give a physical description of the two fictional persons. The agent will observe how the person whose status is being covertly checked answers these questions and whether that individual understands English well. Usually that is sufficient for the agent to decide whether to continue with an overt status determination. (If the suspected illegal appears confused or unable to understand English, the agent switches to Spanish and asks where the person was born. At that point, a covert interrogation has become an official alienage and deportability check.)

Such covert interrogatory conversations can be thought of as a face-saving, foot-in-the-door method of establishing legally adequate articulable facts to justify an official immigration check. They are also used on occasion by plainclothes investigators in the cities, where the ambiguities of status are apt to be even greater than in a border town. The ambiguity arises from the fact that EWIs, and most other immigration violators, are status offenders whose violations are not discrete acts having tangible clues or willing witnesses. Nor are immigration offenses behaviors that INS officers can spot visually, except when aliens are actually observed crossing the border. In most cases, violations can be definitively established only after talking to the individual approached.

Such field practices grow up within the interstices of law and policy because of the unique constitutional constraints law officers are subjected to in our society. But aside from the constitutional niceties, citizens do not like to be stopped and questioned by officers in uniform. Disguised or covert interrogations make it possible for the officers to handle the situational ambiguity arising from the fact that immigration offenses are not *per se* observable. Thus sidling up to a suspected illegal alien and asking the time of day or information about a bus route helps to minimize the personal friction that would arise from resort to direct official inquiries right at the start. (As is noted later, INS officers can easily circumvent the constitutional requirements. To justify a stop, officers can easily claim that they thought the individual was wearing Mexican clothing, behaved furtively, or closely resembled a person they had processed before. Thus, productivity considerations, along with the desire to avoid frictions with citizens, are probably much more relevant to field practice.)

The officers' belief that illegal aliens, unless streetwise or long-term U.S. residents, give themselves away by their dress, grooming, and behavior is a firmly held professional dogma. Officers invariably assert that when illegals see patrol agents, they'll quickly avert their gaze, look down at their feet, or (if they are in a bus or train station) begin looking around furtively for the exits. Or, spotted on a commercial street, they edge up to and along the building walls, as though hoping a door will appear where they need it rather than where it was built. Even when agents can't consciously tick off the articulable facts, required by law before approaching a suspected alien or forcibly detaining an individual who is suspected of illegal alienage, they know, they claim, who is "wet" after months and years of working with illegal Mexicans.

The function of this professional dogma is that it helps to firm up the officer's decision to approach and question individuals who, upon questioning, may turn out not to be illegal aliens. Despite their professional dogma of infallibility, officers know that their determinations of status in advance of interrogation are probabilistic and that mistakes occur. (Indeed, the professional dogma of infallibility applies mainly to Mexicans. In the case of OTM aliens encountered in public places [rather than being specifically sought on the basis of a tip], the officers can rarely make accurate judgments of illegal alienage based on visual observation alone—a fact of which they are painfully aware.)

The arrest of the two men caught near the Nogales border fence illustrates how field officers handle the arrest decision in a context of low ambiguity. The agent I was with believed he had adequate reasonable suspicion both to approach the men and detain them if necessary. First, a nearby sensor had been triggered. Second, he knew that illegals often enter through the hole near that sensor and also knew that these two men didn't belong to the neighborhood. But his strongest articulable fact for forcibly detaining them, which occurred when he ordered them into the car, was their furtive behavior upon seeing the patrol sedan coming toward them.

CHARACTERISTICS OF LINEWATCH APPREHENSIONS

Linewatch apprehensions are among the most highly routinized of the warrantless arrests made by patrol agents. Interrogations are usually brief, and voluntary return under safeguard to Mexican customs is the typical disposition. Although the high productivity is primarily due to the large numbers of illegals encountered, the lessened situational ambiguity confronting the agents is also an important factor because, in most cases, the articulable facts required for an interrogation are easily obtained. Often the time of day (night) and the location (deserted places where illegals are known to cross, places that normal pedestrian traffic would avoid) are sufficient for approaching and talking to an individual. As is discussed in Chapter 4, routinized apprehensions also occur during most farm and ranch checks.

Because of the greater heterogeneity and ambiguity of statuses of the people who can be expected to be moving about, when suspected deportable aliens are stopped during daylight hours in urbanized areas along the border, the field procedure is more likely to resemble that used in the interior. In the cities, citizens, lawful residents, and deportable aliens may all be found working in the same plant—or standing in the same bus line.

Groups encountered back of the linewatch in isolated desert locales usually pose few problems. Sometimes groups numbering as many as 50 to 70 people are stumbled across by patrol agents who happened to arrive before the smuggler showed up with transportation. On the immediate border, they might have tried to make a run for it. But little is gained by running off in a remote desert place. Often the aliens will have arranged with their smuggler to reassemble at a prearranged place and time on the Mexican side if they are caught before they get transportation into the interior. Also, many smugglers agree to deliver before full payment is made. As a result of these factors, a lone agent, or two, can control the entire group. In cases where the aliens have been abandoned by an unscrupulous smuggler, they may be hungry, thirsty, and suffering from exposure. They are glad to be found.

Linewatch enforcement in San Ysidro, the U.S. border town abutting Tijuana, poses certain problems not encountered in the smaller border towns located in less heavily urbanized areas. For one thing, the terrain affords more cover, and the suburban parts of the San Diego metropolitan area are close by. (From Nogales, by contrast, the alien has a 90-mile trek to Tucson, and there are few jobs for illegals in that sector.) Aliens do not have to travel far to lose themselves in the San Diego metropolitan area where border patrol monitoring is more difficult. In consequence, many will run if they think they have a fair chance of getting across the Tijuana slough or Otay Mesa to the residential neighborhoods of Imperial Beach or into the densely covered gullies that lead to the suburbs of Chula Vista.

At night, in the Brownfield linewatch segment of the San Ysidro station, which includes most of Otay Mesa, the agents will wait until the aliens have come up out of Spring Canyon and onto the mesa. Although the canyon is on the U.S. side, it is easier to catch and transport aliens on the mesa top than down in the canyon.

On the mesa top, agents can tell when the illegals are moving up from Spring Canyon because the lights in Tijuana just beyond the rim will begin to flicker in a moving line, like ducks going down in a carnival gallery. After a group has moved up onto the mesa, the patrol vans move into action, sometimes with the aid of helicopters whose noise and searchlights are useful in corralling larger groups. Sometimes an agent will hide in underbrush and wait for a group to pass by. Then, when another agent, the partner, emerges to confront the group directly, the officer who was hidden appears suddenly to block any who might try to run back to the border. According to the agents, the groups are generally smaller now than they were five to ten years ago. This is because of the patrol's altered tactics, particularly the use of agents on horseback and in helicopters.

On linewatch in the western segment nearer the beach, some agents are stationed down in the marshy flats while other agents are stationed on higher ground across the slough where they can act as spotters, pinpointing groups of aliens with infrared scopes. Alerted by radio, the agents down in the marshlands move in on horseback and all-terrain cycles to make the apprehensions.

Aliens who have managed to get past the screen are occasionally spotted by San Diego police, who sometimes hold them until a patrol van can collect them. Cooperation between the local police and the patrol is good in most areas close to the border. Local police believe that illegal traffic poses a crime problem and are glad to assist the patrol. (Although most aliens in transit enter to work, *cholos* [hoods] and other unsavory types often cross over to steal.)

On the Brownfield (eastern) segment of the line, agents on what is called stillwatch do not use the infrared scope, although this is used in the marshy area near the beach. With so many ravines leading up to and away from the mesa, the groups are not as easily spotted with the infrared binoculars. And in a few places, the aliens need only to bound 50 or so yards across the mesa top before reaching the gullies and their covering foliage on the other side.

Closer in to San Ysidro, near the bus depot, young Mexicans will try to push their way through the bars above the wall of the pedestrian corridor leading to the U.S. inspections checkpoint while others remain on the watch for INS and customs officers who might suddenly appear. Along a dirt road that abuts the tall cyclone fence running from the center of town along Tijuana's tough Colonia Libertad neighborhood, the patrol's light green vans are sometimes pelted with rocks thrown by *cholos* trying to distract the agents so a guide can safely move a group up the canyon.[15]

Although once considered a country club station, by the mid-1970s, San Ysidro had become a hard-duty outpost. Levels of violence increased with the rise in drug and alien smuggling. Also, California's rapidly inflating living costs, the increased abuse directed toward agents, and the more strenuous management problems posed by heavier illegal traffic made it less desirable duty for career agents. It is now considered a good place to train green recruits just out of the academy.

At the POE itself, INS inspectors have enforcement problems of their own. On the vehicle and pedestrian lanes, INS inspectors check for both customs and immigration violations and develop the same sixth sense the patrol agents say they rely on to spot tip-offs to drug or alien smuggling.

Some Mexicans with shoppers cards pass through to work in the United States, which is illegal. An inspector who sees a paystub from a local U.S. business sticking out of an envelop on the seat of a car passing through inspection and finds that it belongs to an individual carrying a shoppers card can confiscate the card. Because of the value of the I-186 shoppers cards, many Mexicans mail them back to their Tijuana addresses after they have entered the United States. In the event they are apprehended at work, they do not want the cards found on their persons.

Also, some aliens will try to pass inspection with a false oral claim to U.S. citizenship because citizens are not required to carry documents. Some who worry that their claim might not be believed, arrive with birth certificates. But they give themselves away when the inspectors observe them reading the document too intently in a last-minute effort to memorize the information.

In the ten-year span from 1971 to 1981, apprehensions in the Chula Vista sector increased more than fivefold, from 60,000 to 327,000. And in 1983, they increased to 430,000 apprehensions.[16] Chula Vista accounts for almost half of all southern border apprehensions and about 35 percent to 40 percent of all servicewide apprehensions.

TRANSPORTATION CHECK

In the San Ysidro station headquarters, which adjoins the larger POE inspections terminal and is only a few yards from Mexican customs, a squad of plainclothes border patrol agents are briefed by their supervisor for the evening run into downtown San Diego, where they will check the freight yard, Amtrak terminal, and the Greyhound station. Transportation checks are carried out during those hours when illegal aliens in transit are most likely to appear in airports and bus and train terminals.

Arriving at the Amtrak terminal, the agents mix casually into the crowd of waiting passengers and scan those who appear to be candidates for a check. When a northbound train to Los Angeles arrives, one of the agents boards and returns with a young man. Though his dress is similar to that of the other passengers boarding, something about his behavior triggered the agent's decision to talk to him.

The patrol agents then move on to San Diego's Greyhound depot. They no longer work the residential neighborhoods because doing so can lead to unpleasant confrontations with citizens and immigrants of Mexican descent, some of whom will rally to the defense of the illegal aliens in their neighborhoods. Teenage gang members add to their reputations if they can knock down a patrol agent in a street brawl.

There is another reason for staying out of the neighborhoods. As one agent explained: "If you start picking people up in neighborhoods, you'd wind up with whole families. That's messy, administratively, because there's a detention problem." According to the agents, even though those apprehended might be deportable, illegals who have settled in have less likelihood of being sent back to Mexico. If they have resided in the United States for any period of time, they are likely to have acquired equities and may insist on hearings.

The first agents to arrive at the Greyhound station amble about casually, playing the role of ordinary passengers waiting for a bus. They watch for the cues of behavior and dress that indicate who in the crowd is apt to be illegal. As a rule, nobody is approached until the rest of the squad has arrived. The key to a smooth operation is to have sufficient agents on hand to achieve effective control. Illegals are less likely to scramble for the exits if they believe they are outnumbered. Besides being a nuisance, a physical chase may bring unfavorable public attention and possibly complaints. Most Americans have little familiarity with the work INS officers do. Plainclothes officers tell about citizens who, not knowing what was going on when officers were trying to arrest an alien, tried to intervene because they thought the officers were mugging an innocent bystander.

Because of the lack of public awareness of INS enforcement combined with the fact that officers deal with status violators whose offenses are not so readily visible, officers in plainclothes prefer a low profile. Their snub-nosed .38 revolvers are tucked out of view in waistband holsters covered by a sports coat or windbreaker. At one time plainclothes officers were required to wear business suits. But in the old days, fewer aliens had to be chased, wrestled down, or pulled out from dusty and sometimes dangerous hiding places. Most officers wear leisure-style clothing now.

The officers develop perceptions of the modal behavior patterns they can anticipate in certain locales, and these shape their field tactics to an extent. Illegals traveling in a group to catch a train often avoid bunching up together when they arrive to purchase their tickets. The one who knows some English will buy the tickets while the others wait outside. Should the one purchasing the ticket be approached by an officer, the others will still have a chance to make a dash for it—a good reason for thoroughly scouting a bus or train depot before moving to make arrests. (When illegals are being smuggled by professional rings, a lawful resident working for the smugglers may buy the tickets and may also make sure the way is clear before the aliens are brought into the station.)

Still, most unacculturated Mexican EWIs tend to behave in ways that give themselves away. If they have just crossed over as a group, they will be spotted walking toward the station or through the freight yard spaced three or four yards apart in a single file, just as they walked up the trails from Spring Canyon. They will have bits of brush in their hair or dust on their pants from hiding under "lay up" bushes, or they will have punchbowl-style Mexican haircuts and clothing of Mexican manufacture, such as long-sleeved, button-down shirts and heavy shoes.

When agents approach a Mexican EWI, they try to remember not just that the alien was wearing Mexican clothing but the specific kind of clothing worn. There is always the possibility, albeit remote, that they might have to justify the apprehension in a deportation hearing or court challenge. As one expressed the problem: "If you say a man looked like a Mexican [national], they'll drop the bomb on you, even though that's exactly what he looked like. You have to spot those specific distinguishing things about them and be able to spell them out."

Professional smugglers, who charge $250 to $600, might try to tidy their clients up, perhaps even groom them sufficiently so that they more closely resemble better acculturated immigrants or citizens, at least at a superficial glance. Also, professional smugglers would most likely arrange for transit by private conveyances through to the final destination rather than letting their clients hang around public transportation terminals, which are the very places the border patrol visits regularly. (When professional smugglers use trains, they may have a man on the inside—for instance, an Amtrak clerk on the lookout to make sure the station isn't under patrol surveillance when the aliens are delivered.)

At the Greyhound station, a group of four Hispanic teenagers is approached and questioned by two agents. Two of the four are allowed to continue on their way, but the other two, a male and female, are taken to a parking lot next to the terminal, where a patrol van is already beginning to fill up.

Although the girl spoke reasonably good English, she had no documents on her. The agents decided to ask her more questions to establish the validity of her claim to green-card status. When they were satisfied, she was told she could go. (Immigration and Naturalization Service officers can spend all the time they require to check out the status of an individual who claims to be a lawful resident if that individual has no card. In the case of a citizen, policy varies. Most agents said they would be reluctant to hold a citizen claimant they strongly suspected of being illegal more than an hour or so, even if they felt their suspicion was well-founded.)

The agents then patted down her male companion. Although the youth claimed to be immigrated, he had no papers. His furtiveness also made the agents suspicious. They called in for a check on the service's central computer, using the surname he had given. The computer check turned out negative (no service alien registration [A-file] number to match the name). Because the computer information is notoriously unreliable, the agents do not assume that a negative check necessarily means the alien has lied about his status. Among other problems, including programmer error, many lawful residents are not listed in the computer, or if listed, their hyphenated last names may have been transposed. Thus, although a positive computer check can help expedite the release of aliens who are lawful (assuming they haven't borrowed somebody's name and number), a negative kickback does not prove that any alien claiming green-card status is necessarily illegal. Because of this problem, most agents rely on further questioning to assist aliens in establishing the validity of their oral claims. They will ask questions that immigrated aliens should be able to answer, such as what procedures they went through to obtain immigrant status. Younger aliens, who are not required to carry cards until they are fourteen years of age, will be asked to supply the names of their parents or guardians and a telephone number or address where they can be reached.

The agent who had taken over the interrogation of the young man asked him to show his wallet so he could check any identification he might be carrying that would help confirm his immigration claim. Upon inspection, the wallet turned up a piece of paper bearing a number the agent recognized as a Mexican phone number because of the arrangement of the digits. Although the youth had told the officer he had not been back to Mexico for four years, the discovery of the phone number strengthened the officer's suspicion that the path of questioning would lead to a finding of deportability. (Often wallets or pockets will turn up an assortment of identification, sometimes in different names. That, plus any other inconsistencies between the paper documentation being carried and statements the individual makes to the officer, will strengthen the presumption of illegal alienage.)

The officer's gut feeling that the youth was bluffing was based heavily on the young man's refusal to make eye contact coupled with the fact that the youth's answers were just not adding up. As he explained, "The kid's carrying a brand new wallet but can't remember where he bought it. He can't remember when his mother and father were born. He claims he's got a green card but there's no record of it in the computer. If the kid's the LPR [legal permanent resident] he claims to be, he should know the age at which he was fingerprinted, which is fourteen years, but he doesn't have the answers to any of these questions."

As the agents view the matter, a bona fide green-card holder would know at least some of the right answers.

The agent was finally able to "break" the youth of the claim when he spotted a trolley ticket in his shirt. Although the youth claimed he had not been back to Mexico since he immigrated with his parents four years earlier, the ticket suggested to the officer that he had just come up from Tijuana and was lying. Using this discovery as leverage, he asked the youth why he had lied, and at that point, the youth conceded that he was not the green-card holder he had earlier claimed to be. Although the agents are not as a rule angered when an alien makes a brief attempt to evade arrest with a false claim, this agent did become irritated because the youth had stonewalled for close to half an hour.

Afterward, the arresting officer said he tried to exercise care with a green-card claimant because, as he explained, "If you bust someone who's an LPR, then you have the whole Hispanic activist community down on you, which is why I try to give them enough time to explain their situation." However, agents face a dilemma when they encounter younger aliens (fifteen to nineteen years old). Youths may have legal status but may not be giving the right answers, either because they are frightened or because they cannot get their stories right—perhaps because they lack the requisite knowledge about their immigration status to pass the field interrogation.

Because the youth was not carrying his green card as required by law, the officer had adequate probable cause to make an arrest for the misdemeanor offense of nonpossession (if the youth was eighteen or over). However, because when they reach the station, the misdemeanor charge is almost universally waived under a blanket waiver policy, most officers prefer to avoid an arrest if they can satisfy themselves that the individual is a lawfully resident alien. The dilemma is that the pressure to resolve suspect claims in the field before taking an individual back to the station may lead to errors. Agents do occasionally apply psychological pressure in the form of strong language, and in consequence, it is conceivable that some lawful residents who lack identification might decide to agree to voluntary return rather than try to persuade an agent who is obviously deeply suspicious of their claims.

Thus the possibility always exists that nervous or disoriented lawful residents who cannot get their story straight might agree to accept voluntary return to Mexico. It is not known how often this happens, but when it does occur, it is probably not because the officer intended it but because the alien's story was hard to believe. Agents operate under field pressures that drive them to achieve speedy resolution of claims, some of which they know from experience are used to evade apprehension.[17]

To rationalize the verbal or psychological pressure an officer may have used to break a claim, the officer may reach beyond the alien's eventual admission of deportability, citing other incriminating characteristics of the alien's behavior to substantiate his or her official judgment that the alien was indeed deportable and did not admit to it merely because of verbal persuasion or psychological pressure.

Thus, in the Greyhound bus station arrest just described, the agent pointed out that the youth was streetwise because he had a kind of tattoo web on his thumb that Hispanic gang members wear. Also, citizens and lawful residents of Mexican descent are, according to the officers, more likely to be offended and tell the officer not to bother them when approached. As the arresting officer explained, "Gang members from the Mexican side don't come on that strong. And this kid wasn't even able to look us in the eye."

Although the agents refer to their sixth sense (to an unerring ability to sort illegal aliens from other people in preinterrogation visual spotting), they know they cannot be absolutely sure a person is a deportable alien until they have questioned that individual. For example, I watched while an agent approached a man at a drinking fountain in the Greyhound station. The agent had assumed the man was Mexican. When he showed him his INS badge, the individual calmly explained that he was a Filipino and pulled out his green card to prove it.

At this stage, a mistake in approaching an individual is rarely a problem because no adverse legal consequences will follow if it turns out that the person is a citizen or lawful resident. Only if the person is forcibly detained (prevented from leaving the scene or ordered into the van) might problems arise and at that stage, the agent had better have had very strong probable cause. If a citizen is seized, there can be public relations as well as legal troubles. (Even in the case of aliens who may technically be deportable, agents know they can be called on the carpet if they mistakenly return an alien who is, for example, under deportation proceedings or who has benefit adjudications pending.)

Although transportation checks in urban areas usually involve more situational ambiguity than is found on the linewatch, much depends on the setting. Ambiguity is apt to be higher in public terminals than, say, in freight yards, where only illegal aliens, hobos, and occasionally reservation Indians are apt to be found.

Agents also try as a tactical matter to separate the individuals they approach so they can be interviewed one-on-one or even two-on-one. Agents claim that, because of their macho culture, Mexicans who try to bluff with a false citizenship or a green-card claim are much more apt to persist when accompanied by friends who are able to overhear them. Thus breaking a false claim is easier when the individual is questioned out of earshot of others. In addition, there is less likelihood that others in the group might get the same idea of trying to bluff their way out of an arrest. Although false claims are numerically infrequent, they are viewed as a serious enforcement problem because they reduce the agent's field productivity and carry a risk of legal jeopardy for the agent as well.

TRAFFIC OBSERVATION

The border patrol's traffic observation function accounts for approximately 15 percent of officer hours (according to 1983 figures) ranking just after linewatch (40 percent) in terms of the allocation of officer hours to all enforcement activities. The objective is to interdict smuggling loads. This is achieved either at fixed checkpoints on highways that lead away from the border or by agents riding the highway on roving patrols.

At fixed checkpoints that have heavy traffic volume, such as San Clemente, which straddles Interstate 5 along the Pacific coast, heavy traffic requires that officers expedite the flow. (The same constraint applies at busy

POEs, where inspectors view their function as facilitating the entry of bona fide travelers in addition to interdicting mala fide entrants.) Thus agents can be observed waving vehicles through without necessarily asking any questions of the occupants. They stop and talk only to those drivers whose behavior, companions, or model of car (combined with other facts) lead them to suspect a smuggler's load car. In the fifth circuit, which includes Texas, patrol agents do not need reasonable suspicion to order a vehicle over to the side of the road for a secondary check of the trunk or other compartments at a fixed checkpoint. In the ninth circuit, which includes California, Nevada, Arizona, and Hawaii, citizens are not required to answer questions about their nationality and, indeed, are not required to stop at the checkpoint at all. In consequence, at fixed checkpoints in California, agents must have specific articulable facts that suggest that the vehicle may be ferrying illegal aliens before they direct the driver over to the roadside shoulder. In the ninth circuit, if the defendant's attorney can persuade the court that the arresting agent did not have adequate articulable facts to warrant the secondary inspection, the criminal case against the smuggler may be dismissed.[18] And in that case, all the patrol agent would net would be any deportable aliens found in the car, all of whom would normally be returned to Mexico after being interviewed. (For stops by roving patrols, the reasonable suspicion standard applies nationwide; agents must have articulable facts that the vehicle is carrying a smuggling load if they hope to prosecute the driver.)

However, the Fourth-Amendment constitutional standard for a stop and seizure, an essential prerequisite for criminal prosecution, is only one reason why agents rely on articulable facts. In view of the trivial sentences meted out to most smuggling load drivers, it may not be the most important one at that. Patrol agents conducting highway observation appear much more intent on getting adequate articulable facts so as to avoid unnecessarily inconveniencing citizen and other authorized travelers. (Indeed, a citizen or lawful resident who is stopped while traveling at high speed in a car is much more apt to resent the inconvenience of a stop than a pedestrian.)

That expediting traffic flows at fixed checkpoints takes priority over making smuggling arrests is indicated by the fact that during certain periods—at night, during inclement weather, and at times of peak traffic, such as weekends or holidays—the agents stationed between the marked lanes will move off the highway and onto the shoulder. From their vantage point on the shoulder, they will look for cars that appear to be carrying illegal aliens and then take off in pursuit.

When the agents are standing on "point" between the marked lanes and spot a car meeting their profile of a smuggler's load vehicle, they will motion the driver to slow down. They will ask a question or two before deciding whether to direct the car to the side or wave it on. Based on the additional facts generated by the brief questioning, the agent can decide whether a closer inspection is warranted.

However, most illegal aliens smuggled through a fixed checkpoint during hours when the agents are stationed out on the highway will be hidden from view. When illegals are seated in the car, it is more likely to be at night when the agents have moved onto the shoulder of the road. During daytime hours, the agents look for the telltale profile clues of a load car just as patrol agents carrying out immigration checks of pedestrians in public places or work sites look for appearance and behavior cues pointing to illegal status. Thus if a gap develops back in the lane and it appears that a car is moving to the median or over to the shoulder, this tips off the agent that the driver may be deciding whether to dump his load short of the checkpoint, at which point the aliens will pile out and make a run for it. A driver with a pulsating Adam's apple or knuckles white from gripping the steering wheel too tightly suggests to the agent someone who is apprehensive about something—possibly being caught with illegal aliens. In hot weather, a rolled-up window in a car without air-conditioning is another tip-off. (The driver hopes that if the window is rolled up, the agent will not attempt to start a conversation.) As with illegal aliens in a bus station or on the street, who will stare straight ahead as if to pretend that the patrol agent doesn't exist, some drivers will look rigidly ahead. Because they fail to show normal curiosity about the agents, they are more likely to be questioned.

Agents can work from a large assortment of articulable facts, some of which they themselves can generate. Thus, as a car passes by, the agent can give the rear end a light push. If there isn't any give, the trunk could be carrying illegals; then if a look at the rear axle reveals airshocks, the agent understands why the car was not observed riding low.

Given the heavy volume of traffic and the desire to avoid inconveniencing authorized travelers, such profile characteristics allow the agents to narrow down the cars to be checked to those with the highest probability of turning up a load.

Most of the smugglers arrested are small-time, independent (mom-and-pop) operators and *parientes* (drivers smuggling relatives) cases. They are seldom prosecuted on the felony charge of transporting unless there are aggravating factors.[19] Indeed, in heavy-volume sectors, such as Chula Vista, *parientes* drivers who are illegal are apt to be returned voluntarily with the aliens in their load. When independents and *parientes* (Category III and IV offenders[20]) are prosecuted, the cases are apt to be plea-bargained down to the misdemeanor of aiding and abetting illegal entry with sentences of time served (from one to a few days) and suspended sentences. The main problem agents confront is determining whether an apprehended load is a serious ring (Category I or II transporting) case. Many smugglers will ride with the aliens in the back of a van, leaving the driving to illegal aliens who thereby earn part or all of their smuggling fee. Also, smugglers may try to disguise their involvement in a commercial ring operation by having the involved aliens claim they all pitched in to buy the car, which would reduce the agents' interest in prosecution.

At San Clemente, professional smugglers prefer moving their loads through on Sunday afternoons or during inclement weather because the odds are more favorable. The agents will only be able to pursue a small percentage of the load cars and are apt to target those vehicles having the highest chance of carrying smuggled loads—for example, those whose occupants are visibly hunkered down in their seats when the patrol cars' headlamps sweep across as they pass.

For this reason, a typical weekday catch is more apt to consist of amateur smugglers in the Category III and IV classes, such as elderly retirees earning a few bucks to help with their boat payments, *parientes*, or a group of friends who pitched in to buy the car after crossing the border. (As noted, commercial load drivers will often use this as a cover story because they know that the Category III and IV cases are less likely to be prosecuted than the Category I and II ring cases.) Drivers will also sometimes claim they picked up the aliens hitchhiking. This is plausible if the aliens are visible as occupants and the driver did not seem to be acting strangely when approaching the checkpoint.

If the agents believe that the load might be part of a commercial operation, the occupants will be held until investigators in the antismuggling (ASU) unit are able to interview each individual separate from the rest to determine if any are willing to testify, whether gain was involved, and how their respective stories match up.

If one of the aliens in the load has all or most of the money, that individual is probably the smuggler. However, the agents are not likely to have a good case unless they can get one or more of the aliens to testify. Few aliens will do so unless they have been abused by the smuggler or feel they have been cheated. Although establishing gain (a commercial operation) is not statutorily required to charge a driver with felony transporting, it is usually a necessary element for interesting the assistant U.S. attorney in taking the case for prosecution.

Roving highway patrols, some operating hundreds of miles north of the border, pick off smuggling vehicles on highways known to be major routes for illegals seeking agricultural and urban jobs. Closer to the border, agents mainly observe northbound traffic and are alert to cars, vans, and semitrailers that might be candidates for a smuggling arrest. If there are dips in the highway, an agent will follow behind the vehicle to observe how it rides. If a passenger riding up front in a recreational vehicle (RV) when a patrol sedan passed going in the opposite direction has disappeared from view after the patrol car has reversed direction and come up behind and then alongside the RV, the agent has yet another articulable fact that, coupled with any others observed, may justify turning on the red lights and pulling the vehicle over. Some agents say they like to have as many as four or five strong articulables before stopping a vehicle.

The agent may also drive alongside a car and wave to the driver to see what sort of response there will be. If the driver refuses to respond, becomes rigid, or looks at the right-hand side of the road for a place to pull over (and perhaps let people out), there is that much more probable cause for stopping the car. Waving a greeting to test a driver's reaction is analogous to the covert interrogations some officers use to decide whether to question a pedestrian.

As noted, on roving patrol, the agents usually try to reach a higher standard of probable cause than would typically be used to justify stopping and inspecting a car at a fixed checkpoint. For example, while I was riding with an agent in Tucson, Arizona, we passed alongside a Chevy Nova that was "jacked up" (had airshocks) and carried Hispanic occupants. When the agent looked over at the car, its driver and passengers did not exhibit normal curiosity but continued to look straight ahead. Although the agent felt he had adequate probable cause for a stop, he decided against pulling the car over.[21] He reasoned that the occupants were not as shabbily dressed as he would expect illegals to be. Because Mexicans with jobs and more income can get shoppers cards, he assumed they must be locals with either green cards or shoppers cards going to Tucson to shop. If there had been children in the car, the agent said that would have tipped the decision in favor of a stop. Many lawful residents and I-186 shoppers card holders will bring illegal children into the country as a favor to relatives. Had this car appeared at a fixed checkpoint, the presence of airshocks alone on a older American car might have justified a secondary inspection.

Field tactics are shaped not only by considerations of legal requirements or the central trade-off problem confronting INS field enforcement, namely, the need to target efficiently, thus minimizing inconvenience to legitimate travelers. They are also honed by the need to keep violators guessing. Patrol agents believe that the smugglers must be kept off balance, which they do by changing the locale of operations or by a sudden increase in manpower and attention to a different operational function. Thus, agents may be suddenly shifted from linewatch to highway checks back of the line.

Tactics are also elaborated in response to the smugglers' ability to develop protective countermeasures. Thus a professional smuggler may send a decoy car ahead. The driver, a lawful resident, is instructed to behave in a way that will correspond to the patrol agents' profile of a load car. The smuggler hopes the decoy will be pursued, thus diverting attention away from the real load car coming up behind. Or the smuggler may send a scout up the highway to check the road. The scout will phone back and let the smuggler know if the road is free of patrol cars. But a patrol agent attached to an ASU and driving a nondescript auto (often a smuggling car seized in a prior arrest) may be tagging behind the scout. When the scout stops to call, the agent radios to alert agents farther back that a load is getting ready to come through. (In some cases, the scout may return back down the highway to a gas station where the smuggling vehicle is waiting, in which case the agents are led directly to the target.) Such tactics, although not affordable for low-level arrests, will often be used when a Category I or II smuggling operation is suspected.

Agents scouting for load cars on routine roving patrol may not utilize tactics as sophisticated as those used by the ASU investigators, who develop the major smuggling cases (discussed in Chapter 6); on the other hand, they do develop stratagems intended to give them the advantage of surprise. For example, the agents may select a place on the highway just below the rise of a hill and wait to observe how drivers and their passengers behave as they crest the hill and sight the agents. Again, standardized profiles are used to select candidates for a stop. As at fixed checkpoints, citizens are expected to show what the agents call normal curiosity by glancing over at the agents (without suddenly averting their gaze back to the road, which would indicate furtiveness and apprehension). Citizens will also apply their brakes if they are speeding, thinking the agents are local law officers on the watch for speeders. Load car drivers, in contrast, will immediately recognize the light green sedans as border patrol vehicles and become tense. Unless relatively sophisticated, they will immediately avert their gaze.

Heads sighted just above the car window may be adults slumped down to keep out of view. Type of car is also an indicator. Full-sized Buicks, Chevys, and Fords of the 1960s and early 1970s and in poor condition are preferred as load cars both because of their size and their lower value in case they are seized. (According to the officers, when the vehicle seizure program was finally instituted in the late 1970s, smugglers began switching to cheaper, older cars and rental trucks. More than 5,000 smuggling vehicles were seized in fiscal year 1982, and almost 7,000 in 1983.)[22]

While I was riding on roving patrol in California, I observed the following procedure. When a possible load vehicle came over the rise, an agent posted in a stationary vehicle near the crest alerted a colleague waiting farther down the highway, who then pulled out onto the highway and moved up behind the vehicle. He followed to get a second look and to establish whether adequate articulable facts existed for a stop. Unless the articulables were strong, the agent would probably let the car continue. As one agent explained, "We're not out here just to harass people."

Other factors relating to the locale, time of year, and the like also affect tactical decision making in the field because of their relationship to the quality of enforcement results. Thus southbound traffic is unlikely to be observed near the border because it makes little sense to apprehend illegal aliens who are returning home anyway. In California, southbound traffic may be monitored farther up the state because many illegals working in agriculture intend to work during the winter months in Los Angeles rather than return to Mexico. However, southbound traffic has less payoff because the vehicles are more likely to contain friends transporting friends for gas money, often to help pay for a car purchased with the owner's earnings from the harvest. Although the agents think southbound traffic warrants concern, the arrests are less likely to be of interest to the assistant U.S. attorney. By contrast, northbound traffic in the spring and summer will turn up more commercial smugglers bringing illegal aliens up for the planting and harvesting season. In this, as in other areas of INS enforcement, the targeting of resources is calibrated according to anticipations of enforcement impact.

CONCLUSION

As noted, the apprehension of predominantly Mexican EWI aliens in transit near the southern border is the bread and butter of border patrol enforcement.[23] Although apprehensions are also made along the northern border, they are minuscule by comparison. There were only 4,000 northern border arrests in fiscal year 1983, of whom 3,400 were Canadian nationals, compared with more than a million arrests on the Mexican border. To some extent, this disparity is due to the difference in disposition of personnel. Only 300 to 500 patrol agents are stationed along the length of the Canadian border compared with almost 3,000 along the southern border.

The fact that Canadians can enter through POEs without visas is also relevant. (Canadians are required to have visas only if they intend to stay more than six months in the United States.) As a result, when Canadians enter without inspection, patrol agents can usually assume that they strayed over by mistake because many border roads are poorly marked. Hence, unless the Canadian matches the description of a fugitive wanted by the authorities, the agent may decide to point the way back rather than processing the stray-over as an EWI. In the case of other nationalities encountered at the northern border, such as Hong Kong Chinese or Pakistanis, the agents can more reasonably assume they are dealing with willful EWI violators.

Another distinguishing feature of Mexican EWI apprehensions is their highly routinized nature. First, an arrest usually results after a very brief interrogation; second, the processing of the deportable alien can require as little as ten to twenty minutes because the agent fills out a standardized I-213 form that contains preprinted information (fender I-213s). Even so, not all apprehensions are routine. When criminal prosecution is a possibility, as in a smuggling arrest, officers must be sure that they can establish the necessary elements of the offense and that they have handled the questioning and arrest in a procedurally correct manner. In the case of suspected deportable aliens, officers must also confront the complexities that arise when the individual claims U.S. citizenship or lawful residence.

Viewed from the microlevel of analysis, encounters between agents and suspected illegal aliens involve the agents in a series of judgments at each stage. They must decide whether to approach a given person, whether to order a car to secondary inspection (at a fixed checkpoint), or whether to follow and stop a car (on roving patrol). This is done not only to satisfy the legal niceties of meeting the reasonable suspicion requirement but also for reasons of administrative efficiency and good public relations. Then officers must think about how they should begin the initial questioning based on tactical considerations. (The interrogatory gambit chosen will depend, for example, on how certain they are that an individual is a deportable alien.) If an individual claims to be a lawful resident or citizen, officers must decide whether to credit the individual's claim; if there are reasons for doubt, they must decide what additional questions to ask to probe the claim further. If the individual persists with what agents consider to be a bad claim, agents must decide what combination of appeals might work to pry the alien from the claim.

Beyond the microlevel of agents' discretionary management of their operational environment (who to approach, who to detain for further questioning, the questions to ask, and so forth) there are the tactical judgments that agents and their superiors must arrive at concerning resource allocations at the level of the station (the smallest administrative unit) as well as the sector. In contrast with the criminal investigators, patrol agents feel more constrained to produce apprehension statistics: a large number of EWI violators along with prosecution-quality arrests of smugglers. This is because they believe the effectiveness of a station or sector is measured largely in terms of these statistics. (When quality casework is involved, it usually applies to the manner in which smuggling cases have been worked up and presented to the prosecutor.)

Enforcement measures aimed at improving deterrence typically lead to new strategies of circumvention on the part of violators. Thus if load vehicles are being seized in larger numbers, smugglers respond by using cheaper, older cars or rented trucks and/or by engaging in other risk-shifting tactics. As a result, within the parameters of the law and official policy, field tactics are rarely permanent fixtures of enforcement practice but instead are continually elaborated to keep violators off balance.

Unofficial, as well as officially sanctioned or required, adjustments can also affect the individual officer's exercise of discretion in interrogating and arresting aliens. Court rulings that restrict the scope of field officers' discretion are sometimes buttressed by official agency policy requirements, as for example, when officers are required to write on a G-424 card the articulable facts for questioning an individual at the time they first encounter the person rather than later, when they are back at the district office or station. Other adjustments to court rulings, for example those that have tightened the Fourth-Amendment requirements for a stop, may be unofficial. For example, officers may decide against approaching Chinese or members of other ethnic groups with exotic languages. The reason is not favoritism toward Chinese or any other group. Rather, officers know that illegal aliens in these language groups will be difficult to interview if they cannot understand English (or pretend not to). Such an adjustment is not official policy but arises because of the overall policy impact of stricter constitutional standards coupled with the limits on officer time and resources.

And although the literature on "street-level" bureaucrats has amply documented the way lower-level officials can evade administrative policy guidelines stemming from judicially or politically initiated pressures, some of the adjustments INS field officers make to restrictive discretion-limiting policies can have the effect of enhancing enforcement professionalism. However, it can also lead to less equitable enforcement targeting, as is discussed later.[24] The requirement for warrants for area control raids on businesses is a good example. Investigations branch officers claim that employer surveys conducted with warrants are higher-quality enforcement because of the legal professionalism required to obtain a warrant.

The heightened sensitivity among patrol agents to the need for having sufficient articulable facts before stopping a suspected load vehicle is another example of how professionalism can be enhanced by judicial rulings. The agents know they risk losing a commercial smuggling case if they do not adhere closely to the constitutional standards at all stages.[25] But the level of officer concern over meeting constitutional standards will also vary according to how different officers assess the costs of neglect on their part. Thus, for linewatch and even pedestrian arrests in the interior, an officer's threshold of concern is apt to be lower simply because the cost of discovered error on the officer's part is apt to be trivial or irrelevant in the case of EWI aliens and other administrative violators who are unlikely to be prosecuted. Although the officer's grounds for seizing the individual or the manner in which incriminating evidence of deportability was obtained might be raised in a deportation hearing, aliens do not become immune to deportation if it is established that the officer obtained the evidence illegally.

FOUR

INTERIOR ENFORCEMENT AGAINST ADMINISTRATIVE VIOLATORS

Both border patrol and investigations branch officers pursue deportable aliens who have settled into jobs in the United States or who are illegally resident in the United States even if they are not working. Working from tips (G-123 leads) or other sources of information, patrol agents and criminal investigators (CIs) check the immigration status of suspected illegal aliens on farms, in other businesses, and in jails and prisons. Aliens picked up in public places, such as bus stops, terminals, or the street, are usually apprehended on the basis of visual cues picked up by the officers in the course of routine patrolling rather than on the basis of tips. But when G-123 leads are followed, officers typically expect that, in addition to any aliens named in the tip, they will encounter other deportable aliens previously unknown to the INS. (Some deportable aliens may turn out to have a service file—alien registration number—because of a prior arrest, deportation order, or investigation.)

Most of the employed illegal aliens the border patrol apprehends in the interior are picked up during farm and ranch checks, an activity that accounted for 3 percent of the patrol's productive officer hours in fiscal year 1983. Border patrol agents also conduct city patrol, which is comparable to the business surveys carried out by the investigation branch as part of its area control function. However, in city patrol, the border patrol's arrest ratio drops to approximately one arrest for every four officer hours—about the same as the investigations branch's four and a half officer hours per arrest in employer surveys and other area control activities.[1] If measured solely in terms of offi-

cer hours per arrest, the investigations branch's area control is its most productive activity.

This chapter begins with a discussion of several important differences in
the functional specialization and enforcement outlook of the border patrol
and the investigations branch and then moves on to examine the border patrol's farm and ranch operations in depth. The environment encountered by
patrol agents during farm and ranch checks approximates linewatch apprehensions much more than it does the area control activities of the plainclothes investigators in the cities. For one thing, both linewatch and farm and ranch
checks turn up predominantly Mexican EWIs who are usually detained after
brief interrogations and who are much more likely than other illegals to accept voluntary return under safeguard. As a result, the modal arrest usually
involves a brief and uncomplicated encounter, which usually requires less
paperwork and other processing chores. Although this pattern also characterizes some investigations branch employer surveys, such as raids on southwestern construction sites or garment plants that have a high percentage of
illegal Mexican aliens, the plainclothes investigators are somewhat more apt
than patrol agents to encounter either OTM aliens or settled illegal Mexicans.
These aliens will have either more ambiguous immigration statuses (and may
even qualify for benefits) or, because of their higher investment in getting into
the United States, more incentives to resist deportation even if they have no
equities whatsoever. In short, somewhat fewer of the arrestees brought in by
criminal investigators will accept voluntary return and be diverted from the
formal adjudicatory machinery because more have (or believe they have)
equities that will allow them to stay.

THE DIFFERENCE IN SPECIALIZATION
OF PATROL AGENTS AND INVESTIGATORS

Although patrol agents and CIs have several overlapping responsibilities, including investigations of alien-smuggling and counterfeit-document-vending
rings and false claims to citizenship and lawful residence, the patrol agents
and CIs hold sharply contrasting views of their principal organizational mission. Patrol agents primarily "sack up" (chase and apprehend) illegal aliens in
public places and farms. Although CIs also pursue illegal aliens in public
areas, they view as their primary mission doing case investigations that involve the development of leads and other information bearing on alien benefit
and relief applications or on crime or fraud that might subject citizens as well
as aliens to criminal prosecution, or aliens and some naturalized citizens to
deportation. This conception holds even for those investigators who are as-

signed to the area control unit in their district office and who often refer to surveys of work sites and transportation centers as plainclothes border patrol work.

Although as of July 1983, area control activities no longer exist as a separate functional specialization within investigations, during the period I was in the field, it accounted for most of the investigations branch's arrests. In fiscal year 1982, close to 90 percent of the approximately 105,000 deportable aliens apprehended by CIs were picked up by area control officers, in spite of the fact that less than 40 percent of productive officer time was devoted to this function. Close to 30 percent of all investigations officer hours were spent on completion of 13,000 cases of suspected fraudulent benefit applications and 6,300 cases involving lawfully resident aliens (green-card holders) suspected of criminal, immoral, and narcotics activities.[2]

The difference in functional specialization between the border patrol and the investigations branch reveals itself in other ways as well. For example, although CIs may occasionally go out and arrest agricultural workers in districts that have few patrol agents (especially in the Northeast), agricultural workers account for fewer than 10 percent of all investigations branch arrests. Similarly, patrol agents will also occasionally pursue G-123 tips on illegal aliens working in nonfarm businesses, usually in rural areas having a nearby patrol station but few, if any, criminal investigators.

Patrol agents give a lower priority to G-123 tips on illegal aliens in nonfarm businesses than they do to farm and ranch checks for two reasons. First, because patrol agents have lower civil service (GS) ratings on average than CIs, most patrol stations lack officers who have the legal experience needed to prepare a warrant to check an enclosed private business should the owner refuse them permission to enter. (No warrants are needed to go onto open land.) Logistical considerations are also involved, in that an agent might have to travel 50 or so miles to locate a U.S. attorney to approve a warrant. In consequence, when they do decide to act on a tip on an enclosed place of business, they may conduct the investigation much as they would check a bus station, by positioning agents in a parking lot outside to make visual checks on workers arriving at their jobs. Then they would approach and question those they suspected of being deportable. On the other hand, a tip on a waitress working illegally in a cafe might be pursued because a restaurant is a public area and a warrant would not be necessary to enter.

This difference in functional specialization, although partly owing to the fact that patrol agents are accustomed to outdoors enforcement for which warrants are not needed, is powerfully reinforced by the different productivity expectations held for the two enforcement branches. As noted earlier, the border patrol produces close to 90 percent of INS apprehensions nationwide—obtained through high-productivity mass arrests of mainly Mexican EWIs.

Patrol agents know they can get much better output working farms than they can by pursuing single named leads on nonfarm businesses in their areas.

By contrast, CIs are oriented toward investigating cases that involve more time and complexity. An investigator assigned to a third-party sham marriage case can easily spend a couple of weeks gathering evidence to support a prosecutable case. However, although quality casework is urged on the investigators, they often feel under pressure to produce measurable statistics—either in the form of successful case closings or arrests. (With the implementation of the case management system in mid-1983, the concern over showing a high body count in arrests has declined.) During the time of my field work, CIs felt that the time-intensive case investigations could be paid for if the two high-productivity sections, area control and the general section, maximized case closings and arrests per productive officer hour. However, during 1981 and 1982, investigators in some of the northeastern district offices worried that central office administrators might transfer personnel to the southwest because of the higher productivity of area control activities in that region. At the time, an effort was being made to produce apprehensions of deportable aliens at work sites. Immigration service officials believed that priority should be given to liberating jobs for citizens and permanent residents during a recession. Although the CIs knew that quality area control apprehensions (arrests of better-paid illegal aliens) were also important, they felt under pressure to generate as many arrests as possible (make the stats).

One clear effect of such pressures is that officers will give priority to working those areas where they anticipate maximizing their respective enforcement leverage. For patrol agents, a farm check that will net 25 to 50 aliens is more productive than a lead on a single barmaid in town. Investigators assigned to area control also preferred working urban business leads that would result in what they considered a reasonable number of apprehensions (ten to thirty or more), especially if they involved sites that had jobs attractive to unemployed citizens. Given the distance and time involved in going out to a distant rural community to pick up a few agricultural workers, such efforts were not viewed as quality area control by the investigators. In consequence, the outlying rural communities of some district offices might never be visited unless, say, it was a reportable case originating from the central office.

For example, while I was studying an eastern district office, a small-town sheriff two hundred miles downstate called to report that he had picked up a stranded Mexican wandering around the railroad station. Rebuffed when he called the district office, whose assistant director for investigations explained that the manpower could not be spared to pick up someone so far away, the sheriff called his senator. The senator's office contacted the central office, and the district office was promptly told to detail two officers to pick up the alien.

With per diem for an overnight trip and vehicle costs, the assistant director guessed that this apprehension might easily cost $300 or more. The supervisor in charge of area control operations noted bitterly that whenever he and his officers wanted to pick up a few more aliens, all they had to do was send a team to a restaurant around the block. But a congressional-inquiry case always takes priority regardless of the expense (or merit).

Lower-productivity area control apprehensions will occasionally be made on other grounds.[3] The investigators or their supervisor may feel that the time has come for the squad to "show the flag" in a certain part of the city. Most believe that every nationality group known to have illegals in its midst should be looking over its shoulder even though illegals of some nationalities are harder to spot than others. This is because of language barriers and the fact that some nationality groups are more widely scattered and their individual members less easy to recognize. Although most CIs believe strongly that illegal aliens should never be allowed to think they are safe just because they have managed to reach the U.S. interior, considerations of productivity (arrests in relation to invested time) are a major constraint on achieving equitable targeting in the sense of a reasonably uniform risk of apprehension for all groups.

Also, area control CIs occasionally follow up leads on individual aliens (called individual G-123 leads) who are apt to be the only individuals who will be found at the site (unlike business leads where the officers anticipate locating deportable aliens not named in the tip). Such lower-productivity enforcement is justified when leads pinpoint aliens in higher-status occupations or aliens suspected of criminal involvement, but they may also be carried out simply because the investigators believe that area control should be more equitable and bring in more of the OTM illegals.

In contrast, patrol agents are considerably less likely to take the type of job into account when deciding where to conduct immigration status checks. For one thing, their enforcement environment is almost monotonously homogeneous. In farm and ranch or city patrol, the patrol agents will usually turn up unskilled Mexican EWIs because, with the exception of some southeast Asians, other nationality groups are rarely found working in rural California and the rural southwest. To the extent the patrol agents do use a quality as opposed to quantity (body count) targeting criterion, it is most likely to involve alien smuggling. The quality violator for patrol agents is the citizen or alien caught transporting a load of illegals or an alien picked up by the police for drunken driving, shoplifting, or other minor offenses. Also, aliens due to be released from county and state prisons after serving time for the more serious offenses are quality apprehensions. As one patrol agent said, "I'd rather pick up one criminal and see him removed than get ten tomato pickers." (As is discussed in Chapter 6, investigators also view criminal aliens as the highest-quality arrests.)

Although jail checks are typically not as productive as farm and ranch checks, many patrol agents and CIs believe they should receive priority because aliens involved in crime pose an obvious threat to the public; also, administrative action against this group occasions less public ambivalence. There is another reason as well: Illegal aliens who have been convicted of relatively serious crimes are not eligible for voluntary return. Once in the hands of the border patrol, they will acquire servicewide records that contain fingerprints, will be deported, and theoretically could be prosecuted if they return. Also, patrol agents feel they have somewhat more leverage with illegal aliens convicted of minor crimes, for example with aliens who have been released on probation with the requirement that they stay out of the United States as a condition of their probation. In consequence, many agents consider pickups at jails to be better quality arrests, not only because they are returning alien troublemakers but also because there may be some deterrent effect if these aliens know that they may be returned to jail should they return and be caught. But whether minor-offender aliens are truly affected by this is open to question. In the case of Mexicans, many use aliases. As noted earlier, patrol agents rarely have the time to check into the backgrounds of any but a small fraction of those they arrest in routine operations.

During the fall and winter months, when agricultural activity has tapered off, patrol agents stationed in the interior will often shift emphasis to less productive activities, such as traffic observation and transportation checks. They may even do surveys of nonfarm businesses suspected of using illegal workers or may pursue investigations of suspected false citizenship and other claims (and documents) that have been pending from an earlier, more hectic period. Also, there are times when they may have no choice but to pursue lower-productivity activities because of court injunctions or Department of Justice policy directives. Thus, farm and ranch checks were temporarily put off-limits in northern California in 1982 by the federal district court in that area when several plaintiffs brought a suit against the INS alleging that patrol agents violated citizens' rights by using blocking tactics in open fields. And during the 1979–1980 season, farm and ranch checks were curtailed when the Carter administration imposed a nationwide moratorium intended to curb INS mass enforcement actions in residential areas and businesses. (The moratorium did not apply to public areas, such as train and bus stations, or to businesses for which warrants had been obtained.) Although the Carter administration gave as its reason the government's need for an accurate census count, many agents believe the administration's desire to court the Hispanic vote was the real reason because, they argue, the moratorium was extended beyond the time required to complete the census.

FARM AND RANCH CHECKS

As earlier noted, the patrol's farm and ranch checks are among the most productive interior enforcement activity, as measured by arrests per officer hour. Although they are productive partly because less time is required to process Mexican EWIs, who normally accept voluntary return, they also do not require the preparation work that plainclothes investigators must do in advance of area control raids because of the warrant requirement (see Chapter 5). Patrol agents need only scout the fields where, based on their general knowledge of the farms in their area and the kinds of crops being picked, they know illegals are apt to be working. Not needing warrants, they can quickly scan the crews for those appearance and behavior characteristics needed to justify questioning. Decisions on which farm to sweep may be made when the agents assemble in the morning, or a decision might be made on the spur of the moment while patrolling a general area.

Because patrol agents can spot illegal crews while driving on the highway, some farmers put their illegal hands out of sight of the roadway. Visibility is also related to the nature of the crop. Thus lettuce and cotton fields are easier to work than orange groves or cornfields because high and dense foliage provide better opportunities for runners and hiders.

Field tactics depend on the size of the crew, the number of agents and vans available for the sweep, and whether a spotter aircraft will be brought into action. Also, tactics may be adjusted to the control problems anticipated. If there are deep irrigation canals, these can endanger aliens who decide to run and who may drown if they try to swim across. In California's central valley, agents must be positioned near the canals to minimize this hazard. Just as agents on roving patrol may decide to call off a highway chase if a load-car driver appears determined to make a run for it at 90 miles an hour, so too, with other operations: The priority is to minimize the risk of death or injury to aliens and bystanders. Illegal aliens can do unpredictable things and if any should injure themselves or drown because they misjudged a canal's depth, Hispanic activists and local clergy are apt to blame the border patrol.

Tactical ploys are elaborated to handle contingencies. Thus, if there are only two or three agents available and they stumble across a sizeable crew, there are certain to be more aliens who elude them. One senior patrol agent explained that, when he was short of agents, he would try to give the impression that he had more than his few visible agents accompanying him. He would speak into his portable radio while looking around and signaling to the other members of his phantom squad.

The model farm and ranch operation usually involves four to ten agents and several vehicles. When the agents have arrived at the field, they try to encircle the crew by swiftly accelerating the vans out into the field so that they are posted near the corners. Then, two or three agents will move toward the crew in the center while the other agents stay back by the vans. That way, if any aliens run, they can block them off. Runners take priority. This is not primarily because reasonable suspicion is immediately and convincingly demonstrated (which makes the apprehension legally risk-free for the agents) but because of the agents' social control requirements. If a few runners can be quickly corralled, the chances diminish that others will try. Also, green-card holders will occasionally run as a favor to crewmates they know are illegal, thereby decoying the agents away from the illegals.

Although reasonable suspicion of alienage is needed before the agents can question or detain field hands (as it is in any setting), the agents are not faced with the heterogeneity of statuses that arise in busy transportation terminals and other urban settings. In many fields, the unskilled workers are either green-card holders or illegal aliens, or else they are citizens and lawful-resident supervisors and equipment operators. Determining the candidates suitable for a closer check (interrogation) is not as speedily achieved as on linewatch in San Ysidro. However, it is easier than in most factories or public locales in a city.

Whereas, in an Amtrak station filled with citizens, agents are apt to be looking around to determine who might be illegal, in the lettuce or sweet potato field they are apt to look to determine who in the field might be a citizen. (Green-card holders, too, may be recognizable by their more acculturated dress and better grooming or because they are equipment operators. However, talking to them is not problematic because the agents have as much right to approach and question lawful residents as they do individuals they suspect are illegal.) If the crew is large, or if time is short and the agents are short-handed, the agents may neglect to talk to those they think are green-card holders. This may include some they suspect are illegal. The noteworthy fact—and it is a major distinguishing feature of immigration enforcement compared with, say, a crime-fighting law agency—is that officers need not take a maximalist orientation toward their tasks. That is to say, agents are geared to making a level of arrests consistent with available resources. This includes both the anticipated downstream burden of processing work back at the station and the risk of lawsuits and complaints. Ironically, although many agents complain about the low level of support they get from the public, from prosecutors and judges, and from others, the devaluation of immigration enforcement is reflected in their own field operations. If the vans have filled with the number that can be processed and accommodated by the end of the day, that may dictate an unspoken decision that the rest of the field "looks clean," as they say.

Farm and ranch checks pose far less ambiguity for patrol agents than urban targets pose for plainclothes investigators; however, patrol agents still rely heavily on articulable facts when they winnow down the candidates to be checked in a field. As on linewatch, past experience leads agents to expect that many in a particular crew will be illegal because of their knowledge of the owner's employment practices, the kind of work being performed, or the visual cues provided when the agents approach. Although somewhat ritualistic, the articulable-fact requirement must still be met. An agent stationed near the parked vans may be assigned to observe the demeanor of workers who have stayed in the field (are not running). That agent scans the crew, radioing observations to colleagues who are approaching the crew. Dress (for example, glaring colors or color combinations not typical of more acculturated lawful residents) is useful, but never as decisive as behavior. Some of the articulables are highly uniform, and standard across enforcement contexts. If a worker is looking away from the agents whereas crewmates show the normal level of curiosity (mild and sustained interest but without visible apprehension), that individual has triggered the furtiveness cue and will be checked. So, too, a field hand spotted sneaking away from one row of vegetables to a row whose workers have already been approached and checked. Workers who are trying to watch what the agents are doing but look away when the agents turn to meet their gaze also trigger the furtiveness cue.

However, the reason that observance of the legal requirement is ritualistic at this initial (who to approach and talk to) stage is that little harm is done if the agents guessed wrong and the individual turns out to be a U.S. citizen. The individual is free to walk away (as the agents are apt to assert was the case). But even if the person was momentarily detained, which is hard to prove, the agents would have a good-faith defense if they believed they had well-founded suspicion of alienage based on their first observations. For one thing, citizens are rarely encountered in stoop labor. Beyond that, there is certainly honest error about whether, for example, gestures or eye behavior were in fact furtive.

In farm and ranch operations, complaints arising from mistakes made at the first stage (approach and questioning) must certainly be rare; it is otherwise in urban work contexts, as is discussed in Chapter 5.

The second stage, the phase in which the agent has decided to restrain an individual's movement, poses more legal hazard. Agents worry that they may be set up by citizens or lawful residents who decide to behave as though they were illegal aliens in order to create unfavorable publicity for the service or to provide factual allegations that will support a civil lawsuit. But as noted, unless an individual has been handcuffed or forced inside a van, proving detention is extremely difficult. If an individual refuses to talk, the officers have probable cause—if they had the other articulables needed to approach that individual in the first place. An individual who talks will either give satisfactory answers and be allowed to proceed or will not.

At the first (who to approach and talk to) stage, officers probably use the articulable facts as much for reasons of administrative efficiency as because of the constitutional requirement. As noted, having the articulables minimizes unproductive interrogations. Because the agents are usually working under pressures of time and with limited resources, efficient selection is essential to getting the job done. If a small number of agents are dealing with a very large crew of perhaps one or two hundred field hands, the agents may have no choice but to limit their interrogations to a small percentage of the crew. As a rule, more time will be spent back at the station writing the aliens up (either as "dep procs" or voluntary returns) than will be spent making the apprehensions in the field. In addition, if any of the illegals admits to having family members, the relatives will have to be fetched, along with their belongings. If any insist on hearings, still more time will be required for the added paperwork, for calls to the district office for authorization of the order to show cause (OSC) and warrant, and for making arrangements for overnight holding.

Given the high resource costs coupled with the fact that most INA violators are not viewed as serious or threatening lawbreakers, the level of apprehensions often falls short of the potential maximum—that is, the number of suspected illegal aliens who could potentially be arrested if every check were thoroughly carried out. To be sure, most patrol agents would prefer to get every violator in a field, and often the effort to do so will be made. But if they have just five or six agents or can only process 25 to 35 illegal aliens a day, there will be diminishing returns at the margin in trying to make sure no alien has escaped the sweep. Additionally, they may also occasionally neglect to talk to women because they are more likely to have small children who will have to be picked up at home, perhaps miles from the site. If children have to be taken out of schools, this can also lead to unpleasant confrontations with teachers or principals who will demand an explanation or even protest.

Ironically, the articulable-facts requirement can, in such circumstances, serve the agents' need to maintain equilibrium between available resources and the day's optimal arrest quota because it gives them considerable discretion at the first decisional stage (who to approach). If they were ever queried about a decision not to arrest, which is extremely improbable, they could always say they were not certain whether they had sufficient articulables to justify an interrogation. As several agents explained to me, "You never get into trouble for not apprehending an illegal alien."[4] Although some patrol agents view the constitutional reasonable-suspicion standard (at least at the first decisional stage) as a judicially imposed nuisance and assert that their own sense of professionalism leads them to minimize encounters with citizens and authorized aliens, they neglect to consider how the constitutional standard serves their operational need for maintaining equilibrium between their resources and the potential enforcement caseloads that too vigorous an effort might generate. Agents may have discretion to limit the number of initial encounters, but they have much less discretion to decide not to make an arrest once an alien has admitted deportability. However, discretion is not entirely lacking even at this stage. If the alien claims equities or says a benefit request is pending, the agents can divert that alien from an arrest by deciding that the individual is unlikely to abscond. (Indeed, agents can make a warrantless arrest only when they have reason to believe that the alien would be likely to abscond.) One policy consequence is that agents might decide to credit equity claims to reduce the caseload pressure on their office even when they harbor suspicions about the validity of the claims. If the alien is judged likely to insist on a deportation hearing, the incentives for crediting a borderline story are even greater because of the added time that deportation processing will require. (Although this generalization is speculative, it is plausible. My field data are not sufficient to establish how frequently such decisions favorable to aliens with marginally plausible stories are made in the field. Such decisions are of very low visibility and hinge upon subjective judgments that would be extremely difficult to test.)

MANAGING APPREHENSIONS:
THE VERBAL AND PSYCHOLOGICAL CHASE

The physical chase after aliens who run off is a major nuisance for INS officers. Because of this, they may decide to handcuff younger male workers who appear to be keyed up and likely to sprint, although they would probably not do so until they had first obtained an admission of deportability. An older agent wearing heavy boots is no match for a fleeing younger field hand. Runners who fight, throw objects, or struggle also pose physical dangers to agents.

According to the agents, runners are more of a problem today than in the past. Agents speak of the days in the 1950s and 1960s when an agent or two could go into a field and shout their order through a megaphone for all those without *papeles* to come over to the van. The men without papers, often former contract laborers (braceros), would move over to the van, take off their hats, and "*sí señor*" the officers. But this pattern of deference has weakened over the years. According to the officers, illegals now are generally younger and more apt to be urban reared. Also, they have learned in the short span of a generation that patrol agents are not like law officers in their own society, where they will be shot if they were to run after being ordered to halt. As a result, it takes more agents to control a crew, and if the illegals believe there's a fair chance of eluding arrest, they'll run.

The physical chase merely challenges an agent's stamina. It is the verbal and psychological chase that challenges an agent's interactional skills. Though the number of EWI aliens who try to elude arrest by making false oral or documented claims is smaller than the number who will run or physically struggle, INS officers believe they are increasing in number and boldness. Official statistics on the number of false claimants are not reliable because many of the oral false claims are never reported by field officers. Some agents estimate that no more than 1 in 20 or 30 illegals will try to bluff with a false claim. The agents claim that they are able to break almost all such claims, usually by getting the alien to admit to the truth after further questioning.[5]

Partly to avoid the problem of false claims, patrol agents carrying out alienage checks on farms choose their words carefully. So, for example, at the time agents approach an individual, they may simply ask, "*Tienes papeles?*" (Do you have papers?) rather than asking "Where were you born?" To ask something like "What country are you a citizen of?" would be ludicrous in a situation where the probability is close to 100 percent that the officer is dealing with a Mexican who either has papers (is a green-card holder) or does not. As one agent explained, the tactical advantage of asking "*Tienes papeles?*" is that it gets "the flow going the agent's way" and expedites status determinations.

The worker who is a citizen will certainly let the officer know it, and an alien either has documentation or does not. Some who are old-timers and have been through the system before know the score. They may not even bother to answer the question but simply shake their heads and move off in the direction of the van. (This entails a slight risk that younger workers, whose parents are green-card holders but who are not familiar with the game or whose parents have failed to inform them about such contingencies, might walk over to a van because they do not have their green cards with them and do not know the routine.) However, the risk that adult green-card holders would be mistakenly deported is very low. If caught without a card, they should know enough of the required information to convince agents that they are legal. Teenagers (who are perceived as such) will almost certainly be asked by agents how they can contact their parents.

When aliens claim to have left their cards at home, agents will offer to drive them to their residences to examine their documents. If an alien is bluffing, this is a good way to call the bluff.

Although many illegal aliens carry *tarejas chuecas* (counterfeit green cards), they rarely present them to INS officers because they know the officers will recognize a fraudulent card. (Only very high-quality counterfeits might be missed, and then probably only if the officers are working under time pressures.) Aliens use counterfeit green cards mainly for other purposes: to obtain welfare benefits, credit, or other identification (such as drivers' licenses). If they are carrying them when officers arrive on the scene, they usually hide them to avoid having them taken from them. (When aliens are found with counterfeit cards in their wallets, the officers consider it to be an inconsequential offense because the alien did not attempt to use it.) Only when an alien tries to pass off a fraudulent document do the agents consider it a serious (and reportable) false claim attempt. (No doubt one reason that many oral false claims are not reported is that officers consider quickly broken oral claims to be *de minimus* violations.)

THE FRUSTRATIONS OF ENFORCING UNPOPULAR LAW

Although farm and ranch checks resemble linewatch apprehensions in terms of the low level of status ambiguity and heterogeneity encountered, they resemble urban business surveys in certain other respects. Besides the need to block off fields to control runners, the patrol agents are sometimes opposed by landlords. (Criminal investigators' dealings with uncooperative and sometimes hostile businessmen are discussed in Chapter 5.) These confrontations between ranchers and agents can easily turn nasty. The property owner may try to block the road to prevent the agents' entry or exit.[6] If the agents find the gate blocked by a tractor after they have already entered the property, they can point out to the rancher that as long as they hang around, the workers who have run off will not be returning.

Although they may tell farmers and ranchers that interfering with federal officers in the course of their duties is a prosecutable offense, the assistant U.S. attorney is unlikely to go with such a case unless the agent is assaulted and hurt. What frustrates many field officers is their perception that federal prosecutors will not back them up with prosecutions. Agents believe such prosecutorial backup is essential to achieve social control over alien behavior as well as to provide strategic deterrence. When they inform aliens about the potential statutory penalties for failure to carry immigration receipts, persistence in holding out with a false claim, and the like, this is often more in the nature of a bluff that the officers hope the aliens won't call.

Farmers may resist for any number of reasons. They may have advanced the smuggling fee for their illegal field hands but not yet recouped their investment. Or they may be irritated because the raid has disrupted a crew working on perishable crops that are being harvested late. If they have had a bad year financially, they will be even more prone to take it out on the agents. Sometimes they have legitimate grievances because of damage done to irrigation sprinklers or other fixtures when the agents chase illegal aliens. As in the

cities, agents are often treated to epithets such as green Gestapo or storm-
trooper by ranchers and foremen who wish they would chase after illegal aliens someplace else.

Although illegal aliens often return to the ranches they worked for in
previous seasons, or are recruited for a crew by independent labor contractors, some ranchers are known to be actively involved in the smuggling and
harboring (concealment) of illegal aliens. Yet patrol agents encounter difficulty prosecuting such cases, sometimes because they have trouble gathering
sufficient evidence but occasionally even when their evidence is satisfactory.

A good example is the prosecution several years back of a group of Idaho
ranchers indicted for alien smuggling. According to patrol agents in the ASU
in the sector that handled the case, the ranchers had placed orders for aliens
and paid the smuggling fee upon delivery. Unbeknownst to the ranchers,
they had contacted a Mexican who was an INS informant. Undercover ASU
agents arranged to allow controlled loads to be delivered to them and taped
the incriminating telephone conversations for the arrangements. Local politicians were up in arms over the case and Congressman George Hansen wrote
to acting INS Commissioner Doris Meissner to complain about the arrests
and prosecutions of these farmers.

Because of what he considered to be procedural defects, the judge dismissed the case before it went to the jury. Yet the agents who were involved
believed the decision was politically motivated. Had it been a drug smuggling
case, they claimed, there would have been no problem with the way the evidence was gathered. Although federal prosecutors are more immune from
local constituency pressures than such local officials as sheriffs, many have
political ambitions that lead them to mitigate strict enforcement of unpopular
laws in their district. In rural areas, aiding and abetting the smuggling of illegal aliens is not viewed as a serious offense.[7]

Most immigration violators, including many considered to be serious
offenders by the INS, are generally a low priority for most federal prosecutors. (In some districts, such as San Diego, immigration cases are the bulk of
the federal criminal caseload; one result is that they are prosecuted more vig-
orously and competently.) As the patrol agents tell it, when a smuggling case
involves respectable ranchers who are just trying to find willing hands to
bring in their crops, prosecutorial discretion will bend in the direction of dis-
missal or leniency. Agents in California tell about a case that was brought
against a rancher caught harboring illegal aliens. The case was airtight; the
rancher agreed to plead guilty. According to the agents, the federal attorney
told the rancher's lawyer to change his client's plea to not guilty. The U.S.
attorney could then justify declining the case on the grounds that it did not
warrant the expense and trouble of a jury trial.

Some ranchers occasionally violate the law or actively interfere with immigration status checks on their property, but many more resist passively by taking measures to minimize the detection of their illegal workers. They may develop early warning systems and alert their neighbors by citizens' band radio or telephone when they sight the patrol's distinctive green vans coming. Also, sheriffs will sometimes get the word out when they learn that patrol agents are being detailed into their counties. (They may hear about it when the patrol agents call up the sheriff to find out how much jail space they can count on for holding apprehendees. The agents may know the sheriff will alert local ranchers, but they know they will pick up all the illegals they can handle anyway.) At most times, and especially around planting and harvesting time, patrol agents are not welcome visitors.

However, local law officers will often cooperate with the border patrol when a child has been brutally murdered or run over by a drunk driver (or another serious crime has occurred) and the local citizenry believes an illegal alien was the culprit. Then the red carpet may be rolled out and local law officers may well provide assistance, perhaps by helping the agents check out the bars in town. Normally, INS higher-ups prefer that patrol agents not carry out immigration checks in bars because intoxicated patrons are more likely to fight. Besides the bad press that can be generated, federal officers are at a disadvantage in a brawl because, as one agent explained, it is much easier for a local police officer to persuade a city or state prosecutor to take an assault charge than it is for a federal officer to get a federal prosecutor to take such a case. The assistant U.S. attorney's threshold standards are usually higher. In contrast to local courts, the federal courts simply are not geared to handling misdemeanor caseloads.

Labor contractors, who may also have an investment in an illegal field crew (if the rancher is paying them by the job and they are paying off the crew after taking a commission), will post family members as lookouts on hills near the roads used by the patrol. Or they may watch for the patrol's distinctive spotter aircraft, whose flight pattern is distinguishable from that of private aircraft. (Spotter planes are useful to the officers on the ground because their appearance can sometimes provoke aliens to run, which alerts the officers to illegal crews. When directed to fields where the officers are conducting checks, the pilot can help agents pinpoint where runners are hiding.)

Because they so frequently meet with public resistance in interior enforcement, agents often express their ambivalence toward enforcement aimed at honest, hard-working illegals who pose little threat to the society (unless driving while intoxicated or without insurance). The agents realize that ranchers often have difficulty finding reliable field hands for the wages they can afford. Yet although this attitude mirrors the ambivalence of many other Americans ("If I were in Jose's shoes and couldn't support a family, I would be working illegally in the United States too"), it does not erode their commitment to their enforcement role. They may sympathize with the Mexican EWI's plight, but in the same breath, they will explain that EWIs are still violating the law of the land. Thus, whereas they may extend exculpatory rationalizations to EWIs and to the ranchers who employ them, they still come down firmly on the side of enforcement. As law enforcers, they must rationalize the validity of their actions, or they would be incapacitated by ambivalent feelings toward the job. They will argue that, if the ranchers would only pay decent wages, they could find citizens to do the work. They will also recite (and possibly exaggerate) the number of illegals in state prisons or the extent to which illegal aliens take unauthorized welfare benefits. However, in defense of their conduct, they can easily stand on the terra firma of national sovereignty. They are enforcing the laws of the land.

Yet the hostility they encounter and their perception of the public's lukewarm support angers many agents and demoralizes others. It is a major reason why many patrol agents and CIs would prefer concentrating their attention on more serious INA violators. Some drift into cynicism. One seasoned patrol agent theorized that what the public really wanted was controlled management of illegal immigration rather than strict enforcement. As he explained, the public wanted a reasonable level of enforcement, not a full effort. Ranchers need a certain level of arrests so their illegal crews will not demand higher pay; smugglers want enough arrests so there is demand for their services; people living in town want the agents to pick up the illegals involved in crime or other troublemaking. The patrol's anecdotal lore is filled with sarcasm. Some agents relate stories of ranchers who, after resisting them one day, call the patrol the next day to report an illegal alien who the rancher suspects made off with some of the ranch tools or who has made a pass at the rancher's wife.

Ironically, the increasing professionalism of the border patrol over the past several decades may, along with the termination of the bracero program, be largely to blame for the increased conflict occasioned by interior apprehensions. In some areas, during the 1950s, there were unofficially sanctioned policies to adjust law enforcement to the needs of the community. According to some officers, political favoritism was shown to powerful Texas ranchers (or ranch-owning politicians).[8] Even on the eastern seaboard, or so some officers claim, the ranches of some influential senators were off-limits, and the gardeners or cooks of highly placed civil servants or elected officials were sometimes known by the INS to be illegal but were not acted against.

Under a less professionalized regime, where accommodations might occasionally be brokered to meet community pressures for leniency, enforcement might sometimes be adjusted to minimize conflict with those who benefited from using illegals. Today, with the rise of a more professionalized corps of officers, the old style of personalistic accommodation to local economic interests or the political clout of the Washington elite meets more resistance. (Some INS officers claim that illegal aliens not only work in menial jobs on Capitol Hill but also can be found in congressional staff jobs. Such exceptionalism is resented and contributes to officer cynicism toward politicians.)

But accommodations of a different sort must still be made. The rise of the newer civil rights and ethnic group activists exerts pressures that can mitigate strict INS enforcement. Sometimes this is done through court injunctions. If the service agrees to a settlement on terms unfavorable to itself, or if it fails to win upon appeal, additional restrictions may be placed on certain enforcement activities. And the INS's public relations concerns can lead to restrictions not required by law—as, for example, the policy ban on searches of churches or unofficial discouragement of checks of bars and street sweeps in residential neighborhoods. The mobilized pressures exerted by the civil rights activists to minimize INS enforcement often dovetail with pressures from conservative farming and business interests. Their complaints are then taken up by vote-seeking politicians who echo the charges of undue harassment. In the mid-1980s, the surge of new illegal immigrants from Central America has added to the tensions between the INS and some local communities. The sanctuary movement, which began in a handful of churches and has since accelerated and come to include entire communities, has become the new civil rights crusade of the 1980s.

FIVE

AREA CONTROL IN THE CITIES

⊠ Important differences between the investigations branch's area control activities (as it was called while I was doing field work in 1981 and 1982) and the border patrol's ranch and farm checks were discussed in the preceding chapter. After a brief discussion of the organizational structure and role of investigations within the INS, this chapter examines investigations' area control function in greater detail.

Most of the INS's approximately 800 CIs (1982) are assigned to district offices in the larger cities. Some investigators are assigned to border patrol ASUs and some are stationed in satellite offices in smaller towns. The investigators' view of their central mission is shaped mainly by case investigations involving more serious INA violators. These include principals and lieutenants of organized rings (conspiracy cases) as well as benefit applicants suspected of fraud. There are also other cases having specific predications that originate from inside the INS (dual-action cases sent down by other sections) or are based on leads the CIs have obtained from other federal or local law agencies. Sometimes new leads are generated by investigators in the course of routine work on other cases.

The fact that most of the investigations branch's apprehensions involve administrative violators located through employer surveys or G-123 leads doesn't change this perspective. The officers still view themselves primarily as case investigators rather than as plainclothes border patrol agents. Thus, even though area control makes the statistics in quantitative terms, it tends to be devalued compared with casework involving criminal aliens or aliens suspected of fraud. With the exception of occasional G-123 leads on high-status aliens or the gathering of evidence for an administrative warrant to enter a factory, area control work is not usually investigative in the way that the fraud unit or the criminal, immoral, narcotics, and subversives (CINS) unit pursues a case.

True, some of the investigators enjoy area control work. For some, this is because the results are tangible and immediate. By contrast, in many background checks on benefit and relief applicants or in other dual-action investigations, the officers may find themselves spinning their wheels. They suspect the benefit will not be denied even though they have developed sufficient adverse information. Or they know they are unlikely to locate an absconded alien in the time their supervisors will allow them to develop leads and make the arrest.

In contrast, area control has something to show for the day's work: Aliens are apprehended and processed, required to post bonds, returned to the border by bus, and so on. Also, some CIs doing employer surveys will defend what they do by asserting that area control work requires good street skills including Fourth-Amendment expertise. Among other things, they must make quick and complex determinations of an individual's status in the field and develop an intuitive feeling for the people and situations they encounter.

In the largest district offices (such as New York, Chicago, and Los Angeles, which have 100 to 200 investigators), the officers are assigned to specialized units within the investigations section. Officers in the higher civil service grades (GS 11, 12, and 13) are usually found working the more complex cases developed in the fraud, antismuggling, or CINS units. Lower-rated newcomers (GS 9 and below) are most likely to be found working in area control or the general units, both of which require less mastery of the law and also involve more cut-and-dried tasks. (The work of CIs in these other units is discussed in Chapter 6.)

In medium-sized cities, there may be a dozen or so officers assigned to investigations, depending on the size of the alien population (Atlanta, for example, has considerably fewer investigators than Washington, D.C.). In satellite offices in smaller towns, there may be only three or four officers who will be jacks-of-all-trades and will handle investigations, benefit examinations, deportations, and whatever else comes to hand.

Although investigators in the larger offices are more likely to spend most of their time directly on enforcement-related tasks, they are sometimes called on to assist other INS branches. For example, they may help examiners clear up adjudications backlogs or assist the inspectors at an airport during peak arrival times for overseas flights.

Many investigators resent their diversion from investigative work because they view themselves, first and foremost, as law enforcers. Some dislike doing what they refer to as attorney work. Variations in their enforcement routine, however, are usually not resented.[1] This is especially true when the officer is being rotated out of the area control or the general unit into fraud, CINS, or some other unit whose cases are considered challenging and important to enforcement goals. Periodic rotation is done partly to give the newer officers more experience and partly to alleviate the monotony of performing the same investigations day after day. In a few district offices, job rotation is mandated by formal collective bargaining agreements between the investigators' civil service union and INS management; in others, INS supervisors rotate their officers even in the absence of union rules because they believe it enhances officer morale.

The chain of command lengthens as the investigations branch increases in size. The assistant district director of investigations, who reports to the district director, will have supervisors in charge of the various specialized units. In the largest offices, an added layer of squad leaders will be found serving under the area control, fraud, antismuggling, and other unit supervisors. There may also be an additional special investigations unit, which handles third-party conspiracy cases that may involve sensitive or complicated investigations abroad.

Although staffing levels vary widely from unit to unit and are adjusted to reflect shifts in caseload pressures, the area control units had the largest number of investigators in most offices I visited during my field work in 1981 and 1982. That was partly due to the fact that area control was able to produce more arrests per productive officer hour than other units could produce "case closings," but the most important reason was the recession of the early 1980s. Central office higher-ups believed that more jobs should be liberated for citizens, and area control staffing was increased in response. During the Carter administration, by contrast, these units had been cut back drastically, an action that many officers believe arose because urban interior arrests were politically troublesome for that administration. But with the recession and a more enforcement-minded Reagan administration in office, the central office had instructed the districts to put 50 percent of their investigator man-hours into area control activities by the fall of 1982.

In other investigations units, the output measure is case closings, which are less politically visible and sensitive compared with area control apprehensions. Although a case investigation may lead to an arrest, followed (in most cases) by voluntary departure and (in a small percentage) to deportation or prosecution, many do not—as, for example, when an officer carries out a routine character check on an alien applying for suspension of deportation relief or investigates a suspected sham marriage. Success is not easily quantifiable beyond the measure of cases opened or pending in relation to those closed. Thus, in dual-action cases initiated by examinations or naturalization officers, a case can be closed when the officer has obtained the information the examiners asked for in order to justify a benefit grant or denial. But as one investigator said, "What happens afterward we won't know, and frankly, we probably prefer not to know."

Even if the officer cannot obtain the information or cannot locate an alien who has absconded after being ordered to appear for a hearing, the case may still be closed (and counted in the statistics) if certain investigatory steps and procedures to obtain information that would help locate the alien have been carried out.[2]

During the period of my field work, most area control operations were being conducted at businesses and construction sites, although occasionally the officers would pursue working aliens at bus stops or on streets where day laborers were known to assemble. (Illegal aliens who turn themselves in at district offices along with technical violators [crewmen] are also counted in the area control unit's statistics.) When area control arrests occur at residences, it is usually serendipitous. That is, while pursuing a criminal or fraud case investigation, the officers happened to stumble across administrative violators. Immigration and Naturalization Service higher-ups may know that the CIs netted the administrative violators simply because they turned out to be illegal when they were asked questions relating to a case under investigation; however, INS's critics and some journalists, who see the matter differently, will report the arrests as a sweep in a residential area.

In the mid-1970s, central office policy had begun to discourage the CIs from conducting immigration checks in residential areas (unrelated to specific case investigations) because of the legal and political turbulence they could stir up. However, the policy shift could also be justified by the fact that work site arrests were better quality because they targeted employed aliens. Even after the Carter administration's census moratorium, which had put residential neighborhoods off-limits and also sought to curtail farm checks and business surveys, was finally lifted in the fall of 1980, area control operations were not resumed in residential areas in most cities. (Patrol agents may still occasionally work residential streets in smaller border towns because there is apt to be little mobilized activist pressure and enforcement actions have low public visibility.)

The remainder of this chapter focuses on the tactics CIs use in area control operations and on many of the dilemmas they confront. Other aspects of investigative enforcement are discussed in Chapters 6 and 7.

AREA CONTROL IN THE CITIES

As was pointed out in Chapter 4, plainclothes investigators' immigration status checks at work sites resemble farm and ranch checks in one major respect: The officers often meet resistance from the employers of illegal aliens as well as from the aliens themselves. However, at urban work sites, citizens and lawful residents are more likely to be working alongside illegal aliens, including some with possible benefit equities and others whose immigration situation is ambiguous. This means that employer surveys (or checks in public areas) are much less routinized than farm checks and linewatch patrolling.

Before the area control squads began to emphasize workplaces almost exclusively, they sometimes used tactics similar to those used by the border patrol on linewatch and during farm and ranch checks. That is, they would work proactively, often in residential neighborhoods where they knew from experience they could pick up illegal aliens in public view on the street or at bus stops. Investigators in Los Angeles, for example, would take INS vans home at night and make their pickups in Hispanic barrios on their way in to the office the next morning. The vans could be filled after a few stops and the paperwork done by 3 P.M. Adult Hispanics walking along the streets were good candidates for checks because, the officers reasoned, most Angelenos, including American citizens of Mexican descent, traveled by car.

Sometimes the investigators were asked into a neighborhood by an irate apartment house manager who wanted to clean out tenants who were causing trouble. Or local police would enlist the aid of investigators when a neighborhood had a crime problem and it was believed illegals were part of the problem. The streets being public areas, street pickups did not require warrants, and if the agents wanted to check a rooming house, they could usually get the building manager's permission to enter (patrol agents say that any agents who can't talk their way onto private land are not worth their salt). Or investigators might pursue aliens they spotted on the street into an apartment house, where they would encounter and question other aliens. As noted earlier, however, mounting criticism has caused INS policy to prohibit residential area control sweeps.

Although sweeps based on tips from the public (reactive enforcement) had always been done to some degree, the shift to business surveys meant that CIs would have to rely more heavily on leads phoned or mailed in by the public. Such leads are important because, although the officers always knew which industries were apt to turn up illegals, the reduced visibility afforded by business locales meant the officers might need to get a warrant if the owner refused them permission to enter the nonpublic area of a business.[3] Working reactively from tips that named individuals and gave their work addresses was not an absolute necessity for a warrant, but it did assist officers to establish the probable cause the U.S. attorney would want when screening the warrant request before going to the federal magistrate.[4]

This is not to say that proactive area control no longer occurs. Although it has clearly declined in importance, even as late as the early 1980s, investigators in some cities would decide to conduct a sweep at a commercial inter-section known to be a gathering spot for day laborers. And in some cities, they still conduct checks at bus stops and transportation terminals, as border patrol agents also routinely do. Thus at an airport, the CIs visually scan pas-sengers arriving on domestic flights from certain cities because illegals some-times travel by plane after crossing the border. Individuals wearing excess amounts of clothing will be suspect.

At a bus stop known to be used by illegal aliens, a CI may unobtrusively sidle up to an individual suspected of being illegal and will ask in English for the time of day or whether a certain bus has come by. Such an indirect ap-proach can generate additional articulable facts to warrant a forcible deten-tion and more detailed questioning when the individual appears flustered or answers "*Mandé?*" (Excuse me?).

But investigators and their superiors have become more circumspect when conducting alienage and deportability checks in open public areas. For example, if a landscaping crew is spotted and the officers stop, the aliens may run into bystanders or knock over a child on a tricycle as they attempt to flee. Despite policy controls intended to discourage officers from going on private property, when agents are confronted by aliens who defy official authority, who run or throw objects at the officers, this can lead to incidents, such as damage to plants in gardens, that can cause citizens to complain. There is also less control in a congregated urban setting, and hence more risk of injury. In addition, higher-level administrators have valid concerns over officer actions that might provoke new litigation leading to temporary or permanent court injunctions that might further hedge the officers' discretion and the agency's autonomy. Such adverse litigation could further curb what Peter Schuck has called the need for "vigorous decision-making."[5] As one INS officer expressed the problem, "bad cases make bad law." So, too, with bad arrests.

BUSINESS SURVEYS: PROCEDURES

When tips on reported illegal aliens are received in the district office by phone or mail, and if the information is specific and appears credible, the area control investigator who takes the call will fill out a G-123 form. Names and other identifying characteristics of reported aliens are recorded along with their work addresses. In some offices, leads on businesses are distinguished from leads on individuals even though business addresses are given in both cases. In many business leads, the officers assume they will find more than just the named suspected illegal aliens. (Occasionally, tipsters give aliens' resi-dential addresses in their letters rather than their places of work. Leads on single individuals are less attractive, because of their lower productivity, but if a case looks interesting, an investigator might try calling at the residence to learn where the alien works; sometimes the investigators even succeed in persuading aliens to come down to the district office and turn themselves in.)

Because there are always plenty of leads to work on in most offices, selecting them on the basis of credibility (specific rather than vague information) makes good sense, even aside from the probable cause requirement for a warrant, should one be needed. Leads on administrative violators that give a residential rather than business address are, productivity considerations aside, of little use because of the policy against pursuing aliens at residences in most cases. (But these leads may be turned over to other units if they name individuals suspected of being involved in crime or serious immigration violations or if they name individuals who absconded before or after having deportation hearings.)

Usually the area control supervisor or a squad leader will have the final say on which leads to pursue. Like patrol agents, area control officers feel a certain amount of pressure to produce a decent monthly arrest total, which will be entered into the G-123 report. These can be quickly generated by raids on easier targets, such as restaurants whose owners are less apt to refuse entry, or by more carefully planned raids on blue-collar establishments that, although a warrant may be required, will produce a high number of arrests. But a concern over the statistics is only one of several targeting desiderata. As noted in Chapter 4, lower-productivity G-123 leads are often worked either because they involve quality cases (white-collar or highly paid deportable aliens) or simply because many officers believe that targeting should be as equitable as possible. Many officers feel strongly that it is important for the public to realize that Mexicans are not the only enforcement problem.

Targeting decisions can also result from the CIs' perceptions of a business management's attitude toward the service. Although employers currently violate no federal law when they employ illegal aliens, many investigators will refer to certain employers as flagrant or notorious employers (and in an occasional slip of the tongue, even use the term violator in connection with a business), especially if they believe the owners are not only aware they have illegal aliens in their employ but actually prefer them because of the economic advantages.

Criminal investigators point out that some business owners consciously violate federal law by arranging for workers to be sent to them and paying fees to smugglers in advance (aiding and abetting) or by hiding or helping their illegal employees escape during a raid (harboring). Investigators sometimes stumble across secret rooms and other hiding places, such as piles of lumber with hollow interiors. Sometimes they find aliens who have been put in crates that have then been nailed shut by fellow workers. But making a harboring charge stick against an employer is often difficult because it is usually hard to prove that the employer knew these things were going on—and indeed, the employer may not actually have been aware.

When the officers decide to survey a smaller business, such as a restaurant or some other small, service-oriented establishment, they are much less likely to do the advance preparation work they would do when they select a larger business. A two-man team may just drop by to conduct the check while en route back to the office from another assignment. This is possible because they can check the public area of the business without a warrant; also, the owner is more apt to give consent because a quick inspection of a small work force will usually not disrupt operations the way a survey does in a factory, where operations may have to be shut down temporarily. Often, the officers will keep a list of smaller establishments to be checked if they happen to be in the area and have the time. Or, if they have produced fewer than the expected number of apprehensions during a planned raid on a larger concern, they can make up the deficit by surveying one or two smaller businesses on the way back to the office.

Larger firms require more advanced planning, partly because of logistical requirements but also because the officers are more likely to be denied entry. If they approach a firm for permission and are refused, they may strengthen the evidence needed to establish probable cause beyond an informant's lead (if they are working from a tip) by sending an advance team out early in the morning to question persons about to enter the firm. Thus street arrests of illegal aliens in commercial districts are often carried out to bolster the founded suspicion needed for an administrative warrant. Of course, what sometimes happens is that other workers, who see the officers interviewing a man or woman on the street, turn their cars around and speed off. Inside the plant, other employees rush to the windows, see what is going on and wave off friends they know to be illegal who are coming up the street. Or they may rush to a phone to tell a friend to call in sick for the day.

Besides arresting a worker or two, the officers have the satisfaction of knowing that their presence on the street can put a crimp in an employer's operations for the day if other workers have been scared off.

PLANNING FOR THE SURVEY

When the area control supervisor decides on a survey of a firm where the officers anticipate finding more than just the one or two illegal aliens named in a tip, someone will contact the management in advance to determine whether voluntary consent will be given. Owners who consent are informed that investigators will come back at a later time to carry out the checks. The precise date is not given because this would make it possible for owners to alert illegal workers, who would then stay away.

Area control officers will try to accommodate a cooperative management by conducting the survey in a manner that will pose the least disruption. If the firm has a small work force, the investigator who makes the initial contact may decide to interview several workers then and there. In the case of a larger firm, employee payroll and job application records are usually requested. If the owner cooperates and agrees to supply company records, the officer explains that they will not have to disturb plant operations when they return later to conduct the checks.

After checking over employee records, the area control officer who is handling the case will draw up a list of the workers suspected to be deportable. When the officers arrive later, they will usually confine their interviewing to this group, calling in the workers for a brief interrogation in a room set aside by the employer. (But the officers may also try to persuade the owner to let them go out on the floor if they think there are illegal aliens in addition to those on their list, especially if they spot runners.)

Some employers may consent to let the INS conduct a survey but refuse to turn over records, in which case the investigators may seek a court order to subpoena them. If they are working from employer records, the investigators look for a variety of profile clues. For example, workers' Social Security numbers should be consistent with the time when they first started working (as judged by the ages they list), which presumably would be close to the time when they applied for their cards. Many illegal aliens give Social Security numbers that are incompatible with their ages. In some cases, the numbers are genuine but belong to friends or relatives, which means the alien is contributing to somebody else's retirement account. Some simply make up a number for an account that does not exist.

Scanning job application forms, the officers can also spot foreign handwriting, which may be a tip-off, especially if it is linked to a Hispanic or other foreign-origin name. Many illegal aliens provide honest answers on their application forms. Thus they may list the primary or secondary schools they attended in Mexico or overseas or even the town and foreign country they were born in. With names and birthdates, and often the place of birth as well, investigators can pinpoint those they reasonably believe to be aliens (although they may turn out to be naturalized citizens). If the employer requires job applicants to state whether they are citizens or aliens authorized to work and asks for the I-551 numbers of those claiming to be lawful permanent residents, the officers can check both the names and alien registration numbers of these aliens against their service records. If they come up with a valid alien registration number but under a different name (which means the alien is probably borrowing someone's number) or they find no record of the number at all, then that is somebody they need to talk to.

Such prescreening techniques are not foolproof. Illegal aliens who have listed themselves as U.S. citizens and mask their alienage by giving a U.S. birthplace are unlikely to be caught unless something unique, such as a Social Security number that could not exist, has drawn the officer's attention. The INS has no records on citizens and therefore nothing against which to check the name and birthdate of a citizen claimant. (In such a case, the individual would have to be interviewed in person and would be likely to come to INS attention only through an informer's tip.) Also, an alien who has borrowed both the name and alien registration number of another immigrant is less likely to be ferreted out. Given their heavy work loads, investigators lack the time to carry out screening that would reduce positive errors (deportable aliens not screened out) to the irreducible minimum.

If one assumes that resources, being scarce, need to be allocated rationally in terms of unavoidable trade-offs, it makes sense for officers to maximize their leverage by profiling to catch the easier (most apparent) deportables and then moving on to other business. As with immigration checks in open fields and other public places, alienage and deportability investigations that use prescreening profiles obtain better returns on invested time by focusing on those individuals who from all appearances (dress and behavior in an open field or nonexistent service numbers after a prescreening record check) are most apt to be deportable when interviewed. A consistently thorough and probing inspection of every individual or record would quickly lead to diminishing returns; indeed, although more thorough screening might make enforcement more equitable because it would catch more of the better acculturated, shrewder, or less honest deportable aliens, the returns could well become negative as the time available to pursue more serious INA violators correspondingly shrank. Thus, and somewhat ironically, inequitable enforcement against administrative violators may be the way Peter has to be robbed to pay Paul in order to maintain other enforcement commitments.

Nor is this dilemma confined to business surveys. It is systemic in its ramifications throughout the administrative system. Thus an officer may spot, leaving a restaurant, a Chinese cook who, because of white coat and distinctive slippers, the investigator is reasonably certain is an alien and very possibly an illegal one. But if the officer stops the cook, and that individual doesn't understand English (or pretends not to), the officer's discretion narrows and the dilemmas mount. Unless the cook tried to run, the officer who forcibly detained or took that cook in would be on shaky legal ground. Assuming an interpreter could be found in a reasonable period of time, the cook might turn out to be just another lawful resident without a card—in short an unproductive arrest costly in time.

The reasons many employers consent to cooperate with area control officers vary. Some do so for patriotic reasons. Knowing that their fellow Americans need jobs, they would prefer not to hire illegal aliens. Some are genuinely surprised when they learn they have illegals on their payroll and, although this is atypical, may even help the INS by joining in inspection of bathrooms, storage areas, and the like. Often, and this is especially true in larger concerns, the employer, who is not involved in the hiring, may not know. Supervisors, who may be lawful aliens or naturalized citizens, may be in charge of the hiring and may use their positions to hire fellow nationals. (Some supervisors use their hiring authority to extract bribes and even, according to officers who have discovered "paramour suites" in unlikely areas of a building, sexual favors.) And, of course, some employers would prefer to hire citizens or legal aliens but believe (or so they claim) that they could not remain competitive in their industry if they did so.

Officers claim there are even times when employers welcome surveys because their sales have fallen off but they are too good-hearted to lay off loyal workers, or they may be reluctant to fire them for fear of retaliation by the union. The INS can take the blame. Some anonymous tips come from business owners who, officers hypothesize, want to replace the illegals they are currently employing with a fresh batch. Aliens who are being underpaid may have begun to compare their earnings with those of others they know in comparable jobs and, if the comparisons are unfavorable to themselves, will grow restless. As one New York investigator put it, in such cases the aliens "have gotten too big for their pants." Most officers dislike thinking they may be helping an employer turn over his or her work force because, in such a case, their efforts abet the owner's exploitation of employees. But investigators need to work from leads and even when they suspect a tipster's motives, they cannot always be sure their suspicions are correct.

Other business owners are indifferent to whether illegals are employed in their company but cooperate because they know they may be targeted in the future, and perhaps more frequently if they refuse. Under the circumstances, investigators may decide to get a warrant to raid a firm they know will be less productive than some others as a way of conveying to the owner that federal law officers are to be respected. Area control keeps a record of prior surveys on a business; a notorious employer has a higher risk of being surveyed again because the priors on such a firm help the officers bolster their probable cause for a warrant.

Finally, there are employers who have established good relations with their workers and choose not to cooperate with the INS for fear of destroying their employees' trust, or who insist the INS get a warrant because they worry that, if their workers flee and are injured during a survey they have consented to, they might be sued.

When an employer refuses to cooperate, the contacting area control officer explains that, in that case, a warrant will be obtained, and the unit will conduct the survey in a way that suits the INS's convenience, not the owner's. As one officer explained, "Telling an uncooperative employer we'll get a warrant is an inducement because, if we get the warrant, we conduct the operation according to our convenience, not his, and we can close the plant down on safety grounds, during our search and interrogation. That means he'll lose production for that period. Also, he can be required to open any door anywhere. It's more of a hassle for the employer."

With a warrant, the officers can poke through cabinets and inventory, break locks on gates and doors. Instead of a survey conducted on mutually determined terms, the squad will arrive with bolt cutters to conduct a raid. The officers believe they must raid uncooperative employers because failure to do so would stiffen resistance to voluntary cooperation among other firms in the industry.

When a raid has been decided on, an officer is assigned to visit the establishment to learn about its interior layout (if it is possible to get inside the building) and the exits leading from the building, which will have to be covered during the raid. Basic information on the nature of the business, size of the work force, and the nationality and sex of the aliens believed to be working there illegally is gathered so the supervisor can decide how many officers and vans to send, whether a translator should be present, and how much resistance might be anticipated. (Male aliens are more likely to run than females. Also, males who are from more distant South American countries and who lack equities have more incentive to resist because of their heavier investment in getting into the United States.)

If the officers seek to maximize apprehensions, they may pick a payday. If they think most of the illegals on the work force have been put on a late afternoon or a midnight shift, they may alter their usual pattern of conducting a morning raid and go out at night instead.

CARRYING OUT THE RAID

On the scheduled day, the area control squad will be briefed on the details of the operation, usually by the officer who first visited the establishment and who may also be the contact officer for the raid. The contact officer dresses in business clothes and is the one who approaches the management with the warrant.

In larger operations, involving ten to thirty officers, the area control squads and their supervisors assemble at a prearranged place that is out of view but in the vicinity of the plant. Sometimes the area control supervisor will make a quick tour by the plant to see whether the main gate is open and to check for any indications that the management may have had prior warning of the raid. To avoid giving early warning, a car with a state rather than federal license plate may be used. Because notorious employers of illegals are believed to monitor the radio channels used by the officers, destination is not discussed when officers talk by radio en route to the site.

When the signal is given, the caravan of light brown sedans and vans descends on the company. Some of the officers take up positions outside the building to pick up runners and to check other workers who are walking out the exits if, based on behavior and appearance, they appear to be aliens. Meanwhile, the contact officer goes inside to inform the management that a survey is underway.

Sometimes agents will make a call without a warrant, as, for example, in a reportable case that has a prompt call-up date that does not give them sufficient time to gather the probable cause for a warrant. (In a smaller district office, they may do this when they feel they cannot spare an officer to do the workup.)

During one raid that I was able to observe in a midwestern city, the owner professed not to know he had illegal aliens working at his plant when we entered. He invited the officers to have a cup of coffee (this was politely refused) while he went back to talk to his plant superintendent. The diminutive superintendent, a Hispanic female, asked if the officers could wait a few minutes until the midmorning break. That wouldn't be a problem at all, the contact officer assured her. Unbeknownst to the officers, she alerted the workers in the main plant area. When the officers entered, their initial impression was that the plant was clean. But by chance, one officer checked a dark, recessed area in a storage closet and found a worker hiding. Then the officers began a thorough check, poking through bales of raw unfinished fabric, into the restrooms, and under racks of finished inventory, and they began to turn up more illegals. (Often, officers need only look around at the empty workstations with inventory in process to know that illegals are going to be found somewhere.)

At this plant, which stitched semifinished fabric into bedding, the officers were surprised to find that the illegals were mainly Mexicans, although there were also a few Salvadorans suspected of being EWIs along with a Thai. (They had been expecting to find Koreans.) Two of the Mexicans claimed to be visa tourists, but even if that were true, they were out of status because they lacked authorization to work. The one Thai male, his fear visible in his face, was pulled out from under a garment rack and immediately handcuffed. Because the others had also been found hiding, probable cause was immediately reached for an arrest, and they were quickly loaded into a van.

While accompanying investigators on a different raid, this time in a slum district in the Northeast, the supervisor candidly explained as we entered the reception foyer on the first floor that he didn't mind the management sounding the alarm. It made the work of the squads easier because the illegals would automatically separate themselves from the legal workers by running. Sure enough, when we emerged from a freight elevator on the third floor, Haitian and Hispanic males could be seen scurrying through the aisles of sewing machines into adjoining rooms and toward exits at the rear. Some officers immediately went after the runners, and singly, or in groups of two or three, they were led back to a temporary holding area. Besides the fact that reasonable suspicion for forcible detention is reached immediately for runners, they are also helpful in that the officer can later justify a higher bond along with a warrant of arrest on the OSC because runners have, by their behavior, exhibited a stronger likelihood of absconding. (Ironically, however, if they have substantial equities—and a stable job is one—the assistant director for investigation, or the immigration judge, may reduce the bond or release the aliens on OR, despite the trouble the officers faced in the field. Officers resent the fact that holding a good job may be considered an equity for bond purposes because they are conducting these surveys precisely for the purpose of liberating good jobs for citizens and authorized aliens. But it could also be that a district office may decide to shade the bond in favor of the alien [by setting a lower bond or granting release on recognizance] because of the resource costs of detaining the alien.)

At the microlevel of the enforcement encounter, field tactics are shaped and honed by the officers' combination of intuition and experience. First, even though violence is rare, officers must be alert to danger. Does the alien holding a knife or tool intend to use it against an officer? (Males are almost always patted down after the alienage and deportability determination, but male officers will not pat down a woman unless they believe she is carrying a weapon.)

Second, officers must also judge, from experience and collegial lore, how a particular individual should be handled from the standpoints of control and interrogation. While on a raid in a West Coast city, I accompanied an officer who was walking an alien out of the plant to his car for the purpose of checking documents the alien claimed showed he was married to a citizen. All the while, the officer maintained light, but close, physical contact with the alien. He explained that he would place his hand on the inside of the individual's forearm by the elbow joint, with a finger on the artery to check the pulse. Or he might rest his hand lightly on the alien's shoulder to make the same check on a neck vein. If the alien is extremely apprehensive, the pulse becomes rapid, and the officer is forewarned the alien might try to bolt. (The physical contact is, in itself, a deterrent to running.) The officer added that this was also one of the ways he could determine whether aliens were telling the truth about their status—a rapid pulse would suggest that the alien might not be leveling with him.

To return to the raid in the northeastern slum, after the runners were brought back and assembled in a temporary holding area, some of the officers began searching for hiders in cabinets, attic storage bins, the basements, and other places. Investigators acknowledge that some aliens elude apprehension because of the diminishing marginal returns of trying for 100 percent success. At some point, they have to return to headquarters to start processing those they have arrested; also, the vans may be filled to capacity. As noted earlier, this reveals the reduced enforcement concern that applies to INA violators compared with "real" criminals. One cannot imagine DEA agents breaking off a drug raid because they have already filled their cars with suspects or because they worry about having to stay late to complete the paperwork.

Other officers continued strolling through the plant, watching the behavior and faces of workers who remained at their workstations or were moving about (but not running) on the floor. The microlevel tactics for deciding who to question depend not only on officer experience but also on the legal standard, as enforced by local district policy, in effect for that area.

For example, until the Supreme Court's Delgado ruling in the spring of 1984, officers in Los Angeles were required to have "individualized suspicion," much as if they were approaching persons on a public street or in an Amtrak station. They either had to have the name and description of a worker in advance or to have spotted the articulables of nervous behavior and unusual clothing for those not specifically sought but encountered on the scene after they arrived.[6]

Where visual scanning is the preferred or required mode, the articulables are apt to have the same basic parameters as those used in open fields or public places. Officers will look for those who cast furtive looks, break off eye contact, or appear to be shifting from their workstations into a group that has been checked, and so on. Often the characteristics of the work site are determinative to some extent. In some businesses, workers are seated in rows and remain at their benches; in others, they are wandering around on the floor. If time is short in relation to the number of workers to be checked, it is probable that investigators handle the trade-off the way patrol agents sometimes do when they stumble across large crews—that is, they will select on the basis of clear-cut articulables because of the operational need to narrow down the number of candidates to be questioned in the plant. (Indeed, patrol agents may pass up a field where they spot Indochinese at work, on the reasonable assumption they are very likely refugees. As aliens, they could be checked; but if most are refugees, it hardly pays to check the entire crew even though a few who are illegal might turn up.)

Consider the following situation, which will illuminate the microlevel decisions made on the scene. The investigators arrive at a plant where they can reasonably assume almost all of the foreign-origin females working at industrial sewing machines are either legal or illegal aliens. The officers move along the rows to question them and check their papers. An obvious citizen (non-foreign appearance and clothing and absence of accent) might be passed by if one were encountered. The problem arises, of course, that a visual determination of a worker's citizenship status may be made on the basis of physical appearance (European-origin physical features) rather than, say, a more legitimate articulable fact, such as showing normal curiosity toward the agents' presence. Thus, although court rulings prohibit the INS from basing an interrogation on foreign physical appearance or foreign speech alone, officers are quite free to use facial and other physical features for negative sorting (that is, deciding who *not* to talk to). In effect, the courts' Fourth-Amendment reasonable-suspicion standard provides a certain amount of leeway when officers decide not to approach certain individuals because they can easily claim the absence of sufficient articulable facts. (Such field decisions, because they are invisible to superiors, would never come under scrutiny.) However, such impacts reveal the paradoxical effects of the law, especially if the policy intent of the law is to achieve equitable and non-discriminatory enforcement as well as to protect citizens against unwarranted intrusions.

Negative sorting usually occurs because of resource constraints rather than because of any subjective bias for or against a given group or category of aliens. For example, Latino females may be screened less thoroughly than Latino males because of the burdensome task of having to pick up children and the need to provide special accommodations. Sometimes suspected illegal aliens will be bypassed because time has run out. While I accompanied investigators on a raid that pulled out a sizeable group of Haitians and Central Americans, I observed several CIs pass by a group of European-origin workers in a basement area. After we passed, one of the officers said, "They look like they might be Poles," but they were not approached and questioned. The officers may have decided to "make them citizens" because they were winding up the survey. Also, because of the blanket extended voluntary departure being granted to all Polish nationals at the time, arresting illegal Polish aliens would have little meaningful enforcement impact. The Poles would very likely be given indefinite voluntary departure and might even receive INS authorization to work.

LENIENCY DUE TO CASELOAD
PRESSURES AND OTHER FACTORS

Because most INA violations are not serious as a rule, investigators have considerable leeway to exercise field discretion on the basis of caseload pressures, public relations sensitivities, or purely idiosyncratic motivations. Sometimes this can lead to a toughened enforcement posture although it more typically results in either individual or collectively applied leniency.

Thus area control investigators are apt to grow angry when an employer berates them for handcuffing an employee. I observed a survey of a restaurant in a Virginia suburb of Washington, D.C., during which the owner became angry when the investigator arrested her Salvadoran cook and salad girl. She berated him by asking why the INS wasn't arresting people who mug and rob and why the INS was picking on her restaurant. (It was a reportable case. A former cook had written to the U.S. consulate in France that he had not been paid back wages he claimed the owner owed him.) The officer became irritated and responded by explaining that she was violating Virginia state law, which prohibits the hiring of illegal aliens and that he would report the restaurant to the relevant government bureau of the state. (Doing so might make the owner leery about rehiring the illegal cook and salad girl after they were released on bond.) In Virginia, only a handful of employers have been successfully prosecuted and fined; those who were fined had rehired illegal aliens who were former employees and who they therefore knew were not authorized to work. If one generalization stands out in the literature on law enforcement, it is that the use of actual legal sanctions is much less significant than the use of the threat that they may be invoked. One reason (but not the exclusive one) is the need law agents have to keep sanctions in reserve to control offender behavior during and after the field encounter. Even if officers doubt the ultimate deterrence value of the law for curbing the violations for which it was intended, they know from experience that it can often be successfully used to manage the behavior of those they must deal with in the field.[7]

When dealing with aliens and those who employ them, the purpose is not just to extract respect for official authority, although the officers would prefer at least grudging acquiescence to their needs, but to get the job of apprehending illegal aliens done with a minimum of fuss and bother. (Several officers told me that aliens who are respectful toward them may sometimes be allowed to return voluntarily despite the fact that they have been recognized as repeat crossers. Had they been abusive, they probably would have been written up for deportation processing.)

Decisions to err on the side of leniency probably arise mainly from caseload and other pressures. For example, if officers take too much time during area control surveys, they may cause the employer to lose an undue amount of production. They might turn up a few more violators if they continued to search, but at the margin, the effort may not be justified if the owner will complain about the service to associates in the business community or to politicians or will perhaps choose to harass the service with a civil lawsuit. Of course, in the case of a notorious employer for whom a warrant must be obtained every time the officers want to enter the premises, this is less likely to be an important consideration for the officers.

Because the officers would prefer employers to cooperate, even if only grudgingly, they have an incentive to be accommodating—sometimes even when they have gone out with a warrant. Too hard-boiled an attitude can stiffen the resistance of other employers they will want to visit.

During one raid I observed involving a cooperative employer, the officers broke off the survey even before they had finished interviewing the approximately 200 or so workers. When they returned with 20 or 30 aliens in the vans, the area control supervisor, who had remained at headquarters, wanted to know what had happened that there were fewer arrests than had been anticipated. The squad leader explained that the owner had withdrawn his consent. But it is also possible that the raid had been cut short because the owner had begun to pester the agents, asking them when they would be finished so he could get back to full production.[8]

A form of collective leniency may be extended to workers who have not been checked at the time the officers decide to break off a survey or who may have been questioned so briefly that adequate screening of oral claims is impaired. Thus oral claims to green-card status may be credited when the workers claim they left their documents at home. Whereas time pressures may be one factor in determining leniency, a management's cooperative behavior can be another. In a survey of a garment shop that employed mainly Koreans, for example, not only had the management cooperated when the officers made an unannounced call without a warrant but also they had agreed to assist with translation. Because the squad had no Korean interpreter, the survey could not have been conducted without this help. Many of the workers claimed to be green-card holders but said they had left their cards at home. The officers could have taken in those without cards, but as noted earlier, such arrests are not productive. In addition to the cooperation on the part of the management, other factors had tipped the scales: The officers faced a language barrier in a noisy work setting, nobody was available at the headquarters office to handle the computer checks of names and numbers phoned in from the field, and Korean language specialists would have had to be located late in the day for the processing work. The two aliens who were taken out of the plant had caused problems; one had been found hiding, and the other refused to speak with the officers. (It turned out the latter was the relative of a diplomat and had been working without authorization.)

As this example shows, field discretion can be used, within the framework of the law, to sanction those who do not cooperate and to benefit those who do. In the preceding case, the officers may not have been absolutely sure in their minds that all of the Koreans were the green-card holders they claimed to be. But they could rationalize breaking off a survey on the grounds that the employer who has been cooperative is less apt to have something to hide.

THE IMPACT OF STATUS AMBIGUITY

Although some urban area control surveys, especially in such western cities as Dallas (construction sites) or Los Angeles (light industry), will net mainly Mexican EWI violators without equities and show productivity ratios (arrests per officer man-hour) as high as some border patrol operations do, most such surveys turn up a more heterogeneous mix of violators than those of the border patrol's farm and ranch checks.

Thus a business survey may turn up the administratively routine Mexican male without equities who can be written up in 15 to 30 minutes and given voluntary return on the bus that afternoon. However, it can also turn out a broad assortment of aliens, with varying immigration statuses, who will not only take more time to sort out in the field but also will require considerably more time in terms of paperwork back at the office—especially if they ask for hearings.

Those aliens who cannot be released (because they are judged likely to abscond) will be brought in. If they want hearings, they must be written up with an order to show cause, they must be fingerprinted and photographed, it must be decided whether a warrant of arrest must be issued, a bond must be recommended, the assistant director for investigations will have to sign off on the paperwork, arrangements may have to be made for them to call an attorney, and more—all of which can take one or two officer man-hours per apprehension, and sometimes longer if a translator is needed.

Even though mainly Mexican EWIs were turned up, the following case will serve to illustrate the greater complexity arising from more variegated status situations. A survey had been scheduled for a Los Angeles fashion textile manufacturer. The owner had consented to let the agents enter the plant to interview about 25 workers the INS suspected were illegal based on a prescreening check of employee records.

When the agents arrived, the workers were called into an office the employer put at the investigators' disposal. Although those interviewed were predominantly Hispanic females, they were not the recent border crossers that patrol agents routinely encounter but aliens who had settled into Los Angeles.[9] As they were led into the office, several presented Silva-Levi letters based on a federal court ruling that prevented the INS from allocating Western Hemisphere preference visas to Cubans. However by this time, the allocation of Silva-Levi immigrant visa numbers had already been exhausted, which made the letters valueless and their holders (barring other possible equities) deportable. Instead of apprehending the women, the investigators obtained their current addresses and let them return to work. They would be sent a letter instructing them to either report to the district office so an order to show cause could be served or that they could depart voluntarily within 30 days.

The reason given for not apprehending those who had Silva-Levi letters was that, because they had made contact with the service and had applied for the letter, they could be assumed unlikely to abscond. Yet in some cases, such an assumption can become a useful rationale for a nonarrest decision arrived at on grounds of administrative expediency. In the case of women, relatives may have to be contacted to be certain somebody is available to look after their underage dependents until the officers can send somebody around. If they have been in the United States for some time, other equities may surface (perhaps later if not at the time of the field interrogation) and that can mean additional work for examiners and immigration judges. As one agent put it, "Sometimes when you arrest deportable aliens, you may be doing them a favor by encouraging them to initiate benefit applications."

In cases, such as the one discussed here, the Fourth-Amendment stricture relating to warrantless arrests—namely, that aliens should not be arrested unless judged likely to abscond—can serve administrative needs arising from resource constraints because it augments the officer's field discretion. It is a double-edged sword that can be used to rationalize leniency or to bolster a tougher enforcement posture against aliens who cause trouble. Such aliens can be judged more likely to abscond even though motives of social control (situational sanctioning) are also, and maybe primarily, involved.

Other workers interviewed in this plant turned out to have applications pending for suspension of deportation relief; this is not unusual in the interior, given the large numbers of aliens who can elude apprehension for years on end. Most of them were not carrying a copy of the OSC they had been served either when they were first apprehended or at the time they turned themselves in to a district office to apply for suspension of deportation relief. The officers had to question them briefly to verify their stories, just as they do in the case of aliens without papers who claim to be green-card holders.

When aliens are already in proceedings, it hardly makes sense to apprehend them again. But an oral claim to be in proceedings may have to be checked. One of the ironies of re-encountering deportable aliens who are already in proceedings is that they will have de facto authorization to work even if they lack official authorization. In the case of aliens with no equities, a no-work rider is sometimes appended to the OSC, in which case if INS officers were to encounter those aliens again and find that they had been working, their bond status would be revoked (in theory) and they would become subject to detention. But no-work riders are not typically imposed as a bond condition because the service does not want to deprive these individuals of their livelihoods, especially if they have families to support.[10]

Another of the females interviewed at the garment plant presented a baptismal certificate from a city in Kansas. She spoke no English but she claimed to have been born in Kansas and then sent back to Mexico to live as a child. The investigator was suspicious because her name had been on the list with an alien registration number that turned out to belong to another person. A true citizen doesn't need a green card, let alone someone else's. Because of the many different kinds of baptismal and birth records, an on-the-spot check for validity is difficult. Although the officer can check with the El Paso Intelligence Center to see if they have a record of priors on a birth or baptismal certificate, pressures of time often incline them to test the bona fides by asking questions in the field. If the alien does not pass the questioning (that is, inconsistencies remain or the mala fides are obvious), the officer may go a step further. As one investigator described his technique:

> I may explain how they would have to appear before a judge and be prosecuted for making a false citizenship claim and that it's a felony offense. If he has documents on him, I can explain that we'll check these out, make calls to the motor vehicle bureau or the state vital statistics office. But what they don't know is that the service really can't go to the bother of doing all that. They don't know how limited the service's resources are.

As a result, when a claim is not believed, the investigator usually will point out that although those who are making false statements are committing a felony, if they confess to the truth they will still be given voluntary return.

In the case described here, the woman explained to the officer that the reason she used a fraudulent green card was her inability to speak English. She told the officer she used the card because she worried that nobody would believe her when she claimed she was a citizen.

Based on what she was saying and on how she was telling her story, the officer said he thought she might be leveling with him. Although he would check it out later, he decided to let her go in the meantime. She was allowed to go back to work. (Concern over a possible suit for falsely arresting a citizen is the reason officers give for shading a decision in favor of a suspected false claimant, but here too, time and resource considerations may also intrude.)[11]

Assessing the validity of documented claims in the field often depends on the collateral assessment of how individuals are responding and telling their stories at the time. Thus the women who presented Silva-Levi letters and were released after their addresses were jotted down could conceivably have borrowed the letters from others; such letters are not secure documents and do not have the holder's photo. Sometimes aliens will borrow the green cards of relatives and pass them off on officers as their own. If there is an age discrepancy between the face of the alien standing in front of the officer and the one on the photo, the officers will look closely at distinguishing features, such as earlobes. Even so, they cannot always be sure.

Also among those interviewed in the office were a number of other women suspected of having phony green cards because the alien registration numbers they gave the employer were not found during the prescreening record search. When questioned, most conceded their alienage and deportability. They were taken to the office because, having committed immigration fraud, they could be assumed likely to abscond. In such cases, the officers' discretion narrows because they are dealing with self-admitted violators, not borderline cases or suspected false claimants who refuse to tell the truth (or "fess up" as the officers say) and whose citizenship claim may be difficult to investigate.

But more important, aside from self-admitted deportability, the officers feel obliged to bring in all aliens who make oral or documented false claims, even though they may well have equities that may lead to their release later or the grant of a benefit. Perceptions of moral culpability, as well as the constraints of a law enforcer's legal obligation and professional role, quickly firm up the arrest decision. Thus, even though apprehending females imposes greater burdens (and some officers will, in consequence, hope that most of those they encounter will have equities or be judged unlikely to abscond on other grounds), their discretion is nil in the case of a fraudulent lawful resident or United States citizen claimant, just as it is in the case of deportable males without equities, regardless of whether they sought to bluff with a false claim.

That pressures favoring discretionary leniency are strong is revealed by an incident I observed while riding on roving patrol. After another patrol team had stopped a car suspected of transporting illegal aliens, one of the patrol agents came back with a man who had presented a bogus Silva-Levi letter. The agent called over "Well, that was a mistake." At first I thought he meant that his decision to stop that particular car was a mistake because he had netted just one illegal alien out of a load of three or four passengers. But what the agent apparently meant was that, because the man had presented a fraudulent document, he might have to be set up for a deportation hearing despite the fact that he also claimed he was marrying a citizen. That would mean additional processing work back at the station. For that very reason he might decide, the officer I was riding with explained to me, to offer the man voluntary return "if he behaves himself."

Equally troublesome, because there is apt to be no payoff for the time invested, are cases of illegal aliens who claim to be married to citizens (and who may indeed be married to citizens who have not yet petitioned for their spouses' green cards). When the officers cannot test such marriage claims (as when the spouse lives in another state), such aliens may have to be brought in and served with an OSC, after which they might be released OR. Such cases act as a break on productivity (meaningful arrests) even though the arrest may count in the statistics. This is because, besides the added time for deportation processing, such arrests do not always produce departures but start other wheels in the apparatus spinning—processing relief and benefit petitions, for example. As a result, when used with administrative violators, deportation processing is often viewed as an administrative resource waster, and unless the alien insists on it, it will be used sparingly. Moreover, subtle pressure to encourage aliens to accept voluntary return may be communicated from higher-ups in the district office to the patrol agents or CIs because of limited detention space or a desire to keep the caseload of hearings within manageable bounds. On occasion, when it appears aliens are having a hard time making up their minds what to do, officers may try to tip the scale in favor of a decision to take voluntary return through subtle or not so subtle cueing, as by hinting that they might end up spending time in a jail where other inmates don't speak their language.

Even more complexity and status heterogeneity will arise during business surveys that turn up OTM aliens who, in addition to speaking exotic languages, may pose difficulty because of the variety of particularized immigration situations that emerge upon interrogation. Among other things, nonimmigrant visas can vary widely in terms of the conditions attaching to each kind as well as in terms of the outcomes that are likely if the alien is determined to be a violator. Even if the OTM alien is a fairly typical out-of-status violator (for example, a B-2 visitor who has overstayed or worked without authorization), that alien or a relative either may have applied (or be on the verge of applying) for a benefit, or may be acquiring other equities that make it likely that an application will be made soon.

The officer must decide whether it is worthwhile to bring such aliens in or just tell them to go to the district office to get work authorization or apply for a benefit. (If they are working without authorization, but state that their employer has put in an I-140 sixth-preference visa petition, they probably should be written up because that may block their Section 245 adjustment-of-status petition, and they would then have to return to their country to pick up their visas.) With just a few minutes available for each interview in a plant that has a sizeable work force, the investigator will have to quickly sort out the person's immigration status (Is there a visa, and if so, what kind? what equities does the alien have? and so on).

The following raid illustrates the greater complexity of urban business surveys.

When the area control squad in a northeastern district office decided to raid several firms believed to be sweatshops paying illegal aliens as little as $12 a day, the information they had led the investigators to believe they would find mainly Koreans and possibly a few Iranian nationals. Because this was not an industrial city, the officers did not normally carry out surveys on factories, preferring restaurants and construction sites instead. (It was easier to get permission to enter restaurants and to control runners there. Construction sites, although posing more danger and control problems, had high-paying jobs attractive to citizens.)

But this particular raid had priority as a reportable case, having originated from higher up in the INS chain of command. The supervisor in charge believed someone in the Department of Labor had heard about the sweatshops. (Getting the INS to take enforcement action against illegal alien workers as a way of cracking down on employers suspected of violating federal wage and working standards appears to be one of a variety of intradepartmental forms of back-scratching.) At one of the sites, the officers encountered an Indian national who was taken in because she refused to answer the officers' questions. Back at the district office, her brother, a diplomat, explained her status to the officers. It turned out she was out of status on two counts: She had overstayed her G-5 visa and was working without authorization. After being photographed and fingerprinted, she was released. The officers told her she would be served with an OSC later by mail.

At the second site, an industrial sewing shop in a residential tenement building that had been converted to commercial use, the investigators picked up several Koreans and a Pakistani woman. The latter resisted and had to be forcibly taken to the van. At headquarters she claimed she was in a training program and therefore not technically working for pay. As the wife of a diplomat on an A-2 visa, she needed INS authorization in order to work. If it was true that the shop had been operating a training program without paying workers, then INS would notify the Labor Department so they could take any action they cared to follow up on for possible labor law violations. The woman was released after her husband came over from the embassy. She would count toward the apprehension statistics, but no action would be taken because, according to the investigators, the State Department would never revoke a diplomatic visa for such a minor matter, which is how State Department officials view immigration violations—much to the consternation of INS officers.

One of the Korean females apprehended had an F-2 visa as the wife of a student attending college in another state. Knowing she would be violating her visa status if she was found working for pay, she, too, claimed to be in her company's training program. This opened up new options for the officers. If they wanted to go to the bother, they could call the employer to find out if, in fact, she was being paid; if necessary, they could subpoena the company's pay records to find out. Or the officers, curious as to why she would be living so far from her husband, could decide to make a more detailed check of her story, which might turn up other violations. If her husband had changed colleges without asking INS permission, he would become deportable, which would also make her automatically deportable. But because a minor violation can be waived at the district director's discretion, nothing might come from the time spent on the case even if something did turn up. In addition, were administrative action to be taken in such a case, it might have the perverse effect of tempting the alien to seek other means of redress, perhaps a sixth-preference labor certification. Hence the irony: A more rigorous enforcement posture in the interior directed at deportable aliens with current or likely future equities can sometimes add to caseloads for adjudicators as well as for the D&D branch's docket control.

When so much can be forgiven, when there are waivers for so many violators based on grounds of hardship or marriage to a citizen (even when fraud has been committed against the government), and when, as one officer asserted, most of the aliens who are removed from the country are the ones who themselves finally agree to go, it becomes easier for investigators to rationalize reduced screening when they face time pressures and other constraints. Cynicism about enforcement efforts against administrative violators is never far below the surface. Many officers wonder if anyone really cares who is minding the store, especially when, as they view the matter, so many judges and politicians seem to want to give it away. Nor do they feel that they can count on support from higher-level administrators, who are more concerned that field officers will cause legal and political problems for the INS. As one officer put it, "Immigration enforcement is like being in a football game without a home team." [12]

PROCESSING ADMINISTRATIVE VIOLATORS

Before they are loaded into the vans (although sometimes this happens after they have been brought in), the property of apprehended aliens is inventoried, their money counted in the presence of at least two officers, and any potentially dangerous objects removed (belts, matches, and the like). At the district office the investigators call them out of the holding room one at a time so they can be written up on the standard I-213 arrest form. In the case of Mexican nationals, those who want to return to Mexico voluntarily must sign the I-274 waiver form after the I-213 form has been filled out and they have been informed about their rights to a hearing and to have an attorney.

The I-213 form asks for relatively standard booking information. The investigator asks the alien's name, age, sex, place of birth, occupation and earnings, parents' names, and the last date, place, and time of entry into the United States. The officer also asks how that entry was accomplished (with or without inspection), whether there was a smuggler involved (if EWI), if that alien has been apprehended before (and, if so, how many times).

In the narrative part at the bottom of the form, the officer will write down legal justification for the arrest, for example: "The alien was apprehended while running from a workstation during a factory survey." The officer will also provide any pertinent information relating to the alien's deportability because the higher probable cause standard must be reached for a warrant of arrest to be issued. Usually the probable cause is based on the alien's own admission, for example, "subject admitted to having entered without inspection and was not in possession of immigration documents." In addition, the officer lists any aggravating conditions or behavior on the I-213 form because this can have a bearing on whether a bond should be required and what its dollar amount will be.

The alien who insists on a deportation hearing is written up with an OSC/warrant of arrest, or the officers may insist that the alien be written up. The alien who can establish possession of sufficient property, a job, or family equities might be served the order to show cause without an arrest warrant or be released OR after a warrant has been processed. In most cases, however, the arresting officers do not view their job as being one of probing to determine all possible immigration equities that might entitle the alien to a benefit or discretionary relief. Aliens who believe they have adequate equities for a benefit or relief should make their own demands for a hearing.

The concern of enforcement officers is primarily with expediting their caseload. They must be certain that they have not mistakenly arrested citizens, and they must be sure to notify the alien of certain rights (for example, the right to have an attorney and to have a hearing). The officer who believes an alien might be prosecuted in a criminal proceeding will, at the earliest possible time, advise that individual of his or her *Miranda* right to remain silent.

The *Miranda* warning is rarely read to administrative violators in the field unless they are suspected of being smuggling guides (and sometimes not even then if the officer has no intention of charging them with smuggling). The officer's objective is to encourage those suspected of being deportable aliens to answer questions so their immigration status can be established and they can be processed for civil administrative action. If they were to be read their *Mi-*

randa warning at the time of the initial encounter, there is the risk they might refuse to speak. Criminal proceedings are, of course, ruled out if an alien admits, for example, to having entered without inspection absent the *Miranda* advising. But then criminal action is rarely contemplated for EWI offenders, including many who make fraudulent claims; although the EWI offense is formally charged, it is waived under a blanket waiver policy. However, an alien who is to be written up for a deportation hearing would at that point be informed of the *Miranda* right to remain silent and have an attorney, if that individual has committed a violation that could theoretically result in criminal prosecution. (This would not apply to aliens who overstay their visa expiration dates unless the officer believed they had also committed fraud or other INA violations subject to criminal action.)[13]

FACTORS AFFECTING BOND POLICY

When the officer has finished the paperwork, it is presented to the assistant district director for signature. The officer may request a bond in a certain amount, but the final amount is at the discretion of the assistant district director or the district director. It may subsequently be reduced by the immigration judge in a bond redetermination hearing. Deportable aliens who show substantial equities may be released OR, despite behavior in the field (running or hiding) that the arresting officer believed warranted a bond. The bond, officers are reminded, is merely to ensure an alien's appearance at a hearing. However, the amount set is apt to be higher in aggravated cases, such as an alien who struggled or fought with an officer rather than simply hiding in a warehouse loft or who made a serious false claim (presented a fraudulent document) rather than just an initial oral claim that was quickly broken. Serious violators, such as suspected narcotics traffickers, terrorists, or aliens involved in organized crime, are also given higher bonds, if they are allowed out on bond at all. (Sometimes an INS bond can be used as a backup to hold a suspected Latin American drug trafficker who the DEA or other federal law officers are afraid they might have to release at a preliminary hearing because of insufficient evidence. The problem here, however, is that drug smugglers can easily make even the highest INS bonds of $20,000 or more.)

Although individual factors relating to an alien's equities, conduct, or criminal threat potential explain differentials in bond determinations within a district, there can be considerable variations in the average bond from district to district because of the service's need to keep resources in equilibrium with caseloads. In districts having relatively more INS detention space, or having more adequate alien detention and transportation funds with which to rent local jail space, the average bond appears to be higher.

When locally available detention space shrivels up, as happened in the Washington, D.C., district office while I was interviewing there in the spring of 1982, the usual bond amount for most administrative violators was $500, which is the minimum service bond. (The arresting officers might start with a higher bond of $1,500 as a way of making the alien feel lucky when they finally reduced it to $500.) The investigators claimed that the mayor had cut back on jail space for INS detainees—much more so than for other federal agencies; also, jail space in outlying suburbs and counties had been trimmed, apparently because of court rulings aimed at curbing prison overcrowding. (Such actions toward INS are cited by officers as evidence of their poor-step-child status within the Department of Justice.)

The lack of overnight detention posed a dilemma for the district office. If they picked up too many aliens who lacked the equities normally needed to qualify for release without a bond, they might have to be released on their own recognizance anyway. As it was, females were already routinely being released. If the policy had to be extended to single males without equities, word might filter out into the community that the INS couldn't make its bond stick. If that happened, investigations might have difficulty getting anyone to post the bond. Salvadorans, the most numerous nationality apprehended in area control, could easily raise the $500—either individually or with the help of relatives and friends. (They could skip out before or after their hearing, although few did before their hearings because of the time they could gain with an asylum request.) Because most Salvadorans would have to pay $1,500 or more for a smuggler plus transportation costs to get back into the United States, forfeiting a $500 bond was clearly much cheaper. Some CIs in the office thought it functioned as a kind of tariff for working illegally in this country.

THE IMPACT OF CASELOADS ON RESOURCES

It is important to understand the linkages and their multiplier effects within the system taken as a whole. Because available detention space and funds can impact on bonds, they can constrain the level of administrative apprehensions. Earlier, it was noted how the availability of detention space and immigration judges can affect the exercise of discretion by patrol agents. If detention space is short or the immigration court caseloads are overloaded, then patrol agents and CIs have less leeway for writing aliens up for deportation—unless an alien demands a hearing. Their ability to use deportation for those they view as deserving violators diminishes.

Sometimes the resource-caseload cantilever is jerked out of balance by events over which the officers have no control—for example, by an unanticipated event, such as the emergency processing required by the Mariel boatlift from Cuba in 1980. Sometimes it may be thrown out of balance by the officers themselves, as for example, when the area control investigators in New York went all out and apprehended many more violators than the INS facilities could accommodate. They did so because they worried that the central office was contemplating shifting personnel from the low-productivity regions to higher-productivity areas (from the Northeast to the Southwest). The result was that aliens without equities had to be released OR, which can damage the credibility of INS's sanctioning power.

In the Washington, D.C., office, area control arrests held steady in a range of 20 to 40 a month, and were held to a lower rate partly to maintain this essential equilibrium.[14] Other important reasons were the small size of the investigations unit and the need to give priority to dual-action case investigations ("the district director doesn't like to get writs of mandamus"), along with the fact that, because of caseload pressures, the immigration judge gave political asylum cases low priority. These were the cases area control was most likely to turn up. Aliens with marginal asylum claims, or those whose claims were unlikely to result in favorable determinations after review by the State Department (the situation facing most Salvadorans), were in no hurry to have their hearings expedited. This was in sharp contrast to aliens who were relying on private counsel and who were paying the cost of more expensive safaris through the juridical thicket (contests of 212 waiver and 245 adjustment of status denials, requests for 244 suspension of deportation relief).

The enforcement apparatus responds rationally in the sense of allocating resources in relation to external pressures and internal constraints. If political asylum cases are a lower priority because Salvadorans are in no hurry to have their claims adjudicated, it hardly makes sense to conduct area control surveys that may turn up even more of them, especially when they cannot be held in detention should they be unable to post the bond.

The resource-to-caseload cantilever gyrates through orbits that must be calibrated on the basis of unanticipated contingencies (officers may have to be detailed away to Florida to handle a boat lift crisis) or court injunctions (pickups on the street or at bus stops may be stopped until an appellate court rules on a district court's injunction). Micro- and macro-level policy shifts sometimes collide. Thus, in the Washington, D.C., district office, the district director wanted the dual-action backlog cleared up even though the central office was insisting (this was in 1982) that 40 percent of all investigator manhours go into business surveys.

The policy orbits must also be calibrated in accordance, if the metaphor may be extended, to the gravitational pull of other bodies external to the system. Thus the district or regional office may adjust policy out of a concern over the local political impact of certain activities. In Los Angeles, a second raid on stores in the Little Tokyo district was ruled out because of the bad publicity and complaints that had resulted from the previous week's raid. The CIs had targeted Little Tokyo to demonstrate that area control was equitable and did not focus solely on Hispanics. And an investigations branch supervisor in another city was quietly "promoted" to district director in a distant city because, or so officers claimed, his enforcement efforts against Polish nationals had caused political trouble.[15]

Also, although some features of the external environment will remain fairly constant, they can vary widely from district to district. Vigorous area control activity causes fewer problems in more conservative cities that have less well developed activist organizations. Because the percentage of OTMs (and of settled Mexicans with equities) increases as one moves farther into the interior, from the Southwest toward the Northeast, business surveys in those areas are even more apt to build up caseload pressures for immigration judges and examiners because more aliens will demand hearings. Even apprehending more OTMs who agree to return voluntarily can, because of the cost of overseas airfare and a gradual policy shift toward granting voluntary departure even to aliens whose travel is paid for by the INS, cut a deep gash in the alien detention and transportation budget.

Hence to the many microlevel ironies discussed earlier one must add the macrolevel paradox. A too-rigorous interior enforcement policy can, like a too-rigorous regime of physical exercise, damage the organizational tissues long before it can achieve the hoped-for beneficial effects.

It is an exaggeration to say that business surveys have no meaningful payoff. Sometimes abscondees are stumbled upon along with more serious INA violators (this is the usual way most absconded aliens are apt to be found, according to one officer). Most deportable aliens are inconvenienced and may have to go to considerable expense and bother. Because this imposes costs, perhaps it works as a deterrent; yet it is hard to know what the empirical impact is on visa abuse or fraudulent and surreptitious entry. That is, it is hard to know the extent to which the number of violators is affected by a certain level of interior enforcement, which imposes tariffs of its own kind (such as fees for attorneys and the problems that must be faced once one has been apprehended).

Viewed from the standpoint of the gravitational tug most important to the agency's orbit, namely the much larger body of the Congress, area control, farm and ranch checks, and linewatch produce the service's most salient and visible statistic: administrative violators (EWI and visa aliens arrested and ordered to depart). During the time I was in the field, this was thought to be important to appropriations and to individual careers—if inferences can be drawn from the statements and behavior of INS officials. (For the reasons noted earlier, it is less relevant today.) The paradox is that many of the re-

sources may be boiled off to generate the statistics needed to justify and legitimate the appropriations in the first place. What outside observers may not see
is the way in which caseloads generate caseloads without a *meaningful* enforcement payoff. Thus many apprehensions involve much paperwork and
require the costly time of government trial attorneys, examiners, docket control officers in deportation, clerical personnel, and investigators, who will
have to process relief and benefit applications, hearing transcripts, and the
like, without necessarily achieving the most important enforcement goal: the
permanent removal of deportable aliens or deterrence against would-be entrants. Indeed, an alien caught after having lived in the United States for
seven years will probably put in for suspension of deportation relief, which
will require a background investigation. In other cases, aliens released OR or
on bond may go out to look for a citizen spouse, which may generate an I-130
spousal petition and then a Section 245 adjustment of status request, which
in turn—as part of the multiplier effect—may require a marriage fraud investigation. (When an alien under proceedings marries a citizen, that can be
taken as a tip-off factor.) And then, after investing resources in an alien who
was apprehended and given a hearing, the alien may simply abscond and dis-
appear. It is hardly surprising, then, to hear officers occasionally speak of
their efforts as "wheel spinning."

SIX

CASE INVESTIGATIONS

Because criminal investigators view themselves primarily as law enforcers, most prefer cases that have potential for skilled investigation and/or criminal prosecution against INA violators. The potential enforcement pay-off (convictions, with fines or prison sentences) adds to the prestige of working cases that involve major offenders, among them smuggling-ring principals, document counterfeiters, and arrangers of sham marriages. Also, cases involving aliens who pose a clear threat to the society (subversives, terrorists, narcotics traffickers, and other dangerous felons) are considered priority cases, even though the INS may only have jurisdiction over the INA offenses, which may warrant only deportation action on the agency's part. (Aliens suspected of subversion or terrorism fall under the FBI's jurisdiction. Such cases would only be investigated by INS officers upon request by the FBI, and INS's involvement would normally be limited to checking into identities and other background information.)

Adding to the glamour of such cases is the fact that in-depth investigatory work may be required. Thus investigators assigned to the ASU will often work undercover. They might pose as vendors in order to make buys from document counterfeiters or as "businessmen" who arrange to receive illegal aliens from a major smuggling organization.[1] Their transactions would be monitored by hidden recorders (consensual monitoring) or videotaped by a hidden camera. Or they might cultivate informants to obtain leads on aliens and citizens involved in major criminal conspiracies.

Working these serious violators can involve the officers in information sharing and other liaison work with FBI and DEA agents, which enhances the officers' prestige and reinforces their occupational image of themselves as law enforcement officers.

Although investigations of aliens suspected of terrorism or espionage fall to the FBI, one investigations supervisor in the Northeast claimed one of the reasons he preferred working subversives (the top priority case classification) to all other cases was that it involved him in dealings with the "bureau" (FBI). Working with counterparts in the FBI extends the halo of the bureau's prestige to INS investigators.[2]

Investigators in the CINS unit can also develop leads of use to other crime-fighting agencies as a result of the information they gather on aliens. Moreover, the Immigration and Nationality Act gives them a unique advantage. Whereas other local and federal law officers must have probable cause that an individual was involved in a crime (or was about to commit one) before they can detain an alien, INS officers have a statutory right to interview and, if necessary, detain aliens for the purpose of an immigration status inquiry. As one officer expressed it, "Any alien has to talk to us."[3] Thus police, or even the FBI, may be curious about certain aliens (who they are, where they are from, and so forth), but they cannot compel them to talk about their identity or immigration status. (Whether INS officers' statutory advantage over other law agents in investigating aliens is as important as they claim it to be is hard to know.)

PROCEDURES IN CASE INVESTIGATIONS

Case investigations can include a wide range of investigatory duties. Some have no relationship to law enforcement in the sense of information gathering for the purpose of apprehending and charging violators. For example, among the duties assigned to the general unit is the investigation of accidents involving government cars. General unit investigators also conduct the background character checks on some aliens applying for benefits and relief or on aliens for whom private bills have been introduced by Congressmen.[4] (Since mid-1983, many fewer routine character checks are done.) Whatever does not easily fit in with the work of another unit is apt to be dropped in the lap of the general unit.

Although the background checks formerly conducted by the general unit had a potential enforcement outcome, usually a finding of good moral character would be turned up for aliens applying for suspension of deportation relief, naturalization, and the like. Even when the background check turned up negative information, it might be too insubstantial to warrant denying the benefit. Because of the doubtful payoff, some CIs viewed this function as merely going through the motions. Some complained that they simply burned up fuel and time trying to locate up-to-date addresses for aliens or other persons they had been detailed to find and interview. (Background FBI and police checks are still routinely done, but this function falls to clerical workers.) No doubt the low payoff was a major reason these routine background checks were curtailed under the case management system in 1983.

The general unit investigators also receive requests to check out facts pertaining to eligibility claims made by aliens applying for benefits or relief. Thus they may investigate a hardship claim when a lawful resident requests a Section 212 waiver in deportation proceedings. If there are doubts about whether an elderly or ailing citizen mother is dependent on an alien's income for support, that might be checked. Or in a Section 244 suspension case, an investigator might be assigned to determine whether a child does, in fact, have the serious medical problem the parents are basing their extreme hardship claim upon—a problem they allege cannot be treated competently by doctors in their homeland. The alien may bring documentary evidence of these claims into a hearing, but if there is reason to doubt their veracity, investigations might be asked to verify the claim.

In contrast to area control surveys, the cases of the other units usually originate from other INS sections or other government agencies rather than through mailbag tips, as in the case of area control. In the fraud unit, whose work is described more fully in Chapter 7, a dual-action investigation may be received from examinations along with a predication that lists a number of discrepancies that have surfaced in an I-130 spousal petition and that suggest the marriage may be fraudulent. Or an officer in the general unit may conduct a background check sent down by naturalization for a permanent resident applying for citizenship. Such a case may, however, be transferred to the fraud section if there is reason to believe that the alien's prior benefit (immigrant visa) was obtained through fraud. Thus, a Pakistani applying for naturalization may be looked into because, soon after he received his green card some years back, he divorced his older citizen wife. (The fact that she had been twenty years his senior should have tipped off the examiners at the time of the immigrant visa application.)

A case might go to the CINS unit if the alien is suspected of having committed crimes other than immigration offenses. In some cases, an investigator who is not attached to the fraud unit but who turns up a lead that suggests INA fraud may be allowed to pursue the case. This is not the typical pattern, but investigators can sometimes claim jurisdiction for cases falling outside their unit's purview. Supervisors tolerate the practice because it contributes to their subordinates' skill development as well as their morale. Sometimes an agent who is rotated back into area control or general from fraud or CINS will bring along unfinished casework. However, an important fraud case would almost always be assigned to a higher-grade officer (GS-11 or GS-12) if it involved considerable legal complexity or indicated smuggling-ring involvement.

Besides the dual-action cases involving benefit applicants suspected of other-than-immigration crimes, CINS investigators also attempt to track permanent-resident aliens who become caught up in the criminal justice system. They may hear of a lawful resident who has recently been convicted of drug dealing, burglary, or homicide. With a certified copy of the conviction, the officers can initiate proceedings to "bust" that individual back to deportable alien. (Whether this person will, in fact, be deported will depend on the time elapsed since the conviction and the seriousness of the crime, along with hardship factors.) Local police might also alert CINS investigators to an alien who had already been cleared by the general unit's background investigation for a benefit but had just been picked up on a criminal warrant. If the individual is not a lawful permanent resident but was EWI or out of status (and hence, deportable to begin with), the case would be worked by the area control officers.

The D&D officer in charge of docket control (deportable aliens who have been ordered to depart or who are under proceedings, and the like) will alert the general unit when an alien has absconded before or after a deportation hearing. (Cases originating from D&D are not, however, referred to as dual-action cases because, in the case of abscondees, they merely have to be sought out and apprehended; in contrast to an investigation on which a benefit hinges, action by another branch is not pending the outcome of an investigation.)

Occasionally a case investigation may be triggered by information sent in by private citizens or other law enforcement agencies. For example, homeowners may write to convey their suspicion that a house on their block is being used as a drop house by smugglers. Such a letter may be turned over to ASU officers, perhaps after an officer in another section has screened the lead by driving around the neighborhood and talking to people. The ASU officers may then conduct surveillance from a van or an adjoining building to obtain evidence for an arrest.

In most background checks, the general unit officer assigned to the case will obtain a routine check of FBI, CIA, and, in the cities the aliens being checked list as their current homes, local police records to see what gets kicked back. The officer will also review the aliens' files to see what other information has been placed in their folders that might warrant additional investigation. Should prior criminal convictions turn up, those aliens may be statutorily ineligible for the benefits applied for, although this will depend on the seriousness of the offenses and how long ago the convictions occurred. If a check of police records indicates that an alien had been charged by the police for a crime but no conviction resulted, the investigator may want to probe more deeply to learn about the individual's associates or behavior patterns on the assumption that, where there is smoke, there is apt to be fire. Although administrative and federal court precedents have narrowed the scope of discretion open to examiners for denying benefits based on adverse information on an alien's character, negative information that falls short of a criminal conviction may, depending on the circumstances, justify a denial in some cases. (For some behaviors, such as prostitution, despite the fact that they are legal in certain jurisdictions or almost never prosecuted, criminal convictions are not required to justify denials.)[5]

A general unit investigator might also decide to talk to people in the benefit applicant's neighborhood to see if other derogatory information turns up. Any adverse information will be entered into the officer's case report, reviewed by the officer's superior, and then sent over to naturalizations or examinations. The CIs merely gather the facts and write a summary; the decision to deny or grant the benefit rests with examinations.

PRIORITIZING CASES

Aliens involved in crime, unless they are minor offenders, are considered a high priority. Because they are individuals toward whom the public does not feel ambivalent, officers experience little of the conflict they sometimes feel when they pick up honest and hardworking deportable aliens. As one investigator described it, "Apprehending a criminal alien is a lot more satisfying than picking up a seventeen-year-old girl in an area control raid, who begins to cry."

Yet, although the CIs try to monitor the jails and courts to ferret out aliens involved in crime, screening is far from thorough in many districts. During the period of my fieldwork, investigators explained that this was because of manpower reductions coupled with the higher priority that district directors were giving to working dual-action background and fraud investigations.[6] As noted earlier, although external political pressures have impacts on INS resource allocations, there are internal organizational requirements that can exercise powerful constraints on investigator priorities. Even when area control operations were being given priority in the early 1980s, the CIs in some offices still gave dual-action cases priority because they were the district director's priority. (This has, however, changed considerably under the new case management system that has been instituted since I left the field in 1982.)

Abscondees, although officially on the books in docket control, are also a low priority because they are not, obviously, pressing the INS to take action against them. By contrast, a district director knows that, if benefit adjudications are held up, aliens awaiting decisions might get angry and may go to federal court for a writ of mandamus. Many investigators feel strongly that abscondees should be tracked (in part because of the cost they have already put the service to), but the return on attempting to find them quickly diminishes because of the hours that can be spent tracking down a single alien. The fact that the prior resource costs have already been absorbed for apprehending and writing up the alien earlier apparently does not justify an additional heavy time investment, unless perhaps the alien is a serious offender. As time passes, the trail quickly goes cold, which reduces the likelihood that the absconded alien can be easily turned up by an investigator. The CI may be limited to contacting the post office to see if the alien left a forwarding address, checking with the last known employer, or calling the state department of motor vehicles to see if they have a current auto registration (this is usually the best avenue because aliens must give their correct address if they want to receive new car tags by mail).

As noted before, the structure of organizational incentives is sometimes skewed in favor of expediting investigations involving pending benefit adjudications over high-cost enforcement functions that have marginal payoffs. Of course, this is one of the CIs' major complaints. Some felt that their supervisors looked at the statistics on case closings rather than looking at enforcement quality in a broader sense. As one investigator stated, "Investigators can be errand boys for just about anything the district director wants them to do." Although many background checks were unproductive, they had to be done because an alien and the alien's attorney might be awaiting a decision. On the other hand, a heavy investment of officer time can be justified for cracking a major smuggling or document counterfeiting ring because of the enforcement and publicity payoffs.

INS INVESTIGATIONS AND
LOCAL LAW ENFORCEMENT

In the case of aliens involved in crime, who are tracked both by area control (if they are EWI or out-of-status nonimmigrants) and CINS (if they are lawful residents), knowledge of their criminal activity will often depend on whether local police and court officials alert the INS. However, the police may not know whether offenders are aliens (they may have lied about their identity) or the police may know about their immigration status but simply fail to notify the INS. In consequence, area control investigators periodically screen bookings at city and county jails along with state and federal prisons. However, cutbacks in investigators during the 1970s, along with the policy shift in favor of employer surveys in the early 1980s, led (or so some officers claim) to less regular screening of jails and prisons.

Although jail calls were still done in most of the districts I visited during

1981 and 1982, the emphasis on producing arrest statistics through business surveys conflicted with jail calls because the latter were less productive in quantitative terms. Because aliens in trouble with the law are assumed to pose a higher control risk, even though their offenses may have been nonviolent, a two-man team might have to be sent to pick up a single alien.[7]

On the other hand, officers would often accept turnovers from the local police as a favor to local law officers with whom the CIs were on good terms. In some cities, individual police officers were frequently more sympathetic to INS enforcement goals than many politicians were. Reciprocal back-scratching from the police—for example, by helping the INS with crowd control or providing local overnight jail space—justified the INS sending men out to take turnovers even though the alien was an ordinary EWI charged with being drunk and disorderly or with shoplifting. Or the INS may have been alerted because the police pulled over for a traffic violation a driver who could not speak English.

Interestingly, although investigators are armed, they are expected to re-quest police assistance whenever they have advance indication that they will encounter dangerous or armed aliens in the course of an investigation. The reason may be that investigators, whatever their training with firearms, are assumed to be less prepared to deal competently with armed and potentially violent violators because they so rarely experience dangerous arrest situa-tions. Some CIs say they are glad to have their guns because they often pur-sue case investigations in dangerous urban neighborhoods; this suggests that some view their sidearms less as an adjunct to their federal enforcement work than as protection in the dangerous urban milieu.

Another stumbling block for investigators screening court calendars or prison bookings for alien violators arises from the speed with which offenders can often post bail and be back out on the streets. If aliens have registration numbers, finding them may still be difficult because aliens involved in scrapes with the law are more apt to be transient. Also, even when they locate a law-ful resident with a criminal conviction, this does not always mean that the alien will be deported. A serious charge (based on the alien's actual offense) may have been plea-bargained down to a lesser included offense. As one offi-cer explained:

> If I get a 16-year-old boy with a first-offense burglary, I don't bother with that. But a 24-year-old with an assault charge, I'll check that out, get the record from the computer bank in Albany. Arrests that would disturb a per-son's immigrant status are relevant for us. But we have to go by the actual conviction handed down, not the original charge which may have been the real offense. We have to get the conviction record from the court, attested to and certified to process the case for deportation.

Sometimes local police will contact the INS when they are unsure about the identity of an offender but suspect that person may be an alien. Often the police need assistance from the INS to check people they are almost certain are foreign nationals but who refuse to talk. (Iranian students are apparently notorious for standing mute when confronted by local police.) Here, cooperation between the two organizations is not so much an exchange of favors as it is a dovetailing of their respective interests. The police need to know who such people are; the INS will want to know if they are deportable aliens or whether they may become deportable as a result of the charges being contemplated by the police.

Investigators can assist the police in other ways as well. For example, if the police narcotics squad conducts a raid on a drug ring, they may run into individuals near the scene who they suspect might be involved but who may be hard to hold in custody because of insufficient probable cause for an arrest. If they appear to be foreign nationals, the INS can be asked to send someone over. If immigration violations turn up after the CIs talk to the suspect individuals, the INS can arrest them, which may give the police enough time to gather the additional evidence needed for their separate warrants of arrest. However, the problem is that the INS cannot hold on to aliens indefinitely. As one CINS investigator put it, "We'll hold on to a Colombian illegal, but we can't drag our feet—we have to process him and let him go if he posts the bond. If the judge orders him deported, he goes."

It also sometimes happens that, when a deportable alien who has been charged with a crime goes before the court, the defense attorney will seek a reduction in charges or a suspended sentence by telling the judge and prosecutor that this client is a deportable alien who will be removed from the country by the INS. If the crime is relatively minor and the docket is crowded, the district attorney is apt to find the proposal attractive. But then, after the alien has been let go, the attorney may seek to delay deportation by working the system with various motions. Immigration and Naturalization Service officers complain that too many district attorneys and judges use the INS as a dumping ground for petty alien offenders. Local officials may not realize that turning an alien over to the INS is no guarantee that that alien will be removed from the United States. Thus, except when investigators decide to pick up minor alien offenders as a favor to local police officials, they normally prefer that the local authorities prosecute the alien before passing that alien along to the INS for administrative action.

Although the work of CINS investigators, as of most other units, is measured primarily in terms of case closings that pertain to INA enforcement objectives (identifying INA violations or crimes and other behavior that bear on an alien's eligibility for relief or liability to deportation), CINS officers are apt to stress the importance of their work for the crime control objectives of other law enforcement agencies. For example, a CINS investigator working in a northeastern city emphasized his usefulness to the DEA agents headquartered there. He noted how the DEA had arrested a group of individuals who presented Puerto Rican birth certificates but were suspected of being Colombian narcotics dealers. Their defense attorneys argued that because the men were U.S. citizens, their bonds should be lowered. As citizens, their attorneys claimed, they would be unlikely to flee the country. The DEA agents asked CINS to check their immigration status and, if they could establish that they were deportable aliens, put an immigration hold on them if they could. When the officers determined that they were illegal aliens, the higher bond DEA had requested was sustained.

Another CINS officer in the same city prided himself on the fact that he helped get a hard-core drug pusher a 30-year sentence simply by providing evidence that the man had committed numerous immigration violations, including fraudulently claiming to be a U.S. citizen and re-entering the United States after a previous deportation. When the judge learned that the alien had lied to him in court about his immigration status, he was so angry he threw the book at him.

TENSIONS BETWEEN CRIME CONTROL AND IMMIGRATION ENFORCEMENT GOALS

Investigators become highly motivated when they work CINS cases, not only because they view criminal aliens as posing the most serious threat but also because the sanctions of the criminal law are applied to a fuller extent. In an enforcement milieu where criminal sanctions are so rarely applied, even a three-year sentence is viewed as a very good payoff. And although federal prosecutors typically decline most criminal prosecutions for INA violators—often through a blanket waiver policy, which means they never even hear about many of the cases—they will take cases involving criminal violators who falsely claim to be citizens or who have re-entered the country after having been deported previously. And federal judges will sometimes mete out the maximum punishments upon conviction.[8]

However, investigators working criminal aliens sometimes lose sight of the fact that they are expected to produce investigations relevant to *immigration* enforcement (tracking aliens involved in crime for the purpose of establishing their identities and determining whether deportation proceedings should be initiated). Some enlarge their view of their investigatory function by, for example, developing informants in an ethnic community so they can be kept abreast of organized criminal activities. One investigator I interviewed in an eastern district, who was frustrated at having been transferred out of CINS into another unit, discussed how he relished developing information on Japanese, Thai, and Israeli mafia groups involved in gun and drug smuggling.

The problem, however, is that the CIs' expanded conception of their investigatory role comes into conflict with organizational requirements. Their superiors' eyes are on the case closings relevant to immigration activity, and they are evaluated on that basis. (The productive officer hours expended are entered into the G-123 monthly report along with the case closing data.) In 1982, CINS required an average of 16.5 officer hours per case (compared with the investigations branch average of 8.5 hours in that year).[9] Although such time-intensive investigations come much closer to what the rank-and-file CIs feel real investigation is all about, their superiors are apt to insist that they limit their interest to investigating aliens for information pertinent to immigration actions, in which case all the investigator needs to know is whether aliens have been charged and convicted of crimes, where they are serving time, or where they are currently living. Gathering leads on criminal conspiracies can be useful to other federal and local law officers, but it is not the job of the INS. Hence, supervisors prefer that subordinates confine themselves to responding to inquiries from the DEA or local narcotics officers, for example, by checking the identity or immigration status of a suspected drug dealer rather than doing the DEA's work of tracking general background leads and obtaining other information.

Doubtless, part of this occupational identity crisis is owing to the fact that INS investigators have the same 1811 Civil Service classification as FBI and DEA agents, which makes them resentful when they are required to do tasks unrelated to law enforcement. Many feel that they should not have to spend so much time performing mundane chores, such as accident investigations or routine background checks on aliens applying for legal residence—tasks that could be assigned to nonenforcement personnel.[10]

A New York City INS supervisor in charge of fraud investigations, although sympathetic to the investigators' complaints, gave a more balanced view of the problem:

> We spent a lot of time investigating the ethnic crime syndicates. There are Polish gypsies, Colombian drug smugglers, Russian Jews who are into everything that will turn an illegal buck. There are Israeli hit men and Jamaican Rastafarians who are into marijuana, drugs, and homicide. We dealt with DEA and local police intelligence, and we would have no more than one or two cases assigned to one man. This was intensive case work, general intelligence gathering for possible future use. We were like informants to other police agencies. But there was a cost to that. Our unit had the highest man-hours per case closing. The guys loved it because their noses weren't stuck to a grindstone where they had to produce, say, ten cases a month. But

the emphasis has changed now. The management doesn't want us to investigate general criminal activity because it doesn't produce the numbers.

Clearly, because such work may involve an occasional stint out on the street working undercover along with the collating and piecing together of an odd assortment of data from various sources, such work comes closest to what the investigators think of as real detective work. But it is not immigration work. As one officer noted, the "criminal" in their title of criminal investigator was really there for retirement and other civil service benefit purposes.

Another problem with allowing agents to engage in more adventuresome undertakings, such as doing undercover work on organized crime cases, arises from the grade classification system. If a GS-11, the most common investigative field grade, were allowed to work cases rated for GS-12 or GS-13 grade officers, then under the Civil Service regulations, that officer might insist on a promotion to the higher grade. One supervisor, a GS-13, explained that he had once had to go out into the field as an undercover cab driver on a case merely to ensure that the job didn't go to a GS-11, who might then use that assignment to request a promotion. By contrast, in the FBI, field-grade agents are usually GS-12s and GS-13s. In the INS, GS-12 and GS-13 officers are apt either to be supervisors or to be assigned to the elite fraud and CINS units to work criminal cases requiring more legal expertise.

INS: THE POOR STEPCHILD

Besides the role strain stemming from the discrepancy that investigators perceive between their official classification as 1811 criminal investigators on the one hand and the tasks assigned them on the other, strain is also engendered by the vast gulf they perceive in the status of their agency and other Department of Justice agencies, such as the FBI and the DEA. In their view, the INS is the Department of Justice's poor stepchild. The devaluation of their agency reveals itself in very tangible ways—the unavailability of money to use to make buys, to pay informants, or to lease surveillance cars. Immigration service officers drive sedans dating to the early to mid-1970s (often dented and missing hubcaps). Sometimes the electronic and other surveillance equipment used in an antismuggling unit is rigged up and maintained by an officer who happens to have the knack for such work, who has electronics for a hobby. And the officers may use their personal autos for surveillance because they know the service sedans are easily recognized. (When the INS obtained authority to seize smugglers' vehicles in the late 1970s, ASU officers came into a windfall and had their pick of vehicles for surveillance activities.)

Most CIs are aware of the legal and political realities that put cases involving INA violators at a steep discount by comparison with many FBI and DEA cases. The truth of the matter is that immigration violators do not pose as serious a threat as bank robbers, cocaine traffickers, kidnappers, and others. With the exception of a few districts (among them San Diego) whose assistant U.S. attorneys are specialized to handle immigration violators because they constitute a heavy part of their caseload, many federal prosecutors usually give immigration cases a low priority. For example, the assistant U.S. attorney will usually have no interest in prosecuting the felony of re-entry after deportation unless perhaps it is the alien's third re-entry or there are other aggravating factors. And with the exception of the principals and chief lieutenants in a Category I or II smuggling ring, who may get five- to ten-year prison sentences upon conviction, the sentence meted out to most smuggling drivers is apt to be time served and two years suspended sentence; at most, there would be a six-month prison sentence, of which maybe a third will be served. This is hardly the kind of payoff to excite the prosecutor's interest, especially given the added resource costs of providing translators for witnesses and others who cannot speak English.[11]

With the exception of the ASU officers, who are apt to work major smuggling cases, and those in the fraud unit who are working third-party cases, the CIs' perception that the enforcement function is devalued within the INS can have severe repercussions for the morale of some officers. Many investigators complain that higher-ups are too quick to cave in to political pressures and are overly sensitive to public and media criticism. However, they realistically recognize the fundamental political problem the service faces— the fact that whereas Americans claim to support immigration law enforcement in general, their actual support is often weak and ambivalent (except on the border), especially in regard to administrative violators who have settled into the society and are law-abiding workers. The dilemma, they feel, could be resolved if higher management would give them more leeway to work the serious cases having maximum enforcement leverage for the INS. Such cases, they feel, would produce less conflict and also allow them to do quality rather than "wheel spinning" kinds of investigations. Indeed, some express the wish that their branch could be transferred to a more law-enforcement-minded agency within the Department of Justice. However, such a transfer of function would be unrealistic because investigations activity is heavily intertwined with the work of other INS branches.

ANTISMUGGLING

Investigators assigned to the ASUs, which are found in some of the larger district offices and in border patrol sector headquarters, have as their primary goal the disruption of major alien smuggling rings and prosecution of the principals. Much of their jargon and many of their tactics were borrowed from the DEA during the mid to late 1970s. Carter administration appointee Commissioner Lionel Castillo had made the decision to move the border patrol toward a more professional enforcement focus by going after smuggling organizations rather than individual load cars. Agents from the DEA were invited over to the INS to help instruct officers in the use of methods they had developed against drug smugglers.

As a result, many of the tactics used by ASUs are similar to those found in the drug enforcement field. For example, just as local and federal narcotics officers often work their way up to a major drug ring as a result of first arresting lower-level (street) dealers, a smuggling ring investigation often begins with the apprehension of a single load car, although it may also develop as a result of leads provided by informants. If the case for a criminal prosecution of the driver looks strong, the driver may be offered immunity or a suspended sentence in exchange for cooperating with the service. Drivers working for major high-volume rings can earn as much as $1,000 for a two- or three-day run from the border to Chicago. Some earn $60,000 and more a year. (In exchange for their testimony, illegal aliens apprehended in a load may sometimes be offered the opportunity to remain legally in the United States for a specified period of time.) When drivers are "flipped" (agree to become U.S. government informers), they are expected to provide information on the identities of the ring principals, their lieutenants, other drivers, drop houses, and the routes being used. They may be asked to "duke in" an undercover INS agent, often a Hispanic agent, fluent in Spanish, who will be introduced as a friend or acquaintance interested in earning a few dollars as a driver. Such agents are provided cover stories and addresses by the service.

These agents then try to gain the trust of those higher up in the ring by successfully ferrying smuggling loads. The controlled loads are allowed to proceed without interference by agents at the border so the undercover agents can establish their reputations as competent drivers. In the process of running loads, the officers will gather information on the names of other drivers, the routes taken, and the locations of drop houses used along the way to refresh both the drivers and the aliens they are transporting. In some cases, the ASU may employ trusted Mexican nationals (called *cooperating informants*) or use Hispanic officers to pose as smuggled illegal aliens. By observing and listening to the conversations of drivers, load house operators, and the aliens in the load, they acquire additional information on other routes, modes of transportation, and final destination points being serviced. Eyewitness testimony will thus be available when the case is prepared for prosecution.

Antismuggling unit officers then begin tracking both the long-distance calls made to hotels in Juarez or Tijuana, where the aliens assemble before crossing the border, and the calls to drop houses on the U.S. side. These calls are not monitored by wiretap, but an analysis of the toll records allows the agents to analyze the ring's routes of travel and geographical pattern. When charted on a map, the routing of a major smuggling operation resembles that of a major commercial airline carrier and can stretch as far south as Central America, through Mexico City, up to Ciudad Juarez near El Paso, Texas, or to Tijuana just across the border from San Ysidro. Drop houses are usually located on the U.S. side not far from the border so that aliens who have been moved by foot across the border can assemble on the U.S. side for movement by vehicle at an opportune time to their final destinations in interior cities.

Because criminal convictions for felony transporting, along with tough sentences, will be sought for the principals, and this usually means a jury trial, the officers must build as tight a web of evidence as possible. Depending on the circumstances, inside agents may use hidden microphones to record their conversations with ring operatives. A nondescript RV or van that appears to have broken down will be stationed near a drop house; from there aliens being loaded into vehicles will be under surveillance by hidden cameras. (If the smugglers are filmed kicking or in other ways mistreating the aliens, this will, officers assert, give the prosecutor additional bargaining leverage because of the impact that filmed mistreatment will have on a jury.)

In addition to being risky for agents, putting an undercover officer in as a driver is difficult unless the ASU officers have enough leverage against a driver they have apprehended to get cooperation. They have to be certain they can trust the driver not to tip off the smugglers. Also, the driver must have sufficient rapport with ring leaders so a newcomer recommended by that driver will be accepted into the organization. Access to a ring can also be achieved by having a Hispanic agent pose as a lawful resident or a U.S. citizen who wants to bring relatives up from Mexico or by having a non-Hispanic agent pose as an employer contracting for illegal alien workers.

The following example illustrates how a major case can be developed. In a case initiated by the Chicago district office's antismuggling unit in 1982, an agent approached a naturalized Mexican American known to be a go-between for a major smuggling operation. As a broker, this individual accepted orders for aliens at a cost of $500 apiece and made arrangements with the ring to have them brought into the country. The go-between, who will be called Juan, told the undercover officer to have his relatives go to a hotel in Ciudad Juarez. There, the hotel owner would arrange to get them to drop houses controlled by Juan in northern New Mexico. The ASU section then arranged to have the individuals brought up as a controlled load. After controlled loads had been run through this ring for several months, the Chicago ASU section was able to identify more than 70 individuals connected with the ring as drivers, load and drop house operators, or independents who ran their own groups of aliens using the ring's infrastructure.

When they determined that a Juarez hotel owner, who we will call Carlos, headed the ring, the undercover officer who had initially placed the order with Juan for his "relatives," called Carlos at his hotel under a different name, explaining that he had heard that Carlos could help him get his relatives into the United States. The hotel owner denied this because, unknown to the officer, a code word had to be used. Gradually, as he became friendlier with Juan under his other alias, the officer was able to obtain the code word from him. Indeed, he became well enough trusted that Juan invited him to help out with the job of making pickups of illegals at the Amtrak station in Chicago and distributing them to their final destinations in the city. The undercover officer agreed to do this, explaining that he had just lost his job and needed the spare cash. The INS supported his cover story by creating a prior employment record for him at a steel mill.

After explaining to Juan that he had a sick daughter who had been returned to Mexico by "*la Migra*," Juan told him to call Don Ramirez, the code name for the Juarez hotel owner. The officer called the hotel owner, and the arrangements were made. Cooperating informants, recruited from illegal Mexican nationals living in Chicago who had helped the INS in the past and who were known to be good at observing and remembering details, were sent to Mexico. (Their purpose was to identify individuals, memorize license numbers, and the like. Because of the possibility that they might be put on the stand as witnesses at the trial, they had to have clean police records so their credibility could not be attacked.)

In this way, the Chicago officers were able to put together a picture of how the ring operated. Alien clients were expected to pay half of the $500 smuggling fee in advance, with the rest payable upon delivery. The hotel owner took $100, with the rest being paid out to the *guia* (guide) who would take them across the river by foot, the drivers, the operators of load houses en route, and so on. The aliens would stay at the hotel until Carlos received word that the driver for that particular transit route to Chicago had arrived on the U.S. side to pick up aliens going to that city. The driver would leave his truck with the operator of the load house on the U.S. side. The owner of the house would drive the empty vehicle over to the Mexican side. Then he would return with the empty vehicle in the hope that the border patrol would have less reason to be suspicious of it later on.

While the owner of the load house was bringing the truck back from Juarez, his children would scout outside to make sure no patrol agents were in the area. When the way was clear, a signal would be given for the aliens to cross over the river to the house, which literally abutted the Rio Grande. But unknown to the smugglers, ASU agents had staked themselves out in a van that appeared to have a flat tire on a highway overpass within camera range of the house.

When the truck arrived, the aliens piled out of the house on the double and were inside the truck within the space of three to five minutes. The driver took out-of-the-way roads, adding 300 to 500 miles to his route before reaching the motel used by Juan, the go-between, who then put the aliens on the Amtrak train to Chicago. (The ASU officers believed the ring had a clerk on the inside at Amtrak who maintained a lookout for border patrol agents and who also apparently made sure the illegals would get their tickets as quickly as possible.)

Juan later admitted that he moved 50 aliens a week through this station alone. The officers estimated that Carlos, the head of the ring, was moving 700 aliens a week (which would have meant earnings of $7,000 per week at $100 per head).

Getting to the wily Carlos, the prime enforcement target, was not easy. However, the undercover officer managed to develop the rapport necessary to get taken into the ring as a driver, and this eventually made it possible for him to meet Carlos. As he began to successfully run controlled loads up to the United States, Carlos's confidence in his ability grew. To learn more about the routes the organization used, he volunteered to run loads anywhere Carlos wanted. Normally Carlos sought to keep drivers on fixed routes, to reduce the risk of exposing other parts of the ring. But if Carlos trusted a driver, he would give him other destinations, and he had come to trust the undercover officer.

When both the various routes used by the ring and the operators who used them had been uncovered, and sufficient evidence had been developed for a winnable case, the Chicago ASU section finally moved to arrest 38 ring members in a coordinated raid in several states. Knowing that Carlos crossed from Juarez to El Paso to pick up money orders at Western Union (usually prepayments made by relatives of those being brought up), the investigators realized they could arrest him by staking out the Western Union office. Shortly before the ring was broken up in the coordinated operation, the undercover officer called Carlos to let him know he was in El Paso and ready for the next load. Antismuggling unit officers in Chicago arranged to have money orders mailed to Western Union for "relatives" waiting at Carlos's hotel. When Carlos walked into the office to collect his fees, he was arrested.

Besides the fact that major antismuggling cases involve the full panoply of professional crime-fighting skills and employ some of the most experienced officers available, these are also the cases that can lead to prison sentences of five to twelve years. Moreover, some ring members will also become liable to prosecution for nonpayment of federal income taxes.

Yet, although these cases (along with certain fraud ring investigations discussed in Chapter 7) are the cream of INS enforcement efforts, ASU officers nonetheless believe that they have yet to convince judges, juries, and the public at-large that smugglers are organized criminals. As one officer expressed it, "Even though they're not of Italian ancestry, they're definitely organized criminals. That's something we have a hard time getting the organized crime strike force to believe because, unless the last name ends in an *a*, they don't want to get involved. We keep telling them that alien smuggling is lucrative organized crime—more lucrative than narcotics because there's less risk and less overhead."

The problem, as the officers view it, is that, unlike narcotics smuggling, alien smuggling is still apt to be viewed by many in the public as a nonviolent crime. It is true that smugglers do not as a rule carry or use guns; however, they have been known to keep aliens against their will until relatives or friends come up with the balance of a smuggling fee owed. In some instances, they have used violence to recoup smuggling fees. They also abuse aliens on occasion, sometimes intentionally. (When aliens are injured or killed, it is usually because of road accidents, suffocation in a locked trunk or van, or because they have been left stranded at a pickup point.) As the officers view the matter, illegal aliens are just so many "hunks of meat" to a smuggler.

Although violence is associated with alien smuggling, it is not as prevalent as it is with drug operations, and this may be one reason why the sentences handed down to convicted operators are lower. (The possibility that illegal aliens are viewed as less of a public hazard than cocaine and heroin—if indeed, they are viewed as a problem at all—may also be a factor.) Although ring smugglers face business as well as legal risks, they operate in a less predatory environment than major narcotics traffickers. Unlike drugs, which are easily transported and readily marketable, aliens are not a marketable commodity that can be "ripped off." Also, much less cash changes hands at the various transaction points, and the aliens, themselves, do not carry much cash because they fear being robbed by borderland bandits.

Patrol agents' lower expectation of violence on the part of alien smugglers is revealed by how agents respond to situations where they think drugs might be involved. They are more apt to be on the alert when they sense that a situation they encounter (for example, a late-model luxury car spotted at night near the banks of the Rio Grande) involves drug rather than alien smugglers because drug smugglers are more apt to carry guns for protection and may be tempted to use them against law officers.

During the early 1970s when drug smuggling was increasing along the California border, there was an increase in gunplay, and patrol agents, who normally only carry sidearms, sometimes equipped themselves with automatic carbines—and sometimes had to use them. (At that time, it was patrol agents who were intercepting most of the marijuana being ferried over by truck or in knapsacks because in that area, patrol agents were more numerous than customs and other federal agents. Drug smuggling, some officers believe, declined along the California border during the 1970s, in part because the border patrol was being strengthened to deal with illegal aliens. Given the street value of drugs, which drug smugglers themselves have invested in, the increased risk of apprehension by patrol agents apparently served as an effective deterrent, and the smugglers moved elsewhere.)

Besides the enforcement impact of breaking up a major smuggling ring, which officers claim justifies the heavy resource commitment required, arrests involving Category I and II smugglers publicize their enforcement efforts much better than routine street busts of mom-and-pop operators. As the public comes to realize that a major ring can gross millions of dollars and is as organized a crime as drug smuggling—even if perhaps not as violent an activity—they hope judicial attitudes will toughen and higher sentences will result upon conviction. If the public and others in the federal law enforcement establishment move closer to the ASU officers' view, then perhaps ASUs will begin to get the additional manpower and resources needed to pursue the many rings still in operation.

SEVEN

FRAUD INVESTIGATIONS

 Aliens suspected of fraudulent benefit applications are considered to be among the more serious INA violators. In addition to the possibility that their benefit requests may be denied, they may be subject to deportation or even criminal prosecution. In actuality, a very large percentage of benefit requests are approved, which suggests that most petitions are bona fide. For example, in a typical year, approximately 95 percent of all I-130 immediate relative visa petitions are approved. The difficulty, however, is that the INS only knows about the frauds they catch. It is clear that INS investigators miss a larger, but unknown, number of fraudulent benefit applications, in addition to a sizeable number of suspected fraudulent applications that the service decides not to deny—usually because of evidence difficulties.

Although the fraud unit concentrates primarily on immigration benefit requests and claims, aliens thought to have engaged in entitlement (welfare) fraud against other federal or state and local agencies are also investigated by CIs in the fraud unit. Besides the fact that immigration felonies may be involved (for example, false citizenship or lawful resident claims), aliens who obtain unauthorized public benefits impose costs on taxpayers.

As regards fraudulent immigration benefit claims, the fraud may involve the alien alone (as in applying for a nonimmigrant visa), or it may involve both the alien and a knowing citizen sponsor who becomes an accomplice, as in I-130 spousal petitions and some I-140 sixth-preference visa petitions (in some cases, the citizen may be naive about the alien's purpose). In these one-on-one cases, as they are called, a CI's official objective is to develop information sufficient to remove the examiner's doubts about the bona fides of the relationship so the benefit can be either granted or denied by the examiner. However, in practice, investigators who believe they have convincing evidence that a marriage or labor certification application is fraudulent will often try to obtain a voluntary withdrawal by the petitioner. Although fraudulent I-130 petitions sometimes involve the preference visa categories (for example, marriage of a nonimmigrant alien to a lawful resident), most of the fraud occurs in spousal petitions submitted by citizens for nonpreference (immediately available) immigrant visas. (It is more difficult, but not impossible, for aliens or naturalized citizens to fraudulently immigrate parents or children not their own.)

THE DIVERSITY OF IMMIGRATION FRAUD

Because of the large number of aliens wanting to enter and work in the United States, it should hardly come as a surprise that aliens might seek to circumvent the law by either trying to obtain an immigrant visa fraudulently or by seeking to temporarily evade arrest through an oral or documented false claim. Basically, fraud can be divided into three main categories: (1) fraudulent visa applications, oral claims, and supporting documents used to obtain an inspected entry; (2) misrepresentations of immigrant status to an INS officer after having entered the United States legally or illegally; and (3) misrepresentations of material facts in regard to eligibility in a relief or benefit request.

Considerable diversity exists within each of the three categories. As examples of the first type, aliens may obtain a bona fide U.S. visa stamp after making misrepresentations about economic status or other equities to a consular official in their homeland. If they succeed, their visas will appear bona fide to inspectors, but they have nonetheless entered fraudulently. Or they may purchase U.S. passports in which their photos are substituted for those of the original owners. Or they may pay street vendors to forge counterfeit visa stamps in valid passports.

The second type, misrepresentations of status, has been discussed in earlier chapters. Most are investigated by officers in the field at the time the claim is made rather than by the fraud unit. For example, aliens may falsely claim to be citizens or green-card holders; or they may misrepresent other facts about themselves to induce officers to release them in the field.

As discussed in Chapter 2, fraud investigators must cope with a rich diversity of potential immigration situations and statuses that aliens may try to manipulate through fraud (a complexity that reflects the Byzantine labyrinth of the INA), as well as with other extremely ingenious stratagems designed to circumvent the law.

Consider the most commonly investigated case handled by a fraud unit: marriage fraud. A sham marriage of convenience is sometimes accompanied by fraudulent divorces and even deaths. For example, a Filipina arrives in Los Angeles as a nonimmigrant visitor—possibly on a fraudulently obtained tourist visa. She then travels to Las Vegas to arrange a "divorce" from her Filipino husband (who may or may not be aware of what is going on). The divorce must be arranged in the United States because divorce is not allowed in the homeland. (Or she might present a death certificate for a spouse who is still living, although if she does this, it will be hard to revive him should she want to petition for him later as a permanent resident.)

After divorcing her husband, she travels back to Los Angeles to marry a U.S. citizen. After the citizen has submitted the I-130 petition and the alien has adjusted her status to lawful resident, the alien divorces the citizen (who may or may not have realized that the marriage was contrived to obtain an immigration benefit). She then remarries her husband abroad and petitions for his admission as a lawful resident. Indeed, the travel agency in Manila that booked her airline flight may have arranged a package deal, which might include arranging her fraudulent supporting documents to obtain a nonimmigrant visa, her arrangements to obtain a Nevada divorce, and then her remarriage to a citizen. (The INS cannot contest Nevada divorces because, under Nevada law, third parties have no standing in civil divorce actions. The abuse is well known to Nevada authorities, as are the use of winos called in to testify to the length of residence requirement, the fact that attorneys are knowing participants in the sham, and the fact that the person to be divorced has no intention of becoming a resident of the state.)

Faced with declining enrollments, some American colleges have become vulnerable to recruiters who travel abroad to recruit "students" with a supply of blank I-20 student visa applications. Upon investigation, it sometimes turns out that the recruiter has been selling the visas for $500 each to persons who have no intention to study but merely want to enter the United States to work.

Because unmarried children of lawful residents have preference over married children in getting a visa, a married child of a lawful resident may divorce his or her spouse, enter the United States and then remarry the spouse after obtaining a green card. Even though the divorce may have been valid under the law of the alien's homeland, the purpose was to obtain an immigration benefit, and if the INS can establish that the benefit was the motivating or sole purpose, it can deny the application. But proving intent is easier said than done.

Or aliens may become Buddhist priests simply by setting up lanterns, shrines, and other religious paraphernalia in and around their apartments along with a register of their "congregations" (relatives and friends who sign in when they visit). Aliens who can establish that they are religious ministers become special immigrants, a numerically unrestricted category that does not require certification by the U.S. Department of Labor. (For most other occupations, aliens must have a U.S. sponsor who agrees to employ them; depending on the labor market in the state, the employer may have to demonstrate to the satisfaction of the Labor Department that it is not possible to find qualified citizens or lawful residents for the job.) The absence of this requirement for religious professionals naturally creates tempting incentives for religion fraud.

However, marriage fraud remains preferred, not only because there is no numerical limitation on visas for immediate relatives of citizens but also because it is probably easier to camouflage a sham marriage than it is to create an airtight paper trail that would establish one's occupation as a religious professional.

Although the complexity of the provisions and guidelines relating to certain INA benefits (relative petitions, temporary worker visas, and the like) explains the intricacy of some fraud investigations, usually the investigators' main problem is simply finding sufficient evidence at a reasonable cost in terms of time and effort to establish the basis for a denial. In theory, the proof burden falls on the alien and petitioner, but examiners cannot arbitrarily decide that a benefit claim is fraudulent. In all but the most blatant cases, the bona fides of eligibility have to be checked out. The difficulty and cost of doing so must be balanced against the return anticipated from the investigation. For example, in cases where the fraud is almost impossible to detect, it makes little sense to investigate the unknowable. Aliens who apply for nonimmigrant visas as visitors or students, but who had it in mind to adjust their status to lawful permanent resident after they arrived in the United States, obtained their visas fraudulently but would be almost impossible to catch. Such fraud comes very close to being technical in nature, arising more because of the quirks in our immigration law than from an absence of good moral character on the alien's part. Yet according to the law, any aliens who entered as nonimmigrant visitors but intended to immigrate at the time are guilty of bad faith dealings with the government even though they may have obtained their nonimmigrant visas in a wholly legitimate way and even though they may have sought to adjust their status to lawful residency in a wholly legal (nonfraudulent) manner after arrival. Technically, they are as much fraudulent entrants as the alien, for example, who enters with a counterfeit Puerto Rican birth certificate. (Occasionally, evidence of aliens' lack of good faith dealings with the United States will surface when they request nonimmigrant visa applications and investigators compare what they told consular officers against what they have done after arriving in the United

States.) Much the same applies to students who request work authorization and who may tell little white lies about their parents' financial difficulties to persuade an examiner to grant work authorization.

The alien who may have committed this kind of technical fraud (it is not viewed as technical by INS officers) is not seen as being as morally culpable as the alien who seeks to immigrate fraudulently by, for example, paying a U.S. citizen to participate in a sham marriage. This may be due to the greater importance and benefits attaching to an immigrant visa (compared with work authorization) or to the more deliberate planning required on the alien's part.

In addition to being hard to detect in the absence of "paper" (bogus supporting documents or statements made and written down at the time of the visa application), nonimmigrant visa fraud has a low priority for INS investigators because, by the time CIs get around to working these cases, the involved aliens might very well have returned home. If they have not left, they have become visa abusers, which means that they are already administrative violators and may eventually be picked up and processed for deportation as such. Investigation of their nonimmigrant visa fraud might be warranted if they made application for lawful residence and sought to adjust their status or if, after living underground for the required seven years, they resurfaced to apply for suspension of deportation relief. Evidence gathered on their earlier nonimmigrant visa fraud would be added in with any other adverse information on their conduct in the United States and might help justify a denial of the benefit; this, however, would be at the discretion of the adjudicator.[1]

Normally, the rational allocation of investigative resources dictates that nonimmigrant visa fraud be worked only when aliens are suspected of other more serious violations, such as involvement in immigration fraud for gain, or when they are thought to be involved in other serious crimes. Moreover, the investigators may decide to devote the time required to unearth evidence of aliens' nonimmigrant visa fraud if evidence on their involvement in other criminal activity is considered insufficient for criminal prosecution or for the denial of an INA benefit. If the examiners and investigators sincerely believe that an alien really is an undesirable, it makes sense to get every piece of adverse information they can put their hands on into that alien's file. Because many benefit and relief requests are discretionary, even if the alien meets the statutory eligibility requirements, the accumulation of adverse information may tip the balance in favor of a denial by an examiner or immigration judge.

By contrast, in the case of a visa abuser who the officers just happened to stumble across in the course of a business survey, evidence that that alien obtained a nonimmigrant visa fraudulently would be most unlikely to result in criminal prosecution. It might, however, justify deportation (rather than granting the option of voluntary departure). But even this is not a certainty because of the pressures on the immigration courts.

FALSE CLAIMS

In addition to nonimmigrant visa fraud, which is usually too inconsequential to warrant investigation, INS officers encounter many aliens who make misrepresentations about their status. Because the subject of false claims has already been discussed, little more need be added here. Suffice it to point out that the thousands of fraudulent claims to legal residence and citizenship annually made to officers in the course of alienage and deportability checks are usually unsophisticated and easily dealt with. Most, in fact, are broken within minutes in the field. In such cases, the fraud investigation rarely takes more than several minutes to perhaps an hour or so of questioning, and the overwhelming majority are terminated by the alien's agreement to withdraw the claim. Ironically, although the documented false claims are considered to be the more serious and are the ones most likely to be reported in official statistics, investigators and patrol agents claim that they are the easiest to break. The reason is that anything on paper provides added leverage once the officer can show the alien that the document is phony or is inconsistent with other things the alien has said or with other papers the alien was carrying. (Perhaps documented false claims are considered serious because it is assumed that an alien who invests in a document has a more durable intention of passing as a citizen than one who may have made an oral false claim on the spur of the moment.)

Several factors determine the extent to which officers will investigate a citizenship or green-card claim beyond just a brief interrogation to check out the claimant's story. The ease with which officers can locate additional information is one important factor. For example, if aliens claim to have left their green cards at home, it may take just a few minutes to drive over to look at them. If they claim to have married U.S. citizens, which might warrant releasing them because probably their spouses will eventually petition for them, it may require just a single telephone call to check that out.

The legal risk confronting the officer is another factor. If aliens claim to be immigrated, the officers have much more leeway because, unlike the case of a citizen claimant, aliens encountered without immigration papers can be held as long as it takes to verify their immigration status. And in the case of a lawful resident claimant, there will be a service file somewhere. If the officers consider the case important enough and nothing turns up in the computer, they can ask for a hand search in either the district or central office. (By contrast, citizens are not required to carry documents or even talk to INS officers.) If they do agree to talk and tell the officer the county or state they were born in, their claim is not disproven if no record turns up in the state in which they claim to have been born. Also, if they present a birth certificate and it turns out to be false, finding the true holder of the birth certificate does not disprove their citizenship claim although it may make liars of them for other purposes of the law. (In theory, but infrequently in practice, they could be prosecuted for making false and misleading statements [8 U.S.C. 1001].) Absent their admission, their alienage can be verified only by locating a document of their foreign birth or by obtaining affidavits from reliable witnesses establishing their foreign nationality.

Finally, other aspects of the suspected false claimant's status or behavior are also highly relevant to the decision on how much time to invest in the case. If the alien is a suspected drug trafficker, and if the officers have strong reason to believe the claim is mala fide, then they may spend all the time necessary to establish that claimant's true identity and status.

As with every other aspect of enforcement, in addition to any legal or other risks of error, INS officers must take into account the payoff to be anticipated from an investigation in relation to the time that must be invested in the case. Thus, in the case of an alien who is picked up in a lettuce field and who is suspected of carrying a relative's green card and claiming that relative's identity, the officer might call the district office that has the alien registration file on the green-card holder. His purpose is to get enough information on the background of the true card holder to be able to determine if the alien in custody is the person shown on the card. But because of the time that will require, the officer's hope is to be able to break a false claim just by informing the alien that this will be done. The officer must also consider the costs this investigation will impose on the district office that has the file and weigh them against the likelihood of success in getting the person to tell the truth. (The alien who does will be granted voluntary return.) If the suspected false claimant will not confess, still more resource costs will be imposed if the individual must be written up for a deportation hearing (another call to the district office for authorization for the order to show cause/warrant of arrest, detention costs if the alien cannot post bond, and so on). There is also the risk that the district office may not authorize the order to show cause anyway, in which case the officer who threatened the alien with being written up for deportation processing will look bad.

In the case of suspected false citizen claimants, this can lead to an interesting paradox. The policy of a district office may be one of authorizing an order to show cause only for an alien who has already conceded a mala fide claim. (It may, however, grant authorization in cases where the claim is patently fraudulent on its face, as when a birth certificate has "deceased" written on it, or where there are other aggravating factors.) The reason relates partly to the costs of deportation processing but also to the fact that either the assistant district director for investigations or the officer who handles the liaison with the patrol station must evaluate the case by phone at a distance and may not want to run the risk of authorizing the arrest of someone who might turn out to be a citizen. Yet, the officer in the field must use the threat of deportation processing to get the alien to concede alienage and deportability. Thus an alien who persists with a false claim, even beyond a reasonable time, may still receive voluntary return upon finally admitting to alienage because the officer may have to use an offer of voluntary return to pry loose the admission.

As a result, some officers decide to release suspected false claimants who refuse to back down on a claim. They can rationalize such releases by saying that they can always check the claim later when they have the time. How frequently these claims are checked after release is unknown. Given the transiency of many aliens, one suspects that many such investigations have a low probability of paying off and are, in consequence, tabled.

Although officers dislike having to "cut loose" suspected false claimants, their decision rules are a rational adaptation to caseload pressures and legal risks. They must husband their time for investigating the claims of those aliens suspected of being criminals or major INA violators. When a run-of-the-mill EWI offender is involved, as one officer explained, "Why spend several hours trying to break one false claim when in the same period of time you can go out in the field and pick up ten to fifteen illegal aliens who won't cause any problems?"

But there is no invariant rule. Sometimes ego and professional pride come into play, and the officer will press the issue. The supervisor in an eastern district office described the time he decided to make a case against a suspected false claimant. His officers had picked up a West African who claimed to have been born in the United States in the late 1950s. However, the man's tribal scars, a body odor the officers attributed to exotic culinary tastes, and his heavily accented English made the claim highly suspect. A check with the vital statistics office in the state he claimed to have been born in failed to produce a positive report. Because the officer knew he could not hold the individual for more than 24 hours without a legal instrument (warrant of arrest) and because he had not yet met the proof burden he knew would be needed in a deportation hearing, the man was allowed to leave. In the meantime, his office did some checking around and came up with a lead that indicated the man had passed through customs into the United States a month earlier. When they checked with customs, they found a record of a Nigerian who had entered with a visitor's visa using a slightly different name. A comparison of the signature on the customs form with a handwriting sample obtained at the time of the suspect's apprehension revealed striking similarities, and a handwriting expert verified that it had come from the same hand. On that basis the man was reapprehended. At the deportation hearing, the investigators had what they called a "paper case" sufficient to meet the required clear, unequivocal, and convincing proof burden of alienage based on the handwriting comparisons. If the West African had admitted to the fraud at the time he was first encountered, he would probably have been given voluntary departure. But because he put the INS to considerable trouble, he was officially deported.

Most false claims to U.S. citizenship and lawful resident status can usually be disproven on the basis of documentary evidence if the investigators are willing to spend the time needed to track down the individual's identity. But because of the heavy costs of doing so, most officers try hard to obtain voluntary withdrawals. For a routine administrative violator, the chance that the alien would be criminally prosecuted is very small.

On the other hand, if a case warrants, INS officers can get at a false claimant through prosecution for 8 U.S.C. 1001 (fraudulent claims and misrepresentations), which is often easier than trying to track down the alien's true identity. For example, a New York City woman suspected of having entered illegally from Jamaica had adopted the identity of a U.S. citizen. When the INS located the true citizen, the suspected Jamaican illegal said that she had adopted the identity because she had been the product of an interracial rape and didn't have a family name. As a Jane Doe whose claim to be a U.S. citizen could not be determined without finding out who she was and where she was born, she was convicted of making a false statement in writing (claiming to be a citizen whose identity she had borrowed). Although most federal prosecutors are reluctant to take these cases, the INS officers successfully lobbied for prosecution because of the aggravated circumstances of the case. First, the woman had misappropriated the identity of a living citizen, which could have caused problems for the citizen. Second, the woman had married an alien and was applying to get him a green card as his citizen spouse, thus creating the hazard of a compound benefit fraud.

In another case in New York City, investigators worked hard to make a case on another Jamaican, this time a man who belonged to the Rastafarian drug cult and who had a long arrest record that included drug-related homicide. He remained unknown to the INS for years because he had successfully passed as a U.S. citizen when apprehended by New York City police. Only when he applied for a U.S. passport was the INS finally alerted. When questioned by INS officers, he held firm to his citizenship claim. Because of the threat posed by the offender, the officers not only went to the trouble of locating the citizen whose identity he had borrowed but also sent an officer to Jamaica to establish his true identity and therewith his alienage. On that basis, he was charged with the 18 U.S.C. 1542 felony of making a fraudulent passport application. For some reason, passport fraud is taken more seriously than the fraudulent use of U.S. birth certificates or mere oral claims (this is probably because passports are federal rather than state documents).

Although establishing a positive identity on a false claimant is not easy, neither is it impossible. If the officers know where a suspected false claimant lives or works, they can usually obtain sufficient leads to start with, although in a full-scale investigation, they may have to detail an officer to travel abroad to obtain birth records. (Getting documentation of an alien's foreign birth will help cinch the case from the standpoint of the "clear and convincing" standard required in a deportation hearing but is not an essential element for the government's case.)

ENTITLEMENT FRAUD: THE EASY PAPER CASE

Cases involving aliens with nonimmigrant visas who fraudulently apply for government-backed student loans (which only citizens and permanent residents are eligible for) are very easily made. In this type of dual fraud (also called *entitlement fraud*), as the INS refers to it, students misrepresent their status as citizens or lawful residents. In such cases, the aliens themselves supply the required evidence because, when they apply for the loan, they sign their names to their misrepresentations of their immigration status. (Most students use their real names because they want their diplomas in their true names and also because a loan officer is apt to check with their college.)

Although the fraud is not for the purpose of obtaining an immigration benefit, INS investigators often work these cases in liaison with the Department of Education because these aliens can more easily be deported as a result of their misrepresentations. This will complicate their efforts to re-enter or immigrate legally in the future. Such cases are also attractive to CIs because they are apt to be attractive to state and federal prosecutors, who find them easier to prosecute. But as one investigator in New York pointed out, a fraudulent student loan application involving a few thousand dollars is still small potatoes for federal prosecutors accustomed to white-collar fraud cases involving millions of dollars.

DUAL-ACTION BENEFIT FRAUD:
RELATIVE-VISA PETITIONS

Despite the considerably greater investigative effort put into them, the dual-action cases are often much harder to crack than most of the false claims encountered during routine field operations. In the first place, the alien is apt to have a stronger commitment to the fraud because of his or her investment of time and money. As noted in Chapter 2, these dual-action cases surface in the course of benefit applications in which the alien, besides having gone to the trouble of having made a formal application, may also have hired an attorney and invested time, as well as money, in wooing a citizen (in the case of I-130 marriage fraud). Some aliens are known to have paid as much as two to five thousand dollars for an arranged marriage. If it is a one-on-one fraud, an alien (usually male) may have showered meals, flowers, gifts, and the like on his betrothed. If she is unattractive, he may have had to go much farther to cultivate the relationship. (Officers refer to this situation as "earning the green card.") Male citizens wooed by female aliens can also benefit. A hotel porter accustomed to 50-cent tips can make a good match with an attractive, younger, female alien desperate to immigrate.

A male citizen's return is apt to be sexual favors. When the citizen is female, she may be content with courtly attention and economic support, although sexual relations may also be part of the deal. Thus the barriers erected by the law make citizenship an equity from which a modest return can be wrung among those citizens (and sometimes lawful residents) unscrupulous enough to want to trade on it. (Although there are also fraudulent marriages to lawful residents, second-preference visa fraud is less common because the alien may, depending on the country, have to wait some months or years for a visa number.)

In the case of a naive citizen who did not see through a phony courtship, there will be disappointment and anger when the spouse receives the green card and then leaves. Many enraged female citizens (and occasionally males) come into INS offices to complain. Wanting to get even with the alien, they will ask the INS to rescind the green card. But there is little the INS can do. If they married and cohabited as man and wife, proving fraudulent intent will be almost impossible. Indeed, even in those cases where the citizen was aware of the fraud and tells the INS she received money to marry the alien, it will just be her word against the alien's. He can simply say that he married her for love, but the marriage did not work out.

Although the examiners can deny a benefit request on the ground that the petitioner and alien have failed to meet their burden of proof for establishing the bona fides of their marriage, and so on, obtaining denials has become more difficult for the INS because of recent administrative and federal court decisions, especially in I-130 spousal petitions, that effectively require the INS to prove fraud from inception.[2] When examiners interview an alien and citizen whose discrepancies in age or cultural background are substantial (for example, the alien is an educated university student from Jordan whereas the citizen is a black woman on welfare) and who, when interviewed, appear not to share or know in common what a married couple could be reasonably expected to share, they may try to persuade the citizen spouse to withdraw the petition voluntarily, just as the investigators will do if they are unable to establish the bona fides when a case is turned over to them. If the spouse withdraws, no further action need be taken. By contrast, a formal denial of the petition will have to be justified and may lead the petitioner to request a special hearing, which can impose further costs on the service. By simply having an attorney, the alien can signal to the INS a willingness to fight a denial, which means that the service will have to reckon with the potential resource cost of litigation.

In cases in which the petitioner cannot be induced to withdraw the petition by an examiner and/or the examiners decide to send the file to the fraud unit, the investigators must, in theory, find the information that will support either a grant or a denial. Two decades ago, before INS investigations sections were squeezed between rising caseload pressures on the one hand and declining investigative manpower on the other, a case might be sent to investigations just on the basis of a gut feeling that something was off. Now, according to one investigator, the mala fides must be fairly obvious or "on paper" (for example, major discrepancies in a sworn question and answer statement) to justify a case investigation.

When a case is turned over to investigations, the CI assigned to it may decide to interview the couple's neighbors or apartment house manager to see if the couple lives together and maintains an appearance of wedlock. Income tax returns and bank statements might also be looked at to determine if a working spouse claims the other as a dependent or if they hold joint banking accounts, and the like. The records of the city marriage bureau might be checked if the investigator has reason to think the citizen is currently married to somebody else.

Finally, the officer may decide to do a "bedcheck" to determine if the couple is living together. If they are found living together, this will usually make it easy to close out the case because, according to the officers, cohabitation usually resolves any doubt about the bona fides in favor of the applicant no matter how much the officer may still believe that the marriage was contrived to obtain an immigration benefit. In short, if they contracted a legal marriage and are cohabiting, then they are married.

The constraints facing the officers can be illuminated by looking at some fairly typical investigations.

During one I-130 spousal investigation, a woman from South America had been given the option of departing voluntarily after being found deportable by the immigration judge during a hearing. Two days before she was due to leave, she married a U.S. citizen, a black male with a history of common-law relationships. When the examiners got around to interviewing the alien and her citizen spouse separately in 1980 (four years after the woman had been found deportable), their stories did not mesh, despite their claim to be living together. The examiner sent the case to investigations and two investigators went out to the low-rent district where the man had an apartment.

As they explained to me while we drove to the apartment in the early morning hours, the standard procedure during a "bedcheck" is first to determine whether the man and woman are sharing the same quarters. If the alien spouse is absent, they can ask to see the absent partner's clothing. If there are just a few items of clean clothing, they may ask to see the person's dirty clothes or personal effects. (If some of the clothes are there, they may check to determine whether the clothing is of the right size because it may also belong to a paramour or to the citizen's real spouse.) Sometimes the couple may be occupying the same apartment but not sleeping in the same room. Sometimes the officers will find bedding that has been folded and placed on a sofa in the living room and that may still be warm to the touch—which suggests to the officers that the couple is trying to keep up appearances. (But it is also possible that the couple may have had a fight or that there may have been an overnight guest.)

In this case, when the investigators arrived and found no evidence that the woman lived in the apartment, the man readily admitted that they had been separated for a couple of years, and he agreed to withdraw the I-130 visa petition. The woman, he claimed, had since moved to Texas.

In such cases, the investigators' objective is no different from that pursued by officers confronted with suspected false claims. Although the official purpose is to gather evidence sufficient to justify a grant or denial, the officers' hope is that once they have satisfactory evidence that the marriage is a sham, they can persuade the petitioner to agree to a voluntary withdrawal, preferably on the spot. Just as in the case of false claims where officers seek, as they say, to "catch the person in a lie," in visa petition fraud, the officers develop factual inconsistencies and use them to persuade the respondent (petitioner) to withdraw the petition. Most individuals will not persist with a deception when confronted with obvious discrepancies. Thus, if the petitioner states that the absent spouse's clothing is at the laundry, the officers can ask which laundry, indicating that they intend to check. Or if the petitioner states that the absent spouse is visiting relatives, they can ask where these relatives can be reached, and so forth. Sometimes the game is up when the officers telephone the citizen and find themselves talking to a person who is the real spouse rather than the alien that citizen claimed to have married.

An investigator can also obtain leverage in a suspected marriage fraud simply from knowledge that the citizen is a prostitute (obtained from police records) or from information indicating that that citizen has been involved in attempted marriage fraud before (from service records). If the citizen is a woman on Aid to Families with Dependent Children, the officer may inform her that the welfare office will have to be notified of her marriage. (Some officers are not certain, however, whether the welfare office will, in fact, terminate a recipient's benefits even when notified that a recipient has married.) As a last resort, the officer may point out the serious felony penalty for making false and misleading statements on an official government application. Although pointing out the legal hazards will work in some cases, it can backfire in others. The threat of a legal sanction may lead the alien and citizen to work harder to keep up the front. Still, officers claim they are successful in getting voluntary withdrawals in a majority of cases—65 percent to 75 percent of them, by the estimates of the fraud investigators I interviewed. (There are no official statistics to settle the point.)

If, however, the citizen and alien do not withdraw the petition but persist in their claim, the options available to the investigators narrow considerably. One investigations supervisor claimed that, during his eight years' experience in his district office, no more than perhaps 1 percent of the suspected fraud cases he and his investigators had worked on (but presumably were unable to obtain voluntary withdrawals on) had led to benefit denials. And he could not recall a single investigation that had resulted in the recision of a granted benefit based on evidence that turned up later of fraud having been committed.

Of course, it is hard to know whether such a low figure is accurate or whether, even if accurate, it reflects INS's servicewide experience. Although there are statistics on benefit denials, it is hard to judge their meaning because the relevant base against which to compare them, namely, the total of suspected fraudulent applications sent down for investigation, is not available.

The investigators believe that some fraud investigations are merely pro forma because the mala fides they do manage to dredge up will be insufficient to overcome the proof burden the service must meet if the petitioners change their minds and decide to go ahead with their applications, which is more likely to occur if they are assisted by attorneys. Thus, in the case involving the South American female and male U.S. citizen discussed earlier, the investigators pointed out that their efforts would be wasted if the alien got back in touch with the man and said, "I really love you," and he came back into the office to refile. Perhaps the examiners might still deny the petition based on the investigative report. However, if the alien and citizen appeal, the INS may be required to establish fraudulent intent from the inception of the marriage (unless the citizen had earlier admitted to fraud).[3]

The following case illustrates what happens when a citizen petitioner refuses to withdraw. The case involved a marriage fraud investigation in a western district office. The predication stated that there were significant (material) discrepancies between what the alien beneficiary, a South American female, and her citizen husband had said when asked the same questions during separate interviews.

When two investigators went out for a bedcheck, they found the alien, but not her citizen spouse, at the address. Nor was there any indication that he had lived there. The woman said that her husband lived with her but had left for the university early in the morning. When asked about his clothing, she said it was at the laundry. She became nervous during the interview, a fact the investigator jotted down in his report. Neighbors in the apartment building were interviewed, but they told the investigator they had no recollection of ever seeing the alien's spouse around. The building manager said the alien told her that her husband was in the Peace Corps and traveled all the time.

The citizen was finally located at another address in the city. He explained that he had two residences and occasionally stayed with his spouse at the second address. The investigator then showed him a copy of a paper describing the 8 U.S.C. 1001 felony for giving false and misleading information, at which point he became very nervous. After the investigator left, he called his attorney. He then called back the investigator to state that if there was no prosecution, he would agree to withdraw his petition.

But then he had a change of mind. Five days after he had called to say he would withdraw, the INS district office received a letter in which he affirmed that he did not marry his wife in order to get her an immigration benefit. He acknowledged that his personnel file at the university did not list him as married, and he agreed to see to it that this oversight was corrected. He admitted that he had been having some marital difficulties but added that these difficulties were compounded by the INS's harassment of him and his wife. If the INS had any further questions, he concluded, these should be sent to his attorney. Shortly thereafter, his attorney mailed in a picture of the couple standing next to a wedding cake along with documents showing they had a joint bank account. There were also some store receipts showing the woman using her married name. A reputable immigration attorney would play no part in dressing up a phony marriage this way, but not all attorneys are reputable, and a number are known to assist fraudulent applicants. Some have been prosecuted for actually participating in arranged-marriage rings.

In the G-166 investigative report, which closed the case as far as the investigator was concerned, the investigator concluded, "Upon completion of the investigation, it appears that subject and her spouse entered into a marriage of convenience. Although no one interviewed gave any definite evidence that the subject married her spouse for immigration purposes, the fact that they reside in two separate residences and see each other occasionally would lead one to believe that they do not have a bona fide marriage." The investigator went on to add that after he revealed to the citizen that his wife had not been listed on any of his employment or school records, the subject had agreed to withdraw the petition, but then later changed his mind after talking to his attorney.

However, the investigator explained to me that he was pessimistic that the I-130 petition would be denied. He assumed that examinations would approve the I-130 petition because, even though the evidence leaned heavily in favor of a denial, it would be hard to prove fraudulent intent in this case. Moreover, even though it could be shown that the couple had made misrepresentations about their relationship, these falsehoods would not necessarily be considered material if the petitioner took the case to a hearing or into district court.

Until the mid-1970s, service examiners had considerable leeway to determine whether a marriage was viable because the Immigration and Nationality Act had put the proof burden on the petitioner. Indeed, the statute states explicitly that, if a marriage dissolves within two years, the presumption is that the marriage was not valid for the purpose of obtaining an immigration benefit, and the alien and citizen, not the INS, had to overcome that presumption. But in an important court ruling, it was decided that INS officers were not qualified to determine the viability of a marriage. Nor could they hold an alien and his or her citizen spouse to a higher standard of viability than could be expected of other American married couples. With the profusion of innovative and, some would say, rather off-beat marital life styles in recent years and the increasing frequency of separation and divorce, what makes a viable marriage is practically beyond definition. In effect, this means that INS examiners are left having to establish fraudulent intent from inception. In one-on-one cases, this usually means that unless the CIs in fraud can get one, and possibly both, of the parties to admit that the marriage is fraudulent, they probably will not have a case for a denial. Although the examiners might decide to delay approval, a couple willing to wait it out is likely to eventually pry loose the grant of the benefit.

However, law enforcement agents can devise circumventions that will achieve their objective when they believe that the legal environment has turned against them unfairly or generates frivolous rulings that do not accord with their practical experience. Thus some officers may decide to break a false citizenship claim (when they are almost 100 percent sure that the claim is fraudulent) by telling an alien that there is no record of birth after checking a phone directory or by pretending to call a vital statistics office when in fact the state office is closed on a weekend. The officers can rationalize such tactics as a necessary foil against the lies and bad faith dealings they encounter among violators. Thus, in the case of a suspected sham marriage, the investigators can decide to drag their feet in investigating the case. Although as a rule, dual-action investigations tend to take priority because aliens are awaiting a benefit and may go to the district court for a writ of mandamus to force the service to make a decision one way or the other, there is less pressure to close a case when fraud is strongly suspected. With passing time, the investigators know they have a better chance of "making" the case because the alien and citizen will have difficulty keeping up appearances. If it was a commercial transaction, then the citizen may demand more money for legal and other expenses or for continuing the ruse of living together. If the citizen was naive (unaware that the alien had married him or her solely for the benefit), there is a fair chance the marriage will break up as the cultural differences between the two begin to erode a relationship that came into being only because the alien had an immigration problem, a relationship the alien has begun to tire of. If they do fall out, the citizen may withdraw the petition without any prompting by the INS. If the petition has not been withdrawn, but the citizen is no longer living with the alien, the investigators are apt to have better luck getting a voluntary withdrawal. Thus the officers operate from a quasi-sociological theory: Marriages of convenience are just that. The personal relationship, far from deepening, is likely to deteriorate with passing time.

Just as false claimants are more easily pried loose from their claims when officers can point to inconsistencies in the documents they present or the statements they make, so couples who misrepresent their living arrangements (as when a couple claims to be living together but, in fact, lives apart) also provide investigators with better leverage for obtaining withdrawals. In fact, the alien and citizen stand a better chance of approval if they describe their living arrangement as it really is because INS officers will have a harder time denying the benefit based on their judgment of the relationship's viability. (Analogously, false claimants would probably be allowed to go free if they simply stated that they were born in the United States and said nothing more. Absent inconsistent information or papers, officers have much less leverage for breaking a claim.)

Although some marriage frauds are thought out well in advance of an alien's arrival in the United States, many frauds are contrived as a kind of last-ditch remedy to deal with an immigration problem. Threatened with deportation, a desperate student will seek out an American friend to help him find a way out of his dilemma. He may have finally run out of plausible reasons the INS will accept to extend his visa. However, he has found a good job and doesn't want to return home. He prevails upon a friend to introduce him to an American woman, who might then marry him as a favor, perhaps with the understanding that a sexual liaison will not be required of her. She is told about the student's plight and, her feelings of sympathy aroused, goes ahead with the arrangement. (She may not realize that what she is doing is against the law.)

In other kinds of suspected I-130 relative visa petitions not involving marriage to a citizen, the difficulty confronting the investigator arises less from the proof burden that must be met to establish intent than from the complexity of both the statutory provision and a determination of the alien's eligibility in the light of both U.S. law and the law of the alien's homeland.

For example, I accompanied an investigator on a call at the apartment of an Ecuadoran female being investigated for possible visa fraud. She had arrived in the United States in 1976 with a second-preference visa as the unmarried child of her father, a lawful permanent resident already living in the United States. She then applied for an immigrant visa for her husband, who she claimed she married in 1977 after arriving in this country. The possibility that she had immigrated fraudulently did not come to light until she petitioned for her husband. What tipped off the examiner was the fact that she had a child who was using her husband's name before the time of her marriage in 1977. When the investigator checked with the U.S. consulate in her home country, he learned that she had actually married in 1973, which would have made her ineligible for an immigrant visa as an unmarried dependent of her lawfully resident father and would thus invalidate her application for her husband.

When we arrived at the apartment, the woman admitted that she had altered the date of her marriage but claimed that her marriage in 1973 was invalid under the law of her country because she had been underage at the time. Her grandfather had stood in at the religious ceremony rather than her father. Her father had brought her, she claimed, to the United States to break up her marriage because he had disapproved of it. The investigator had already spoken with her father, who claimed that he had had no knowledge of his daughter's marriage.

The investigator explained to me that what he had to do next was establish whether a father's knowledge and consent are required for a valid marriage under Ecuadoran law.

Children born out of wedlock abroad are also a snare for investigations of first- and second-preference visa petitions suspected of fraud because of the complex family laws in some countries as well as the difficulty often posed in determining the bona fides of familial relationships. Given the unreliability of documentation (or their nonexistence, as in the case of births that are not officially recorded) along with the ease with which civil servants and religious authorities can be bribed to provide oral or documentary testimony in many countries, this is no easy task. State Department officials and overseas INS officers can check into some, but hardly all, suspicious claims. Another problem arises from the omissions that sometimes exist in an alien's record. Although at the time they immigrate, adult aliens are required to list both their legitimate and illegitimate children, some later seek to bring in children they had not listed when they first entered. They claim they omitted their illegitimate children because they feared listing them would hinder their chances of qualifying for an immigrant visa—perhaps on the ground that they might be judged lacking in good moral character or likely to become a public charge.

The reverse problem also occurs: At the time they immigrate, some aliens list children or "brothers" and "sisters" not belonging to them as their own. They may subsequently sell the preference visa slots they have created to somebody else or make them available to relatives. Such artificially created slots become especially valuable once the alien has become naturalized because there are no quota limits for that citizen's immediate relatives who want to immigrate.

DUAL-ACTION BENEFIT FRAUD:
I-140 VISA PETITIONS

Investigations of I-140 sixth-preference visa petitions comprise only a small percentage (10 percent or less) of a fraud unit's caseload. This is because sixth-preference visas are a small percentage of preference visa petitions overall. (I-130 relative visa petitions take most of the available quota slots in any given year, and the wait for a sixth-preference visa is therefore apt to be longer.)

When an alien seeks to immigrate to the United States on the basis of occupational skill, an American employer puts in an I-140 petition for the intending immigrant. To qualify for I-140 visas, aliens must show that they have the skills required, that, for example, they are the specialty cooks or auto mechanics they claim to be. Then the Department of Labor must certify that citizens and lawful residents are not available (or willing) to take the job in question (this is easily satisfied for many specialty cook positions) and that the wages and working conditions being offered are comparable to what citizens and lawful residents receive for similar work. Except for a small number of jobs the Department of Labor has precertified, an employer is usually required to advertise the job opening to establish that citizen workers in that part of the state have not come forward (or are unqualified) for the job. Once the Department of Labor has approved the labor certification, the alien theoretically arrives in the United States to accept the job. Many aliens, however, are actually found to be already working here illegally, which often—and in the officers' view unfairly—gives them the experience to qualify for a sixth-preference visa over other foreign nationals waiting abroad for their visas. In short, labor certification serves as an inducement to illegal immigration. As one immigration judge summed up the problem:

> Labor certification presupposes that an employer will recruit an individual who is abroad and whom he has never seen. What employer would take such a chance on somebody halfway around the world? Also, it takes one to two years to get the application approved. But for cooks, domestic maids, and the like, that's too long. Who will wait that long? So, it's hardly surprising that people would come here first and job hunt and then put in for labor certification. The fact that they've been working without authorization isn't any problem. They just return home to pick up their immigrant visa.

The immigration judge also noted that many do not stay long in the jobs for which they were certified.

As in the case of I-130 fraud, I-140 immigrant visa petitions also involve a citizen petitioner and an alien beneficiary. And they pose much the same dilemma for the investigator, to wit: Can it be proven that a petition that appears to be a sham is, in fact, fraudulent? The main difference between these two visa investigations is that the fraud in an I-140 case can often be documented with paper. If the alien has fabricated an occupational past, INS examiners will have no trouble denying the petition because the misrepresentation can be documented. For example, if an alien claims training and occupational experience as a mechanic in Seoul, Korea, the investigator can ask the consulate to check it out.

In some I-140 frauds, aliens get an employer, often a friend or relative from the home country, to agree to sponsor them for a job although they have no intention of holding that job. Less frequently, the alien will fabricate the job offer by submitting an I-140 petition using stationery taken from a U.S. company. The owner's signature is forged on the forms. Because the employer's signature has been forged, a denial of the benefit is easy to obtain once the investigator contacts the employer.

In other cases, employers may have been contacted about hiring an alien but may have had no knowledge that they are being asked to participate in an effort to defraud the government. Employment agencies may call, for example, and ask if they would consider hiring a good mechanic from Korea. As with citizens who are asked to "sponsor" an alien (and who learn only later that they must "marry" them in a sham ceremony), employers may be led to think that they are only being asked to consider a prospective job candidate. Since they believe they have nothing to lose, they sign the forms put before them. The representative from the employment agency handles the rest.

In one case investigated by an officer in an eastern district office, the owner of a small pizza parlor was applying for a woman from a Middle Eastern country as a specialty food cook. Based on information obtained from the examiner handling the case, the investigator was skeptical about the bona fides. He told me that when we arrived at the shop and met with the owner, we would probably find Egyptian dishes prominently displayed on the menu. Those would have been added on after the owner had learned from the woman's attorney that preparing pizzas wouldn't qualify the woman.

There were two tip-offs that the certification might be fraudulent. The examiner who sent the case to investigations stated in the predication that the woman was a relative of the owner. Another tip-off had inadvertently been supplied by her attorney, who had told someone in the district office that his client was very wealthy. "Why," the investigator asked, "would she want to work for the salary listed in the application, $240 a week, making pizzas?

And her fashionable Baltimore address isn't where you'd find a pizza cook living." Still, if the investigator found her working in the kitchen when we arrived, she would probably have to be approved for the visa. Because she had applied for an I-485 petition to adjust her status in the United States, she had been given permission to work. (Normally, an alien here on a tourist visa could not, as an "intending immigrant," work.)

The investigator had already gone to the pizza shop once before and had not found her working. As part of the investigation, he had also requested employment and tax records for the business from the state of Virginia. Still, proving fraud would not be easy. If she did not turn up on the company's payroll, the owner could say he was paying her in cash. The investigator could call the manager into the office to take a sworn statement and threaten him with lying under oath. But he pointed out that, even if he lied, it would be unlikely that prosecution would result.

The investigator considered other ways the case might be handled. Fraud might be proven later if another employee could be found to testify that the woman never worked there. On that basis, the green card might possibly be rescinded. On the other hand, the owner could state that she had showed up but failed to work out on the job or that she decided she really did not want to work after all, and because she had enough money, she did not have to. As the investigator summed up the situation, "It can smell and look like a fraud and be in every respect a fraud, but unless you can prove fraudulent intent you can't prove fraud."

When we arrived, Egyptian dishes were indeed prominently listed on the wall in the shop. After the investigator talked briefly with the owner, he learned that the woman had not worked there for some months. The owner explained that the woman had a rash on her arm that made it hard for her to cook. Because it had been more than a year and a half since she had been authorized by INS to work, it was quite possible that she had spent a short time working. Of course, she may have simply gone through the motions to establish her bona fides, just as many aliens who "marry" citizens do to pass "bedcheck" and other inquiries in an I-130 investigation.

In this kind of investigation, some of the facts suggested strongly that the labor certification was a fraud: (1) the woman's status in relation to the job, (2) the fact she was a relative of the owner, and (3) the somewhat lame excuse given for her having abandoned the job. Proving fraud, however, would be difficult in the absence of testimony by either the owner or the alien.

Faced with this dilemma, the investigator mulled over the possible kinds of leverage that might pry loose an admission from the owner. For example, if it turned out that there were no payroll records for her during the time the owner says she worked, he might threaten to inform the state of Virginia, on the basis that the owner had probably violated Virginia's workers' compensation law or some other employment provision. Whether that would work, he said, "depends on who the guy is most afraid of, the INS or the state of Virginia."

Although some labor certification fraud is premeditated by aliens and their sponsors even before they have arrived in the United States, in other cases it arises as a result of an employer's desire to help an alien who has become a good and loyal worker but who lacks the equities to immigrate. Such employers may try to cut what they think are only a small corner or two of the law by redefining the alien's job so it will be approved by the Labor Department for an I-140 petition. The aliens may also falsify their past work history in their homelands because they must show that they not only have the necessary skill but also some past job experience. Thus a Hong Kong Chinese whose real duty in an electronics firm is testing equipment may become a translator/correspondent because the latter occupation has a better chance of qualifying.

Sometimes I-140 petitions alert the INS that something may be amiss even though the petitions appear to be bona fide. When the examiners in a district office note that they have been receiving batches of I-140 petitions from the same firm or labor recruiter, it may indicate that an organization is serving as a conduit for illegal immigrants, who enter as nonimmigrant visitors or as fraudulent entrants. So, for example, if petitions come in for twenty Korean machine operators from the same firm or recruiter, the INS may request the consulate to investigate whether the aliens being petitioned for are working at those jobs back in Korea as claimed in the petitions. (If they are not, their I-140 petitions will be invalid. Also, chances are good that, upon investigation, they may prove to be already working in U.S. firms, which would make them deportable.) Even if nothing turns out to be amiss after the consulate has carried out its checks, there may still be enforcement payoff for another government agency. The INS can notify the Department of Labor that a possible garment sweatshop is operating in the city and suggest that their wage and hour division might want to check for labor law violations.

One could argue that, when a federal enforcement agency finds its own efforts blocked (or too costly to pursue, given the likely payoff), it may turn the enforcement problem over to other agencies on the basis of potential violations of their regulations.

THIRD-PARTY FRAUD CASES

Fraud cases involving third parties, such as arranged-marriage rings or agencies that recruit workers from overseas for jobs that are either nonexistent or involve misrepresentation on the part of the alien or of a third-party inter-mediary, provide the best enforcement payoff for investigators. In the first place, the government's proof burden is much easier to make, regardless of whether the CIs anticipate a criminal prosecution as distinct from a denial of the immigration benefit. There is also substantially more enforcement lever-age because, if a third-party organization is involved in the fraud, it will often have handled dozens or even scores of aliens, whose visas can then be re-scinded. Interestingly, although these cases are easier to obtain denials and prosecutions for, they are assigned to the more skilled GS-11 and GS-12 agents. This is because the stakes (criminal prosecutions) are higher, and con-sequently, more legal care must be taken in developing the evidence and other aspects of these cases.

Although aliens who avail themselves of third-party arrangers are gener-ally aware that they are circumventing the law, this is not always the case. For example, a Polish national who has entered as a visitor and needs a Social Security card to get work may be introduced by friends to an individual ex-perienced in immigration matters, usually a fellow national who speaks good English and who claims to know how to get the visitor through the bureau-cratic maze. (Individuals from socialist, Eastern bloc economies, besides being skilled at "working" the system, no doubt have many fewer scruples about pushing red tape to the side.) The go-between accompanies the alien to the Social Security Administration office as a guide and translator. He ex-plains to the clerk that the Pole has a student visa with work authorization and that he has come along to help his friend because his friend does not yet understand English very well. He then hands over a fraudulent student visa with a forged facsimile INS work authorization stamp on the back, without having explained this to his Polish "friend." Of course, many aliens do know what is going on (or may harbor suspicions that the individual helping them is circumventing the law) but decide to look the other way because this is what they have to do to work in the United States.

Often the INS catches on to third-party frauds simply because the prin-cipals have been operating for a period of weeks or months. The quick and easy money causes the principals to abandon caution, and the examiners will note how the names of the same attorneys, ministers, or notaries public ap-pear with surprising regularity on a series of I-130 petitions. Often, too, aliens and their spouses are not only mismatched by age, education, or ethnic and racial origin but also according to a fairly predictable pattern. The ring may be matching aliens from the Middle East, for example, with females from a certain ethnic group or part of the city.

Arranged-marriage rings are vulnerable precisely because they are third-party transactions, which makes plausible-appearing matches between the aliens and the citizens recruited as their spouses harder to come by. In addition to the visible mismatching, such couples will have a difficult time getting through a second interview during which each will be queried separately from the other about matters they should know in common.

Because arranged-marriage ring principals are fast-buck operators, the alien and spouse may have had only a couple of hours together. If an attorney is involved in the ring, an effort may be made to prepare them for the interview, based on the attorney's experience with the kinds of questions the examiners routinely ask. Because of this, examiners often vary their questions.

Third-party cases pose relatively few evidence problems, which is a major reason assistant U.S. attorneys accept them. The other important reason is that they are organized criminal activities and sometimes involve attorneys. Sometimes there is documentary evidence, such as records of the fees received from aliens and paid out to citizens. Usually, citizens can be induced to testify against the principals in exchange for having the charges against them dropped. Most citizens, even though they may have been tempted to circumvent the law in order to earn a few dollars (or obtain an inexpensive maid) still do not relish going to court or having their names publicized. According to the investigators, it is the fear of adverse publicity, much more than the likely criminal sanction (usually a suspended sentence), that pries loose their testimony. Some citizens also become angry with the principals because they were paid less than they expected or because they were not fully informed of the legal risks they would be taking (as when they were told they would only be sponsoring the alien). A recruited welfare woman, for example, may get just a few hundred dollars out of a total fee of $1,500 or more—plus the legal fees, if an attorney is involved—paid by the alien to the arranger.

There is additional enforcement leverage because, in the process of breaking a ring, the service can work back and deny lawful residence to perhaps as many as 30 to 70 aliens. In the case of those who have received their green cards, the service also stands a good chance of getting benefit recisions and deporting the alien beneficiaries.

In I-140 petition fraud, an employment agency may have been set up for that purpose or may have become involved in fraudulent labor certifications as a sideline, just as some travel agencies help their clients obtain fraudulent visas or photo-substituted U.S. passports along with airline tickets and tours.

For example, a citizen might contact an employment agency to request a maid. The agency has a file of aliens looking for shortcuts to a green card and says it knows of a Jamaican who wants to come to the United States and who would be available. The citizen may not know that this Jamaican is currently working illegally in the United States as a B-2 visitor and has been looking for a sponsor who would immigrate her so she could work legally. The citizen agrees to sponsor her and submits an I-140 petition for a maid. When the visa application arrives in Jamaica, the woman's family notifies her and she returns to Jamaica, picks up the documents and goes to the U.S. consulate. The consular officials have no knowledge that she has been working without authorization in the States.

The citizen pays the employment agency $500 to $600 to handle the paperwork for the labor certification, which will probably be deducted from the maid's wages. She may not mind because it is the green card that she really wants. Once it is granted, she will leave domestic service for a better job.

In one case prosecuted in New York City, a law firm serving a predominantly alien clientele was found to have been charging its clients $750 to $1,500 to locate employers who would sponsor them even though the firm knew their clients lacked the requisite skills for the jobs for which they would be certified. They told their clients to obtain fraudulent letters of reference from their home countries to establish the bona fides of their past work history. Then, under an agreement the law firm had with an employment agency in New York, the agency sent out runners to get signatures from employers on blank labor certification applications. These were sent to the law firm, where they were filled out and then sent on to the Department of Labor. In some cases, signatures were forged when the owners refused to play along. The employment agency got a $250 fee and the runner $50 for each signature.

EIGHT

THE DILEMMAS OF
IMMIGRATION LAW ENFORCEMENT

Enforcing the immigration law presents the INS with numerous dilemmas. First, agency policy has often had to adjust to pressures originating from the larger political milieu, especially in regard to interior enforcement. Although political pressures to mitigate tough enforcement were accommodated to a much greater extent during the Carter administration, they continue to impact INS policy even under the more enforcement-minded Reagan administration. In the interior, many well-organized interest groups want weak immigration enforcement. In consequence, a tough, no-holds-barred enforcement policy would have been difficult, even if the INS had all the officers, detention space, and other resources required for an all-out effort against INA violators.

Many examples of how political considerations affect INS enforcement have already been discussed. And there are many more; INS officers could, for example, get warrants to enter churches whose congregations openly defy the law by harboring aliens or aiding their smuggling. But such action would probably provoke public antagonism that would not offset the gain in arrests and prosecutions.[1] The INS avoids raiding hospitals for the same reason.[2]

The INS is certainly not alone among regulatory agencies in having to consider such political trade-offs. In his study of the Nevada casino industry, Jerome Skolnick observed that the Gaming Control Board's audit division avoided overly aggressive monitoring of the industry for the simple reason that a thorough and rigorous enforcement effort might turn up too many problems, and that in turn might call into question the casino industry's hard-won image as a clean industry.[3]

There is yet another factor. According to James Q. Wilson, regulators tend to be risk-averse. They are more concerned with avoiding scandals that might provoke criticism from legislators than they are with expanding their bureaucratic domains. They prefer security to the uncertainties of rapid growth and change.[4] However, although bureaucratic aversion to risk-taking may explain why regulators pay careful attention to the cues they receive from legislators and other political actors, it does not tell us whether they will favor a tough (maximalist) rather than flexible (lenient) enforcement policy. The attitude taken depends on several factors, among them the availability of resources to meet organizational objectives, but especially the public's perception of the social harm or costs that might result from lenient enforcement (or, conversely, from too draconian a policy).

In the case of INS enforcement, the risk of public scandal or damage to official careers would be minimal in the event the press or other watchdog groups were to publicize, for example, the agency's failure to round up illegal aliens in the *X* garment plant after receiving several tips. By contrast, an agency such as the Environmental Protection Agency (EPA) would run considerable risks if it became known that officials had been alerted to a hazardous toxic waste problem in a community and failed to investigate in a timely manner. When the INS gets into political trouble, it is often because it *did* decide to apprehend illegal aliens at some plant. Whereas environmental watchdog groups worry that the EPA might go easy on violators, most interest groups concerned with immigration issues are apt to complain because INS officers are enforcing the law.

VALUE INDETERMINACY AS A
CONSTRAINT ON RESOURCE OPTIMALIZATION

Besides the need to take into account the political ramifications of enforcement actions, the INS must grapple with internal trade-offs that arise from the agency's need to make more optimal use of resources. Although, in theory, the agency could justify practically any resource allocation on the basis of its statutory mandate to enforce the law against a wide variety of INA violators, its limited resources require assessments of the payoffs that can be anticipated from different enforcement activities. For example, would resources be better used by having the investigations branch devote more time to entitlement (welfare) screening rather than work site apprehensions of administrative violators? Should officers pursue more abscondees or screen more jails? How thoroughly should investigators look into suspected fraudulent marriage petitions in one-on-one cases? If too many officer hours are devoted to those cases, less time will be available for investigating more serious third-party conspiracy cases, and so forth.

The problem is that resource allocations often occur in a knowledge vacuum. As Colin Diver has pointed out, regulatory agencies face value indeterminacy. Although a rational enforcement policy would maximize the social utilities of enforcement (public harms prevented and net social welfare increased in relation to expenditures), Diver notes that these utilities can rarely be calculated with any precision. In consequence, agencies must resort to proxy measures of their performance, which in turn can easily lead to goal displacement. Because it cannot easily assess its impact on the general objectives set down by legislators (such as the number of uninspected violations known to have been deterred), an agency may decide to tabulate successful prosecutions, civil fines levied, prison sentences meted out, and so forth.[5]

The INS is no exception to this generalization. Agency officials cannot know how many sham marriages are deterred by publicized prosecutions of fraudulent marriage arrangers; nor can they know the number of Mexican and Central American aliens not working in the United States because Category I smuggling rings X, Y, and Z were recently busted. True, baseline indicators of a sort can be found for some enforcement activities. For example, INS officials assert that the number of illegal aliens who try to obtain unemployment benefits declines after a major screening project involving the INS and a state's unemployment compensation agency. (Such claims may rest on anecdotal evidence—"We heard that applications from aliens declined during the following weeks."—or on a follow-up audit of alien applicants after the earlier screening operation.) Or the INS can project the dollar savings to taxpayers, based on the specific number of illegal aliens uncovered multiplied by the average dollar amounts that recipients are granted.

However, these indicators are not totally reliable measures of deterrence even when they can be expressed in quantitative terms. For example, aliens screened out of welfare programs may simply try again under different names and with different sets of identification. Or just as some immigration benefit applicants are known to do, they may move to a jurisdiction whose welfare officials screen citizenship and lawful residence claims less thoroughly. Also, because aliens may simply hold back until the INS shifts attention and resources to other problems, the durability of any deterrent effect is hard to know.

In the absence of empirically verifiable indicators, agency officials tend to rely on educated guesses of deterrent impact ("taking down organized smuggling rings is much more disruptive to illegal traffic than busting individual load cars"), or they may justify allocations based on what they do have in hand, or can reasonably estimate—in short, on the specific actions taken against known violators. These proxy measures of agency effectiveness— aliens apprehended and returned under safeguard, vehicles seized, savings to taxpayers in welfare dollars, convictions and jail time meted out, and the like—become the agency's product because there is little else to deliver.

But the absence of better performance measures is also due to the agency's failure to devote more resources to evaluation research. For example, the INS could assess how effective an intensive farm and ranch check operation would be in inducing farmers in a given locale to prefer lawful alien and citizen workers. Doing so, however, would require that border patrol activities be planned and directed in accordance with the statistical sampling requirements of the researchers. Also, the farmers in the area selected would very likely complain to their legislators about harassment. Higher-level officials might worry about criticism from Congress.

In earlier years, the agency had less need to be concerned with measures of enforcement leverage because resources were more plentiful in relation to caseloads. It could justify any level of enforcement activity simply because it was the agency's job to pursue INA violators regardless of the social harm that might be attributed to different categories of violators.

Today, however, resource constraints require the agency to address these issues. Although the case management system introduced in the investigations branch in 1983 is indicative of the agency's interest in improving its performance measures, the INS has yet to develop methodologically adequate studies of the deterrent impact of various activities. For example, under the new case management system, the agency does not try to calculate the social costs posed by different categories of INA violators. Instead, the agency sets thresholds for assigning cases on the basis of two factors: (1) the seriousness of various offender groups, which is usually determined according to a legal-gravity criteria and which may or may not correlate with the social costs or harm they pose for the society, and (2) the likelihood that an investigation will result in success (acceptance of the case for prosecution, the probability that an abscondee will be located or that a benefit being sought will be denied, and the like). Only in the case of employer surveys is there an effort to assess whether close monitoring of notorious employers has deterrent effects; that is, whether repeat surveys incline the employer to prefer legal rather than illegal labor. (As of 1983, no impact studies were yet available.)

On the other hand, because the INS has multiple enforcement goals (diverse categories of violators and diverse constituencies served), it is unlikely that it could ever pursue a perfectly utility-maximizing strategy of the kind Diver describes for a rational regulator—even if the net social utilities of its various activities could be estimated. According to Diver, "The rational regulator will concentrate his efforts initially on violations that involve substantial risk of harm but are relatively easy to detect and prove."[6] One could hypothesize, however, that under a fully rational policy, rather than the minuscule 3 percent of officer hours (as reported in 1983) devoted to screening aliens un-authorized to obtain welfare benefits, a large percentage of INS investigators would be assigned to work with state and local welfare agencies on that project. In addition, conceivably no officers would be assigned to apprehend illegal aliens reported working at low-paying jobs. (This hypothesis is by no means farfetched, if it can be demonstrated that deportable aliens make a net economic contribution after all social and economic impacts have been com-puted.) But such a "rational" policy might then subject the agency to charges of nonenforcement or underenforcement of the law by those groups that benefit (or believe they benefit) from enforcement. There *are* citizens who write to legislators complaining of illegal aliens working in such-and-such a plant. Thus, on political grounds, just as the agency must underenforce the law selectively in certain contexts (and forego enforcement altogether in a few), it cannot avoid at least occasional enforcement against almost all catego-ries of violators. The INS will not raid hospitals and churches. But neither can it forego altogether surveys of work sites where low-wage illegal aliens are employed, even if there were no demonstrable social harm from illegal aliens in these industries.

THE CALCULUS OF ENFORCEMENT POLICY

Whether consciously articulated or not, political factors are often closely in-tertwined with considerations of optimal resource allocations in the agency's effort to achieve what it considers to be the most advantageous enforcement strategy. As noted earlier, productivity from linewatch and farm and ranch checks is much higher than that obtained from urban area control. Mexicans caught near the border are much cheaper to process and transport back to the border than other-than-Mexicans apprehended in the interior.

Viewed from the macrolevel, a policy that generates large numbers of cheap and untroublesome arrests is clearly politically advantageous for the INS. A million Mexican border arrests is much more impressive than the roughly 100,000 arrests produced in the interior because most congressional representatives are probably content to look only at the agency's bottom-line statistics. But a politically attractive product may be meaningless from the perspective of a maximally effective deterrence impact. Investigations branch officers assert that southern border apprehensions are not meaningful be-cause they include so many repeat EWIs who are undeterred, whereas the investigators claim that they are doing "quality" case investigations. Catching an alien who will be delayed only for a few hours or days in getting up to Salinas (California) to pick artichokes is not as important in their view as deterring a fraudulent applicant for lawful permanent residence who, if undetected, becomes eligible for welfare and other benefits.

Yet the issue is not so easily disposed of. Although linewatch apprehensions will not deter determined aliens, it may after all create tariffs that do deter many aliens unable to afford the tariff. If this is true, then border enforcement may select for a more productive group of workers, which in turn means that it may also serve to reduce public welfare claims in the communities of destination.

It is not clear how effective the investigations branch is in deterring fraudulent benefit applicants. Illegal aliens caught trying to arrange a fraudulent marriage may simply court another local citizen and work harder to dress up the marriage the next time, or they may try again in a different district. Aliens deterred from obtaining valid Social Security cards sometimes turn up in district offices to petition for immigrant visas based on marriage to citizens.

To put the matter bluntly, the INS operates in a void of knowledge about the deterrent impacts of its activities. The proxy measures of performance— the number of smuggling rings busted, vehicles seized, aliens arrested and returned, and the like—is the statistical veil. It proves that enforcement is being accomplished but doesn't tell us to what purpose.

If the INS had a more strategic sense of its mission and better performance measures, it could achieve much better enforcement leverage. A strategic sense of mission would lead the agency to assess the social costs imposed by different categories of violators. The agency might ask, for example, whether a greater net benefit would accrue to our society from large numbers of Mexican apprehensions rather than, say, deterring more immigration frauds, screening more welfare applicants, or ferreting out more aliens serving prison sentences. The reason Mexican EWI arrests currently account for 95 percent of all INS apprehensions has much less to do with estimates of the social harm resulting from illegal Mexican entry than it does with the fact that most border patrol agents are stationed at the southern land border. Resources that are in place heavily influence what the agency's product will be, and the rationale for these dispositions is lodged in the policy decisions of the agency's past institutional history.

Efforts at resource and political optimization can dovetail when the agency adjusts policy in the light of changing political and economic conditions. Changes in INS enforcement policy in the late 1970s and early 1980s offers a good example.

In the late 1970s, when the INS decided to focus area control almost exclusively on work sites, many officials doubtless anticipated a double gain: (1) improvement in the agency's net political working capital (widespread approval by a public concerned about unemployment along with reduced hostility from those groups angered by the neighborhood sweeps that were once part of area control operations in some cities) and (2) an improvement in the overall quality of apprehensions arising from the more selective targeting of employed illegal aliens.

As it turned out, although the polls showed that the general public approved of the step-up in work site apprehensions during the early 1980s, vocal activists remained critical of any interior enforcement against administrative violators and resorted to lawsuits and complaints to the media and politicians in an effort to curb INS business surveys.

The INS shifted policy gears once again in 1983. Emphasis shifted from making large numbers of arrests to a more selective enforcement strategy aimed at deterring notorious employers of illegals. The unrelenting hostility from ethnic activists and civil rights critics appears not to have been the motivating factor, unlike the decision to cut back interior enforcement a decade earlier. In the first place, the agency knows that the civil rights activists remain hostile, no matter which group of administrative violators the INS decides to target. When investigators raided Los Angeles's Little Tokyo district in 1982 in an effort to persuade Hispanics that area control was equitable, Little Tokyo's residents complained bitterly about harassment. When investigators raided high-tech industries in California's Silicon Valley in 1984 to prove the same point, namely that Hispanic garment workers weren't the only objects of enforcement concern, city politicians in San Jose also lambasted the agency. Almost all ethnic groups (and the local politicians who take their cues from their leaders) complain that the INS is unfair. But the crux of the matter is that any enforcement, no matter how equitable, will be resented by those who are its objects. The INS cannot escape this dilemma as long as it pursues administrative violators who are not troublemakers but productive workers.

More relevant to the 1983 shift in interior enforcement were the serious logistical bottlenecks that had come to plague the agency as a result of rising arrest caseloads. With limited detention space and funds, which were being crowded by the growing numbers of Haitian and Central American EWIs, too many administrative arrests jeopardized the quality of overall enforcement, especially when violators without equities had to be released on personal recognizance. (In New York City, during a period in which investigations went all out to make area control arrests, the only aliens required to post cash bonds were those who struggled or ran during area control surveys. The available long-term detention space had been taken up by Haitian detainees awaiting exclusion hearings.)

Another important factor was the agency's awareness in 1984 that the Simpson-Mazzoli bill might finally be passed by Congress and signed into law. Had the differences between the House and Senate versions been resolved by the end of 1984, the INS's case management system would have been much better suited to the new policy changes. For one thing, there would be much less pressure to pursue hundreds of thousands of administrative violators because it could be assumed that many of these would be granted amnesty. Also, flagrant employers, the new priority for employer surveys under the case management system, would also be a major enforcement concern under Simpson-Mazzoli's employer-sanctions provision.

SELECTIVE UNDERENFORCEMENT:
WHERE'S THE HARM?

A major finding in this study is that the INS must engage in selective enforcement, and even underenforcement, of the law. As already noted, this is done partly to accommodate interest group pressures that are inevitable in a democratic polity. Still, one wants to know why INS enforcement is uniquely beleaguered by such pressures in comparison with some other federal regulatory agencies.

As noted earlier, the INS's dual service and enforcement functions require trade-offs that would rule out a maximalist enforcement posture even were the political environment more hospitable. Port of entry inspectors must try to deter mala fide entrants, but they must also expedite entry by authorized travelers. Patrol agents could doubtless turn up more smuggling loads if they stopped and checked more cars. However, if they did this, it would inconvenience many travelers who are not ferrying illegal aliens and who would be mightily irked. Indeed, if they were too thorough in their role as enforcement screeners, they might generate arrest caseloads larger than the ASU officers in the sector headquarters or the assistant U.S. attorneys in the district would be prepared to cope with. Moreover, the quality of the enforcement effort as measured by conviction rates or sentences and the like might decline as the number of cases rose in relation to available prosecutorial and court resources.

The prosecutions officer might then justify dropping more cases on the grounds that the evidence to hold smugglers on transporting charges was insufficient. Procedural or evidence insufficiencies could also arise, paradoxically, from stepped-up enforcement efforts because, among other things, ASU officers would lack the time needed to build up the evidence for a case. As a result, an all-out enforcement effort would not only trigger political antagonism—in this case, from ordinary citizens inconvenienced by a maximalist policy—but also, barring increases in resources, would damage the enforcement issues as well.

The main reason the INS can engage in selective underenforcement by lowering its screening thresholds or disposing of prosecutions caseloads through offering very favorable terms to violators and the like, arises from public perceptions of the net social utilities involved—namely, the harm anticipated from underenforcement coupled with the costs that would be incurred by a maximalist effort. To state the matter bluntly: Few illegal aliens are dangerous people; to the contrary, most are productive workers. However, if very many of them were believed to be armed terrorists or dangerous fugitives, highway checkpoints would not be lifted simply in order to accommodate heavy traffic, and a business survey would not be cut short simply because the vans were already full or time was running out.

As Eugene Bardach and Robert Kagan have noted, officials in other regulatory agencies may be compelled to adopt a rigidly uncompromising enforcement posture—to "go by the book" as Kagan and Bardach express it—because their agencies would risk public embarrassment and their careers might be jeopardized were they to lower their guard and investigate less thoroughly. This is especially true for agencies charged with monitoring violations whose neglect could cause catastrophic public harm, as for example, in the regulation of toxic chemical waste disposal, mine safety, or the testing of new drugs.[7] Unlike officers of the Environmental Protection Agency, the Food and Drug Administration, the Occupational Safety and Health Administration, or other agencies that are preoccupied with obvious public hazards, INS officers are able to engage in selective underenforcement precisely because the danger or harm posed by most INA violations is much less obvious—if indeed one can even speak of danger or harm at all. (The INS does take suspected alien terrorists very seriously and would give such cases top priority in the event the FBI wanted INS assistance.)

This problem can be viewed from yet another angle. Consider INS's efforts to screen applicants for immigration benefits. In the case of a welfare agency, a lax screening policy will penalize the taxpayers and the agency itself if ineligible people receive benefits. By contrast, erroneous grants of immigration benefits to ineligible aliens do not impose monetary costs on the INS.[8]

Moreover, the cost to U.S. taxpayers of granting ineligible aliens lawful residence or other benefits (internalization of costs by the society) may also be trivial, if indeed there are any costs at all. (Many lesser immigration benefits clearly impose few, if any, costs on the society, such as extensions of time for students who have yet to graduate.) But even when major benefits (immigrant visas or naturalization) are granted in error, whether because of fraud by alien applicants or because of oversights on the part of INS examiners, the recipients will, one assumes, more likely than not turn out to be productive and useful additions to society.[9] Even in the case of ineligible aliens who elude screening and who are not productive (who take more in welfare than they pay in taxes for example), the costs imposed may be indirect or of very low public visibility, as when aliens become public charges some years later or are found to have been receiving supplemental Social Security benefits illegally because they have returned abroad.[10]

However, one cannot so easily extrapolate from the present into the future. Many illegal aliens may now avoid taking public welfare only because they fear coming to the attention of the INS. If this is so, there may well be important, if indeterminate, social utilities from maintaining some level of interior enforcement activities. There is concern, for example, among some policy analysts that both legal and illegal Mexican immigrants take more in public services than they contribute in taxes. As knowledge of the INS's vulnerabilities increases among illegal aliens and their fear of arrest declines, unauthorized use of welfare by illegal aliens might grow.[11]

If it could be shown that very few aliens who become lawful residents, whether because of fraud or agency error, take public welfare or engage in crime, then important incentives for tight benefit screening are weakened. This comes back to the point made earlier in the first chapter. Although a welfare cheat evokes little public sympathy, the apprehension of a "good" alien—even though that person may have committed fraudulent misrepresentation or absconded after a hearing—often leads citizens to mobilize in that alien's defense.

This rather unique aspect of INA enforcement will explain one other. Many enforcement officers, especially those in the investigations branch, would prefer that INA enforcement be prioritized according to the social harm or costs imputed to different categories of violators. Although their awareness of the INS's limited resources is partly responsible for this attitude, the investigators' view of themselves as law enforcers and their preference for criminal rather than administrative enforcement is also involved. They know that many Americans are either hostile or indifferent toward administrative enforcement. Given this fact, those aliens who commit serious nonimmigration crimes or impose other costs on American society should, as many investigators view the matter, be served first from the tray of available resources.[12]

MAINTAINING EQUILIBRIUM
AS AN ORGANIZATIONAL IMPERATIVE

Political and other trade-offs are clearly relevant to enforcement policy. But probably the most important engines of policy are the caseloads that resource allocations in place would generate in the absence of official and unofficial policies that maintain equilibrium between arrests (or benefit and relief requests) and available resources.[13] The idea is well expressed in the satirical lore of the field officers: "They must be citizens because we didn't have time to stop and talk to them." As was pointed out, in many district offices, the level of area control arrests is a function not of the number of illegal aliens who come to INS attention but of judgments on the number of aliens for whom detention space is available (if they cannot post bonds), along with anticipations of how additional administrative arrests might further congest immigration court calendars. Pressures to limit the number of aliens who might demand deportation hearings also arise from resource constraints. In some cases, officers will try to induce aliens to accept voluntary return, sometimes by persuading them that they have no chance of obtaining benefits or relief through a hearing, despite what a street attorney may have told them.

Some of the policy adjustments aimed at equilibrium maintenance are officially promulgated from the top in accordance with the Administrative Procedures Act before being incorporated into the Code of Federal Regulations. But some of the most important policy adjustments are unofficial and of low visibility, and these are often initiated by lower-level officials. As Michael Lipsky has observed, official policy directives are often inadequate to the task of accommodating many of the problems that street-level bureaucrats confront in their work. In consequence, lower-echelon officials improvise policies that allow them to cope with work pressures or uncertainties that higher-level officials either may not have anticipated or may be constrained from acknowledging. Even when they are aware of these problems, higher-level officials may have difficulty giving their blessing to such unofficial remedies because of the legal or political problems that could arise from publicizing these adjustments.[14] And as Lipsky notes, some of the coping mechanisms developed by lower-echelon officials may be basic to the organization's survival, even though they are contrary to official policy.

In the case of the INS, illustrative examples are readily available. These include the techniques officers occasionally use to break suspected false claims in the field. Deceptive techniques (such as pretending to call a state vital statistics office to check out a birth record or allowing an alien to think that a telephone directory is a birth registry) could never be officially sanctioned policy. Nor could higher officials condone efforts by patrol agents to induce Mexican EWIs to take voluntary return by explaining how uncomfortable it will be to spend time in jail with people who do not speak Spanish. Yet agents can be driven to use such devices when middle-level officials must encourage them to minimize the number of aliens written up for deportation processing because of inadequate detention, and so forth. Decisions to require bonds for single men but not for women with children, although prompted by resource constraints rather than an intentional policy to discriminate, might be thought by some to be a discriminatory exercise of official discretion under the law. (Indeed some officers have expressed the concern that discrimination in bond and detention policy might evoke a new outburst of litigation against the INS.)

The inequitable use of discretion at earlier stages, for example, in officers' decisions not to question certain groups of suspected aliens for reasons of administrative expediency ("Women with children take more time to clean up." "If we bring in deportable Poles, they'll just be given extended voluntary departure with authorization to work.") might also be subjected to public criticism. However, decisions grounded in administrative expediency can jeopardize the agency's effort to win public legitimacy if various groups believe its enforcement policies are inequitable.

The prototype policy adjustment, in which Peter the Enforcer was robbed to pay Paul the Facilitator occurred in the mid-1960s, when uninspected entries began to escalate and important social control tools had to be shelved. Whereas before, Mexican EWIs might be detained for a couple of weeks until the FBI was able to complete their fingerprint checks, the border patrol finally had to abandon the policy of routinely fingerprinting all aliens. Expedited voluntary return directly to the border emerged as the most frequent administrative action for most violators. Although the lenient policy of voluntary return had been resorted to in most cases, even during the 1950s and 1960s, it became even more prevalent as the arrest caseload at the border escalated.

The threshold requirements for criminal action also rose. In the 1950s, simple EWI cases were sometimes charged and prosecuted for the 18 U.S.C. 1325 misdemeanor because federal magistrates apparently had the time to take such cases. Even in busier sectors, during the 1950s and 1960s, repeat EWIs might be fined and given jail time. By the late 1970s, however, the 18 U.S.C. 1325 charge had come to be reserved almost exclusively for plea-bargaining purposes in smuggling cases.[15]

It is true that some enforcement activities were strengthened during the 1970s. Commissioner Lionel Castillo sought to professionalize antismuggling efforts by directing investigators to develop more Category I and II organized ring cases; however, on balance, the potency of sanctions weakened in order to keep caseloads manageable. The dramatic increase in EWI entries was mainly responsible for this, but federal court decisions also exacerbated the problems INS field officers faced, as is discussed shortly.

Nor was this imperative to maintain equilibrium confined to enforcement policy. As adjudications caseloads rose, the INS's critics and benefit applicants complained about bureaucratic red tape, delays, and unfairness.[16] The agency responded by expediting benefit adjudications through speedier processing at front desks, special task force projects, and sending excess adjudications work to other offices (called remoting). It is hard to know the precise impact of these managerial innovations on the thoroughness, hence quality, of benefit screening. To the extent that expedited adjudications involved the less important benefits or could be prescreened to ensure that only clearly eligible applications were being expedited in this manner, such innovations may have required little in the way of screening trade-offs. If speedier, front desk adjudications merely reduced the number of personnel involved in handling benefit applications, it doubtless improved service to many bona fide applicants—an important goal for an agency that provides service as well as enforcement. Also, it might even be argued that earlier screening policies were sometimes wasteful during the period when adjudicatory caseload demands were more modest in relation to INS staffing. More bona fide petitions may, for example, have been needlessly investigated. One examiner recalled how decisions were made to send I-130 spousal petitions to investigations in the past:

> Five to ten years ago, you might send one down even though [the alien and citizen spouse] had answered all the questions right. But you thought, "let's take another look at it because it's a Catholic marrying a Moslem." I used to send a case to investigations saying "I've got a hunch about this one," but now they would toss it back in your face. What we're telling the examiners now is that they have to develop the individual aspects of a case, not just rely on profile factors before sending it to investigations.

Some INS officers believe that efforts to deter fraudulent applications had to have suffered simply because examiners had much less time to competently review and investigate the rising number of benefit applications. In addition, federal court and Board of Immigration Appeals decisions that shifted more of the proof burden to the agency for recisions and denials may also have reduced incentives for thorough screening of I-130 and I-140 immigrant visa petitions.

JUDICIAL INTRUSION
AND THE EQUILIBRIUM PROBLEM

Most INS enforcement officials believe that, during the 1970s and early 1980s, expeditious and effective enforcement was being hampered by the decisions of a number of district and circuit courts. There is some evidence that judicial expansion of alien rights may have increased the bargaining power of aliens in relation to the INS, primarily because of more burdensome procedural and other requirements imposed on officers. However, this generalization must still be considered speculative. First, the empirical evidence that would verify the resource impacts of judicial decisions remains sketchy. For example, the *Miranda* rule greatly limits patrol agents' ability to prosecute individual EWI violators for the entry without inspection misdemeanor—as does a court ruling that allows the INS to prosecute EWIs only in the district where they actually crossed the border.

Yet the *Miranda* rule is really irrelevant because the substantial costs to the government of criminal prosecution mean that very few EWI violators could ever be prosecuted anyway. On the other hand, the ninth circuit's requirement that all aliens found in a smuggling load be detained by the INS as material witnesses clearly did handicap smuggling prosecutions in the Chula Vista sector for a short period in the early 1980s, until the Supreme Court trimmed back the requirement.[17] Also, it is conceivable that some court decisions may have eased the burden on INS resources, as is discussed later.[18]

But the trends of the 1970s, whatever their impact, are being reversed. In 1984, decisions by the Supreme Court, along with some important lower court rulings, suggested a dramatic trimming of the sails, compared with the adventurous tacking and unfurling of the due process and equal protection canvas observable through most of the 1970s. It is not just that the Supreme Court has continued to affirm Congress's plenary power over immigration, a trend that remains largely unchanged since the first important rulings of the late nineteenth century. The Court has also become increasingly receptive to taking immigration cases on appeal from the agency. Given that the Court accepts only a very small percentage of cases on certiorari, it is noteworthy that the justices have been highly receptive to those that the solicitor general and the INS believe would have adversely affected immigration enforcement.

For example, in the spring of 1984, the Supreme Court overturned a 1983 ninth-circuit ruling that would have allowed the exclusionary rule to apply to deportation proceedings.[19] Because the ninth circuit includes California, which accounts for almost half of all INS arrests, had the ninth's ruling stood, it could have had dramatic effects on INS enforcement. If aliens in proceedings had been able to contest a government finding of deportability, either because evidence of their illegal entry had been illegally seized or because they had been detained and questioned without adequate reasonable suspicion (thereby tainting any admission of illegal entry they might have made), INS officers would have been required to appear at deportation hearings to testify as to the founded suspicion they had at the time they questioned an individual. Because an alien's deportability is a continuing offense, any finding that an admission to an officer had been illegally obtained would not have spared the alien from deportation.

Had the exclusionary rule been extended to the INS's civil proceedings, it would probably have been seized on by attorneys as an additional weapon with which to gain time for clients. As a harassing strategy, activists could have used it to hamstring the INS because, if very many aliens decided to challenge their arrests, field officers would have been called to testify at hearings, and they would have that much less time to carry out apprehensions. It would also have given aliens an incentive to demand hearings, which would have increased the burden on detention facilities and the immigration courts.

Civil suits alleging that INS officers violated the Fourth-Amendment rights of citizens and lawful residents in the course of business surveys as a result of unreasonable seizures (blocking of exits to prevent runners or questioning of workers in a plant without individualized suspicion that they were illegal aliens) were also being used by activist legal aid groups and employers to harass the service. Although plaintiffs and their attorneys were alleging civil rights violations of citizens and lawful aliens, one suspects that many of these suits were motivated by a desire to curb INS tactics the agency considers relatively effective. The INS has consistently maintained that, when its officers block factory exits to prevent illegals from slipping out or when officers approach and question workers who turn out to be citizens, any intrusion on the rights of citizen and lawful aliens is minimal. Exit blocking is also justified on safety grounds, as a means of minimizing the risk of injury posed by aliens who try to run.

Apparently this view was shared by the Supreme Court because it overruled the ninth circuit's finding in *ILGWU* v. *Delgado* that blockage of exits and a visible show of authority by INS officers constitute an unreasonable seizure.[20]

Ironically, any tightening of the Fourth-Amendment standard means that field officers must have stronger reasonable suspicion of alienage (or individualized suspicion of illegal alienage) before they approach, question, and detain an individual. Had the ninth's ruling in *Delgado* been sustained by the Supreme Court, officers would have become even more conservative than they currently are. They would probably have limited their interrogations during routine patrolling or business surveys to those persons who provide the most clear-cut articulable facts for questioning. Effectively, this means that Mexican EWIs, especially those who are less acculturated in dress and comportment, would run a higher risk of being questioned. This is not because of any prejudice toward brown-skinned people, as critics allege, but because, in addition to the fact that they are able to speak Spanish, INS officers can list scores of established articulable facts to justify stopping members of this group but very few for other nationality groups.[21] In essence, the insistence that the privacy of citizens and lawful aliens be protected from intrusive questioning by INS officers conflicts with the demand that the agency try to be as equitable as possible in targeting different nationality groups for alienage and deportability checks.

As regards the INS's detention and parole policy, the eleventh circuit's

1984 *en banc* decision in *Jean* v. *Nelson*, a much publicized Haitian detention case that originated in Florida's South District, constituted another important victory for the INS. In reversing the earlier finding of a three-judge panel that had ruled in favor of the Haitians, the eleventh circuit reaffirmed the government's right to detain persons being held in exclusion proceedings on the basis of their nationality although not on the basis of suspect characteristics, such as race. (The three-judge panel had ruled that the INS had not used racial classifications to discriminate.) Moreover, the eleventh also ruled that the government was not required to inform aliens in exclusion proceedings of their right to political asylum.[22]

Despite these well-publicized court victories in favor of the government, some other less publicized cases that have gone against the agency during the past decade, and that the agency did not appeal, have added to the INS's costs. For example, in the Northern District of California, to be able to accept turnovers from local jails and prisons, INS must conduct face-to-face interviews with aliens within 24 hours of placing detainers on them. Before, officers would make alienage and deportability determinations by talking over the telephone with individuals who had been picked up by local law officers. If they admitted alienage and deportability on the phone, detainers would be put on them and the officers would go out to pick them up at the time of their release, at which point the I-213 arrest form would be filled out. Now, however, the officers may have to make two trips, one for the personal interview needed for a detainer and then a second trip to pick up the alien upon release. Whenever more officer hours are required for an activity (jail calls in this case), incentives can shift in favor of other less costly enforcement activities.

In 1982, the California Central District Court issued a preliminary injunction (*Orantes-Hernandez*) requiring the INS to inform all Salvadorans of their right to apply for political asylum at the time they are informed of their right to have a hearing and to have legal counsel represent them at their own expense. The injunction has since been applied nationwide. In Texas, a district court also ruled (*Nunez* v. *Bolden*) that apprehended Guatemalans must be advised of their right to apply for political asylum. Although many Central Americans already know about this right (they may know about it through the grapevine even before their arrival in the United States), if INS officers are required to read it to every Salvadoran or Guatemalan, it is reasonable to think that more aliens will lodge asylum applications. (Some INS officials question the fairness of such rulings. Why, they ask, should Salvadorans be advised of the political asylum option, but not Mexicans or other nationalities?)

The dilemma lies in knowing whether the net impact of certain of these decisions is necessarily adverse for the agency. Consider the efforts by the courts to liberalize the INS's parole and detention policy—prior to the eleventh circuit's *en banc* decision in *Jean* v. *Nelson*. If the parole requirement for Haitians is liberalized and many are ordered released pending hearings, then the INS is spared the cost of detaining them. On the other hand, the INS might eventually have to pursue those who fail to appear for exclusion hearings or who abscond after all appeals have been exhausted.[23] The INS can avoid having to shoulder this burden, which would fall to investigations, simply by assigning a low priority to abscondees—which was, indeed, the policy during my period in the field.[24]

As regards court decisions that require the INS to inform aliens of their right to apply for political asylum, the impacts may also run in opposing directions. Consider what happens when Central Americans are caught entering without inspection through Mexico. Unlike Mexican EWIs, they cannot as a rule be returned directly to the southern border because the Mexican authorities refuse to take them, even though Mexican officials may have been bribed to permit their transit through the Mexican interior in violation of their visas. Central American apprehensions have increased dramatically along the southern border in recent years, which strains INS's detention capability. Although some agree to return voluntarily by air, those unable to pay their fare will cost the agency $200 to $300 per individual on average. Given the limited alien travel and detention funds available in heavily impacted districts, there are short-run advantages to the INS from a policy that makes it easy for Salvadorans and other Central Americans who enter EWI to file political asylum claims and be released on minimum bonds. (Other than processing expenses, there is no cost to the INS when it releases aliens on bond. However, as with granting parole to aliens in exclusion hearings, these costs may merely be deferred. At some point, the agency may have to pursue those who abscond from their hearings or may have to pick up the travel and other expenses of those who have exhausted all appeals and agreed to return home.)

Granting extended voluntary departure on a blanket basis to an entire nationality group, such as Poles or Lebanese, is another way in which a potentially large caseload can be cheaply deferred to the future—although such a grant is not made because of caseload considerations. When extended voluntary departure is revoked for a nationality, then in theory, the INS should pursue those who fail to depart after having been notified. But because of the high cost of tracking down individual aliens in the interior, the potentially burdensome caseloads can simply be shelved by assigning these cases a low priority.

However, the question remains: If apprehended violators can achieve unreasonable delay, does this weaken incentives for law-abidingness among aliens still abroad, who learn through the grapevine that a reduced risk of apprehension and a reduced likelihood of removal through deportation are being created because of a judicialized extension of alien rights? Because time is equity, decisions that tie down INS resources create "quasi-benefits" for those who violate the law. Immigration service officers complain that aliens who benefit by breaking the rules effectively instruct others still abroad that the name of the game is to simply get to the United States, whether legally as visitors or illegally as EWIs. To the extent that parole or political asylum policies are liberalized, through either court rulings or administrative policy adjustments, the resource savings may be offset by the incentives generated for further illegal immigration.

Taking the long view, it is clear that the extension of alien appeal and other rights over the years sets severe limits on expeditious enforcement. Field officers must spend more time on processing and other paper requirements at the time aliens are questioned and written up, and this takes time from field enforcement activities. An individual hearing is mandatory, if an alien wants one, and transcripts must be made in the event the alien chooses to appeal. Translators may have to be provided to guarantee that the alien understands the proceedings. If the transcript is not accurate, or if it appears that the alien may not have understood what was going on, a federal judge may order still another hearing. Although adequate guarantee of fair and impartial administrative hearings is an important part of our constitutional heritage, these add to the burdens of law enforcement. They also create equity problems to the extent that aliens who play by the rules are penalized by those who manage to get to the United States, build immigration equities, and capture visas for themselves and their relatives. If we as a society want expeditious and equitable enforcement, we must either provide the resources required or trim back alien due process rights. We cannot have it both ways.

IMMIGRATION CONTROL: WOULD EMPLOYER SANCTIONS WORK?

Although separate Senate and House versions of the Simpson-Mazzoli Immigration Reform and Control Act were approved by the 98th Congress in the fall of 1984, the bill died in conference because the House and Senate conferees could not agree on compromise legislations.[25]

In the event Congress were to approve a new immigration bill, there is a good chance it will contain Simpson-Mazzoli's employer-sanctions provision in some form. For that reason, a brief review of the adequacy of the underlying policy assumptions behind employer sanctions is warranted.

The employer-sanctions provision, which Simpson-Mazzoli's congressional supporters have touted as an effective deterrent to illegal immigration, would penalize employers who knowingly hire illegal aliens.

If new legislation were to include an employer-sanctions provision similar to the one in the 1984 House version, employers would have had a complete defense against possible civil or criminal penalties, if they followed the procedures set forth in the bill for verifying the immigration and citizenship status of workers hired after the bill's passage.

In the 1984 Simpson-Mazzoli bill, it was not altogether clear whether employers would have been required to check worker identification. (The Senate wanted worker verification mandatory for all employers, but the House resisted a mandatory verification requirement.) The problem is that, without a mandatory verification procedure, the INS will have a harder time proving that an employer knowingly hired illegal aliens.[26] Conceivably, some prosecutions might be made on the basis of testimony from illegal workers— if they would agree to testify that their employers knew they were unauthorized to work. But given the proof burden apt to be required of the agency, it is more reasonable to assume that successful prosecutions will be limited to those firms where illegal aliens who had previously been identified by the INS are found working again. This, at any rate, was the state of Virginia's experience when employers suspected of hiring illegal aliens were prosecuted.[27]

But whether worker verification will be mandatory or not in a future bill, employer sanctions could flounder for several important reasons. Employers lack the expertise to make immigration status determinations. They can go through the motions of checking a worker's identification, but they cannot be expected to detect counterfeit or fraudulent identification. Additionally, employers will risk civil rights lawsuits if they turn away workers whose documents they merely suspect are bogus. They can, of course, refuse to hire aliens who admit to being unauthorized aliens or any who refuse to permit their identification to be checked. The likelihood, however, is that most illegal aliens will simply borrow or purchase the identification required. There is also the risk that employers might ask Hispanic or other foreign-appearing workers for identification but neglect to require this of those they consider to be obvious citizens. This would constitute *screening* discrimination, as distinct from *hiring* discrimination, and although it has not been raised as an issue by Hispanic opponents of Simpson-Mazzoli, it would very likely emerge as an issue if a similar bill were to become law.[28]

Employers would be in a difficult situation. Many citizens would resent the inconvenience of having to establish their right to work every time they changed jobs. No doubt, many citizens who lacked the required documents would complain at having to obtain them. Employers who sought INS assistance in checking the papers of workers the employers suspected might be illegal would be unlikely to get prompt assistance from the INS—if they got help at all. Would they defer hiring a worker suspected of being illegal, which could risk a lawsuit? Or would they offer the applicant a job on a provisional basis? This would be an enormous problem for employers in industries with high labor turnover.

The INS will have plenty of problems of its own. First, the burden of employer-sanctions enforcement will fall on the INS's 800 to 900 CIs. At the time Simpson-Mazzoli was under debate, there was no mention in the Congressional Record of additions to the investigations branch for the purpose of monitoring compliance.[29] Considering how understaffed the investigations branch already is in relation to its current caseloads, one wonders where the additional officers would be found. If employer-sanctions enforcement is given priority, investigators may well be taken away from cases involving more serious INA violators, which could severely damage the overall quality of interior enforcement. How many fraud or alien smuggling cases would have to be shelved to assemble the evidence required to slap civil fines on one or two garment manufacturers?

Without a substantial increase in the number of officers assigned exclusively to employer-sanctions investigations along with government trial attorneys and other support personnel, employer-sanctions enforcement might, after an initial burst of agency attention, develop into a token symbolic effort. True, some notorious violators will be hit with stiff fines. A few may go out of business or even go to jail. But unless employers perceive a sufficient risk of both discovery and punishment, employer sanctions are unlikely to deter violators any more effectively than other provisions of the INA currently deter alien smugglers, fraudulent benefit applicants, and false citizenship claimants. Moreover, if the cost in resources to the INS for successfully levying fines on employers is perceived as being too high, INS officers will begin to lose interest and assign investigators to higher priority cases. It happens already with respect to the vast multitude of INA cases that are theoretically open to the service to prosecute criminally.[30]

An analogous situation faced the Department of Treasury's Bureau of Alcohol, Tobacco, and Firearms (ATF) after passage of the 1968 Gun Control Act. The AFT was called upon to monitor compliance with the new law on the part of the nation's more than 100,000 licensed gun dealers. The major purpose of the new legislation had been to reduce the availability of hand guns and other firearms to certain high-risk groups, including convicted felons, drug addicts, minors, and persons who had been committed to mental institutions. But as Franklin Zimring noted, the AFT lacked the resources to adequately monitor a potential caseload numbering several hundred thousand criminal investigations of illegal gun sales and transfers a year (1973)—if all firearms transaction records were properly audited.[31] As in the case of the earlier, unenforceable 1938 Federal Firearms Act, the 1968 Act, according to Zimring, was an example of legislation for which the "symbolism of gun control seemed more important to the vast majority of Congress than the specifics of regulation."[32]

The key to an understanding of how immigration enforcement works is noting how equilibrium is maintained between the various component elements of a very complex and delicately cantilevered system. Disturbing this equilibrium can have far-reaching and unanticipated effects. For example, if the border were to be successfully tightened through the addition of a significantly large number of agents, somewhat fewer Mexicans might try to enter, but incentives would be created for those still coming through to demand deportation hearings because of the increase in the unofficial tariff (inconvenience and/or smugglers' charges). A similar problem could arise if new legislation were passed authorizing amnesty (legalization) for illegal aliens. Because of the ease of obtaining fraudulent documentation to show proof of continuous residence, along with a high probability that the applicant would be authorized to work in the United States pending adjudication of the amnesty application, many more Mexican EWIs might refuse to accept voluntary return.[33] Thus amnesty could have the effect of ratcheting incentives against taking voluntary return, which in turn could leverage the system into a downward spiral by demolishing the service's most important line of defense—its ability to maintain a sufficiently high bond to induce aliens to accept voluntary return.

As more Mexicans asked to have amnesty claims adjudicated (or asked for hearings on whatever grounds), more would find that an amnesty claim would secure their release on a minimum bond of $500 or even on OR. Upon being released on a minimum bond (or no bond at all), aliens would then have the choice of either developing the documentation required to support their claim or going back underground.

One hesitates to publicize the INS's vulnerabilities. But the fact is that the INS will probably not be able to investigate more than a small fraction of amnesty applications for fraud. (Nor would it be a rational policy for the agency to invest heavily in thorough screening of legalization applicants.) The agency would hope that publicizing successful prosecutions of vendors of bogus legalization documents, along with benefit denials to the individual purchasers, might deter fraudulent applications. But it cannot do very much more than that. Individual aliens caught using forged documents to meet the continuous residence requirement will face the same risk of prosecution as that faced by aliens who currently make felony misrepresentations—in short, next to no risk of criminal prosecution at all.[34]

IS THERE A VIABLE POLICY
FOR IMMIGRATION CONTROL?

Overhauling immigration law along the lines proposed by the Simpson-Mazzoli bill is not only unlikely to reduce illegal entry into the United States but might actually aggravate the current enforcement crisis by adding a new and even more intractable enforcement caseload to the INS. It has more chance of destabilizing the delicate equilibrium currently being managed than of improving the enforcement environment.

The options open to the government for controlling illegal immigration are limited. Barring political upheaval in Mexico, it is unlikely that Congress and the executive branch would authorize a militarized southern border with the American equivalent of a Berlin Wall type of solution. (On the other hand, it would be irresponsible of the government not to consider such contingency planning well in advance. Although a Mexican political collapse must surely be rated a low-probability event at the present time, it might happen. If it did, national security considerations would clearly be relevant and might well justify draconian policy measures.)

For the present, and hopefully the future as well, draconian remedies that might stanch illegal immigration will inevitably run afoul of the many political and economic interests that must be accommodated in our polity. Many Americans benefit from having large numbers of foreign visitors. Many also benefit from having illegal alien labor, or at any rate they do not consider their presence sufficiently injurious to mobilize and petition Congress on behalf of a serious enforcement effort, one that would ensure the INS had ample resources with which to deal with the problem.

What is intractable at present is primarily the political aspect of the problem. If illegal aliens were perceived as a serious threat, surely the resources would be found to deter their entry—even if it required 20,000 patrol agents and investigators.

Absent a widespread public perception that illegal immigration poses a major threat to the society, *prohibitory* regulation alone will not work because it is unlikely to receive the level of resources required.

What, then, might be done?

Immigration enforcement should seek to achieve a more optimal allocation of resources by looking at the differential social costs imposed by different categories of INA violators. In interior enforcement, the INS should continue to refine its current new case management system so that aliens who are perceived as imposing the highest costs on our society are served first from the tray of available investigative and prosecutorial resources. Aliens (and citizens) who are involved in organized smuggling, immigration fraud, and document counterfeiting, along with aliens involved in crime or entitlement (welfare) fraud should have priority. In the case of unauthorized aliens who apply for federal or state welfare benefits, the INS can obtain maximum enforcement leverage as well as favorable public response by assisting state, local, and federal agencies with screening.

Congress could also assist by considering tariff regulation as a supplement to the civil and criminal sanctions that, as we have noted, are alone inadequate to the task of immigration control. If more Mexican EWIs were to be legalized on a temporary basis through a generous guest-worker program, the INS could deal more effectively with alien smuggling. Mexican guest workers could be charged for the privilege of entering the United States for a nine- to twelve-month period to work in certain low-wage industries. If the fee were competitive with what smugglers charge, then the unofficial tariffs currently paid smugglers could be converted into an official tariff collected by the treasury. The funds generated could be used to strengthen INS border and interior enforcement at no added cost to American taxpayers.

In addition to a user fee for 2 to 4 million guest workers, an abuser fee could be levied against visa aliens who enter as visitors and students and then overstay or work without authorization. Under such a policy, aliens would be required to post a bond of $200 to $300 before an overseas consulate issued their nonimmigrant visas. Either a flat bond amount might be required regardless of the country or visa classification or the amount might be set according to the assumed likelihood of visa abuse by nationals of a particular country. In any event, aliens caught working without authorization or found to have stayed beyond their expiration dates (without having notified the INS) would forfeit the bond to the government. The funds generated by these abuser fees could also be used to augment INS enforcement activities at a savings to taxpayers.[35]

There would be several advantages to a tariff model of regulation that employed both user and abuser fees. First, the money that aliens pay to smugglers would go instead to support INS enforcement against smugglers and other INA violators. (Research would be needed to determine what part of a smuggler's fee is accounted for by the need to circumvent border patrol agents, as distinct from other services smugglers provide aliens, for example, job referrals or transit through a land whose language is unfamiliar.) If the official tariff is competitive with the "crime tariff," as Herbert Packer designated revenues created by legal sanctions, then smugglers should become a less preferred means of entry.[36] Not only would the INS's resource base be augmented but the agency's enforcement problem should also diminish.[37] Second, a tariff bracero program would be easier to administer than the current, and very cumbersome, H-2 farm worker program. Alien fee payers would be free to work for whomever they pleased as long as they stayed within the industry and job guidelines set by agency regulations. Aliens who played by the rules would be allowed to renew their permits.

Third, although the integrity of the tariff system would require continued border and interior enforcement, the administrative violator category (EWIs and visa abusers) would become a less intense focus of INS preoccupation. The agency would continue to take administrative action against visa abusers or guest workers caught violating the terms of their permits, but the fact that fees have been collected and bonds would be forfeited would mitigate the sense of urgency over this group. In effect, society will have been compensated in part through the fees and bonds collected. The INS will have more freedom of maneuver, as well as more ample resources, to take action against more serious INA violators who impose costs on the society. Improvements in the quality of the enforcement caseload would also benefit the system as a whole. There would be more resources available to enable the INS to investigate and prosecute the serious cases to the extent needed to deny benefits, effect deportations, and obtain convictions.

Although an optimal enforcement policy will require the INS to make more of an effort to calibrate the social utilities to be gained by targeting different violator categories in relation to resource expenditures, it would be wrong to assume that immigration law enforcement is simply a utility maximizing activity. For if that were so, probably almost all enforcement officers would be assigned to screening welfare programs and apprehending aliens involved in crime. Indeed, most immigration enforcement probably constitutes a deadweight economic loss to the nation because most enforcement resources are directed against aliens who probably do not impose costs on our society. The INS should devote more resources to those who do impose costs, but it cannot abandon an enforcement interest in the other violators altogether.

Calculations of the social cost or potential harm posed by different categories of violators cannot alone frame an optimal policy. Immigration law and policy are shaped partly by considerations of U.S. economic and foreign policy interests, but they are more fundamentally rooted in conceptions of national sovereignty. Although national sovereignty may be at a steep discount as a political value among some groups, it is still of vital importance to the polity as a whole. Setting the terms under which aliens can enter and reside among the citizenry is inherent to the sovereignty of the modern state, and although there may be sound reasons why a state might decide to forego a maximalist policy of rigorous enforcement, it cannot abandon its legitimate right to regulate immigration without jeopardizing that sovereignty.

Ironically, the evidence assembled in this book suggests that the INS does indeed strive toward a politically optimal policy, albeit in a poorly articulated and unconscious way. In spite of the fact that immigration policy is probably inherently incoherent in many respects—as, indeed, the inconsistencies in our refugee and asylum policy reflect—much of the agency's behavior suggests an effort to achieve a weighted enforcement outcome, one that will maximize the agency's political capital as well as maintain its imperative requirement for equilibrium. The pirouettes of INS policy mirror the tug and pull of a multitude of competing interests that are in conflict in our society. Where societal consensus is firm, the agency will "go to the wall" despite the substantial resource costs. Conspicuous examples are the strenuous efforts by the INS and the Justice Department to denaturalize former Nazi collaborators and to deport aliens suspected of serious criminal activities. It would be quite in error to say that immigration enforcement has no teeth. The teeth can and will be found when the occasion warrants.

Finally, although immigration enforcement against most administrative and EWI violators is clearly ineffective, the fact remains that the law is enforced against many such violators. Because this is so, INS enforcement provides more than just symbolic affirmation of the important value of national sovereignty. At a minimum, it creates tariffs to entry while also imposing costs and inconvenience for those who have been apprehended in the interior.

But although the INS can engineer numerous policy adjustments that might further improve the quality of its enforcement effort under existing law and levels of funding, the crucial questions must be addressed by the polity as a whole. Is illegal immigration at current levels a sufficiently serious problem? Might certain classes of illegal aliens begin to make greater use of welfare and other transfer programs? If the American public believes that illegal immigration is a problem, then it must persuade Congress to provide the agency with the resources and tools needed to do the job. Absent a willingness on the part of the public to organize and lobby for effective enforcement, and the funding required to achieve it, the INS will continue to muddle through—with enough enforcement to affirm national sovereignty but not enough to achieve more effective control.

NOTES

PREFACE

1. David S. North and Jennifer R. Wagner, "Enforcing the Immigration Law: A Review of the Options" (A report prepared for the Select Commission on Immigration and Refugee Policy, June 1980).

2. Although *deportable alien* is the official term used by the INS, for reasons that will be discussed later, not all aliens who are in violation of immigration laws are necessarily deportable. I have chosen to use the term *illegal alien* throughout this book for several reasons. First, although it is distasteful to some, it is probably the most commonly used term. Second, many illegal aliens are documented. Many arrive legally and carry bona fide immigration papers but subsequently violate the conditions of their visas—by working without authorization, for example, or by overstaying the departure date on their visas. Also, some immigrated aliens, officially called lawful permanent residents, commit crimes that make them deportable. In addition, not all illegal aliens are workers. Many are students or family dependents. The term *undocumented worker* best fits those who enter surreptitiously (enter without inspection) and who come predominantly from Mexico as workers. Still, many of these aliens are later encountered with both fraudulent as well as bona fide identification in the form of Social Security cards, driver's licenses, and the like. Some also have service alien registration numbers and files because of prior apprehensions. In addition, there are some U.S. citizens who are undocumented because, although they may have grown up in Mexico and have no documents when they enter, they were delivered by midwives in the United States while their parents were living here. But, in addition to being a legal misnomer, the main problem with *undocumented worker* is that it implies that foreign nationals living and working in the United States without permission differ from citizens and lawful aliens only by the absence of proper documents. The truth of the matter is that they are here illegally.

CHAPTER ONE

1. A reasonably firm lower-bound estimate of slightly more than 2 million illegal aliens has been provided by U.S. Census Bureau demographers Robert Warren and Jeffrey S. Passel based on special analytical techniques involving comparisons between the 1980 census count of the U.S. population and the number of aliens registered with the INS. Robert Warren and Jeffrey S. Passel, "Estimates of Illegal Aliens from Mexico Counted in the 1980 United States Census" (Paper delivered at the annual meeting of the Population Association of America, Pittsburgh, Pa., April 14–16, 1983), p. 12.

For a discussion of the many efforts to count the illegal population and of the methodological problems of arriving at a reliable count, see Arthur F. Corwin, "The Numbers Game: Estimates of Illegal Aliens in the United States, 1970–1981," *Law and Contemporary Problems* 45, no. 2 (Spring 1982): 223–83.

2. The net illegal flow is the gross inflow of unauthorized aliens less departures. The actual number of illegal entries is much greater. The 200,000 to 500,000 figure, although derived by special demographic techniques, is conjectural. Corwin, "The Numbers Game," p. 244.

3. With the exception of the Alien and Sedition Acts passed by Congress in 1789, there was very little federal regulation of immigration until 1875, when the first acts barring convicts and prostitutes were passed. These were followed by acts barring idiots, lunatics, and persons likely to become a public charge. In 1882, the Chinese Exclusion Act barred a specific nationality group for the first time in our history. For a review of the history of immigration legislation, see Pastora San Juan Cafferty, Barry R. Chiswick, Andrew M. Greeley, and Teresa A. Sullivan, *The Dilemma of American Immigration: Beyond the Golden Door* (New Brunswick, N.J.: Transaction Books, 1983), pp. 39–63.

4. *Fong Yue Ting* v. *United States*, 149 U.S. 698, 711 (1893). Congress's plenary power to forbid the admission of aliens or to admit them upon such conditions as Congress chooses to impose was affirmed again in *Nishimura Ekiu* v. *United States*, 142 U.S. 651, 659 (1892). Nor has the theory been fundamentally altered by the Supreme Court, even to this day.

5. Peter H. Schuck, "The Transformation of Immigration Law," *Columbia Law Review* 84, no. 1 (January 1984): 3–14. In what is clearly one of the best contemporary treatments of the theoretical foundations of immigration law, Professor Schuck notes how one strand of nineteenth-century liberal doctrine informed the judiciary's understanding of how the Constitution should be applied to aliens even as restrictive nationalism based on ethnic and racial prejudice was nullifying other strands of liberal ideology. As Schuck notes, aliens' "natural rights to pursue their self-interest through migration here were now regulated according to considerations of national interest, sovereignty, and power. Consent remained the source of an alien's legal rights and duties, but it was no longer liberalism's consent of freely contracting individuals exercising their natural rights to define their own relationships with others. Restrictive nationalism drew upon the ideological conception of consent-based obligation but re-

shaped it to respond to the dictates of an exclusionary sentiment" (p. 3). In effect, the classical individualistic doctrine of consent-based contractual rights became the cornerstone of *classical immigration law*, as Schuck refers to both the statutes of that era and the legal justifications elaborated by the Supreme Court to support them.

6. In 1904, the Commissioner General of Immigration assigned a small group of mounted inspectors to patrol the borders. Numbering less than 80 officers, they were stationed mainly along the Mexican border for the purpose of curbing the smuggling of Chinese. In 1924, the Bureau of Immigration, which was still part of the Department of Labor, received $1 million from Congress to increase the force of patrol inspectors to 450 men. The smuggling of Chinese and Europeans from Cuba had created a need for patrol inspectors along the Gulf coast as well as on the Mexican border. "The U.S. Border Patrol: The First 50 Years," *I & N Reporter* (Summer 1974): 3.

Oddly, there is no scholarly history of the border patrol. A short, unpublished history has been written by Donald Coppock, a retired former border patrol agent and INS deputy associate commissioner. See Donald Coppock, "History of the Border Patrol" (n.p., n.d.).

7. Whereas the public's demand for tougher enforcement against illegal immigrants appears to be more closely linked to downturns in the general economy, pressures for restricting legal immigration have been motivated by cultural, religious, and other prejudices held toward certain nationality groups along with occasional concerns over economic competition. As Maxine Seller points out, such nativist prejudices toward immigrants can be found throughout American history, including the colonial period. See Maxine Seller, "Historical Perspectives on American Immigration Policy: Case Studies and Current Implications," *Law and Contemporary Problems* 45 (Spring 1982): 140–55.

8. Julian Samora, *Los Mojados: The Wetback Story* (South Bend, Ind.: University of Notre Dame Press, 1971), pp. 17–18, 31–36.

9. Alejandro Portes, "Of Borders and States: A Skeptical Note on the Legislative Control of Immigration," in Wayne A. Cornelius and Ricardo Anzaldua Montoya, eds., *America's New Immigration Law: Origins, Rationales, and Potential Consequences* Monograph Series no. 11 (San Diego: Center for U.S.-Mexican Studies, University of California at San Diego, 1983), pp. 17–30.

10. This has been asserted by several scholars. Jorge A. Bustamante claims that during Operation Deportation, Mexicans were required to prove their citizenship. Those who could not, which necessarily included many lawful immigrants, were expelled. Jorge A. Bustamante, "The Historical Context of Undocumented Mexican Immigration to the United States," *Aztlan* 3, no. 2 (Fall 1972): 257–81.

11. According to Donald Coppock, a retired border patrol agent, such unofficial accommodations in law enforcement were very infrequent. Oral communication to the author, April 1984.

12. Samora, *Los Mojados: The Wetback Story*, pp. 47–50. This version of events is disputed by some veteran patrol agents who served in Texas during this period.

13. This was told to me in the fall of 1983 by a former patrol agent who served in Texas and has since retired. He claims that in his station the senior patrol agent had

instructed subordinates not to make pickups on one ranch belonging to an influential Texas family. The agents, who felt such a hands-off policy was discriminatory, decided to extend this relaxed enforcement policy to all of the ranches in their area of jurisdiction. That left the towns and highways where arrests continued to be made. Other patrol agents I spoke with maintain that the law was impartially enforced in most parts of Texas, although some concede that political pressures were at times exerted to mitigate strict enforcement.

14. Eleanor M. Hadley, "A Critical Analysis of the Wetback Problem," *Law and Contemporary Problems* 21 (1956): 336–39. One reason for the more lenient attitude taken toward illegal Mexican immigration may have been the assumption that Mexican agricultural workers were migrant workers who had no intention of permanently settling in the United States.

Congress's more relaxed attitude toward Mexican immigration was in stark contrast to the attitude expressed by many legislators toward the European refugees seeking admission after World War II and who these legislators felt should be carefully screened and restricted in number.

15. Samora, *Los Mojados: The Wetback Story*, pp. 8–9. According to Philip Martin, only 1.5 million Mexicans participated in the bracero program between 1942 and 1964; thus many of the same individuals were re-entering as legal braceros. Written communication from Philip H. Martin, fall of 1983.

16. Oral communication from a retired former patrol agent, spring of 1984.

17. Although the INS claimed that individuals repatriated into the interior were much less apt to attempt re-entry, the office of management and budget believed the program had been mismanaged and that repatriation by air transport had become too costly. United States Department of Justice, "The Immigration and Naturalization Service: An Agency in Need of Major Reform" (A research report done at the request of Attorney General Griffin Bell, May 1977), pp. 11–12.

18. See Samora, *Los Mojados: The Wetback Story*, pp. 51–53.

19. See "Temporary Worker Programs: Background and Issues" (a report of the United States Senate Committee on the Judiciary, Washington, D.C.: U.S. Government Printing Office, February 1980), p. 51.

20. George I. Sanchez, "History, Culture, and Education," in Julian Samora, ed., *La Raza: The Forgotten Americans* (South Bend, Ind.: University of Notre Dame Press, 1966), p. 9. Also, Vernon M. Briggs, Jr., "Illegal Aliens: The Need for a More Restrictive Border Policy," *Social Science Quarterly* 56, no. 3 (December 1975): 481.

Testimony given in hearings before the Senate Committee on Labor and Public Welfare during the 82nd Congress in 1952 cited the displacement of Texans of Mexican ancestry by illegals. See Hadley, "The Wetback Problem," pp. 344–46. According to Philip Martin, bracero admissions had always been controversial in some quarters. Written communication from Philip L. Martin, fall of 1983.

21. Coppock, "History of the Border Patrol" (tables not paginated at end of paper). Although the statistics include border patrol apprehensions nationwide, the majority would have been made on the southern border.

22. U.S. Department of Justice, Immigration and Naturalization Service, "FY 1983

Report of Deportable Aliens Found in the U.S. By Nationality, Status at Entry, Place of Entry, Status When Found," Form G-23.18.

23. Cafferty, Chiswick, Greeley, and Sullivan, *Dilemma of American Immigration*, p. 60.

For a few years, a small number of Mexican nationals continued to enter legally as H-2 temporary agricultural workers under the Section 101(a)(15) provision of the INA.

24. Immigration and Naturalization Service, "Report of Field Operations: Fiscal Year 1982," Form G-23.1.

25. Immigration and Naturalization Service, "FY 1985 Authorization and Budget Request for the Congress," January 20, 1984, p. 14.

26. Slightly more than 70 percent of mala fide alien entrants were from countries bordering the Caribbean, including Mexico. About 17 percent were from Europe. Based on this study, INS estimated that, instead of the approximately 50,000 fraudulent entrants who were refused admission in 1975, close to half a million would have been denied entry if routine inspections had been carried out with the same care as that exercised by the research team.

The largest single category of fraudulent entrants were Mexican nationals who had I-186 receipts (shoppers' cards) but had violated the terms of their border crossing permits by working. Immigration and Naturalization Service, "Fraudulent Entrants Study" (A study by the office of planning and evaluation, Immigration and Naturalization Service, September 1976), Table 3, p. 15.

27. Legal nonimmigrant admissions to the United States are primarily of three kinds: (1) Mexican nationals who live near the border and have stable jobs may be granted I-186 receipts, which authorize them to travel 25 miles into the United States to shop or visit (but not to work) for a period of 72 hours, (2) Canadian nationals can enter without visas for business or pleasure for up to six months, (3) other aliens, usually from overseas or more distant South American countries, may enter with nonimmigrant visas as visitors for pleasure (B-2) or business (B-1), or as students (F-1).

There are, however, a considerable variety of nonimmigrant visa classifications that cover family members of students, diplomats and their families, employees of corporations having divisions in the United States, foreign workers needed temporarily by U.S. companies, and others.

28. Unlike nonimmigrant visas, immigrant visas entitle aliens to both permanent residence in the United States and most of the nonpolitical welfare and other benefit rights to which citizens are entitled unless such aliens engage in crime or other immoral activities that would make them deportable.

Refugees, who are paroled into the United States until they adjust their status to lawful permanent resident, are also authorized to work and may qualify for a limited amount of welfare during the time it takes them to apply for and receive their immigrant visas. If they have been admitted as refugees in accordance with Department of State and INS regulations, they will almost automatically be granted lawful residence after a year unless they are discovered to have made material misrepresentations about past conduct or actions that would make them excludable. Strictly speaking, aliens who are paroled into the United States have not been officially admitted even though they are physically present on U.S. territory. Others to whom parole is sometimes granted are those apprehended at ports of entry or, as in the case of the Haitians who arrived without documents on the south Florida coast, those who are awaiting exclusion hearings. Foreign nationals charged with crimes in the United States are also paroled in after they have been extradited to stand trial in the United States.

29. In exclusion cases, as distinguished from deportation hearings, aliens carry a much heavier burden of proof to establish their right to remain in the United States. If ordered held in detention pending a hearing, the only legal remedy available to them is a habeas corpus appeal. However, the lower courts have recently been plowing new furrows of opportunity for aliens contesting the government's efforts to expel them. For example, the determination of whether an alien has made an entry, which is crucial for the determination of whether that alien has a right to a deportation hearing with its greater panoply of rights, has become a matter of controversy. The second circuit court of appeals recently upheld a New York district court's finding in which the proof burden, traditionally lodged with the alien, was shifted to the government to establish that an alien had not made an entry. This may well make it harder for the government to hold some aliens for exclusion as distinct from deportation hearings. *Phelisna* v. *Sava*, No. 83–2034 (2d Cir. April 29, 1983).

The Immigration and Nationality Act gives the INS broad discretion to determine the grounds for grants of parole to aliens not authorized to enter the United States. Until recently, some courts sought to limit this discretion. When the INS was found to have discriminated against a group or there were variations in its parole policy that lacked rational explanation, denials of parole were sometimes overturned. See *Bertrand* v. *Sava*, 684 F.2d 204 (2d Cir. 1982).

However, a 1984 *en banc* decision by the eleventh circuit reaffirmed the INS's broad discretionary authority to determine an alien's eligibility for parole and to hold aliens in detention. Moreover, the eleventh circuit ruled (*Jean* v. *Nelson*) that the INS need not inform aliens of their right to apply for asylum and may also discriminate in its detention policy on the basis of nationality. See *Interpreter Releases* 61, no. 9 (March 5, 1984): 164–65.

30. Immigration and Naturalization Service, "FY 1985 Authorization and Budget Request," January 20, 1984, p. 31.

31. See Michael Winerip, "Smuggling of Aliens by Canadian Route to the U.S. Is Increasing," *New York Times*, May 1, 1983, pp. 1, 40.

32. Immigration and Naturalization Service, "FY 1983 Report of Deportable Aliens Found in the U.S," Form G-23.18.

33. Technically speaking, any visa alien who intended to stay on and work at the time of application for a nonimmigrant visa has entered fraudulently even though that person may have entered with a facially bona fide nonimmigrant visa.

34. Nonimmigrant visa aliens who have worked without authorization or overstayed are not liable to criminal prosecution under the INA but are subject to civil deportation processing. By contrast, EWI violators are liable to criminal prosecution. Entry

without inspection (8 U.S.C. 1325) is a misdemeanor for the first offense and a felony for subsequent convictions. For the misdemeanor, the alien can be fined up to $500 and imprisoned for up to six months. On the felony charge, the penalty can be a fine of up to $1,000 and imprisonment for up to two years. However, EWI aliens are referred to as administrative violators because the 8 U.S.C. 1325 misdemeanor is so rarely prosecuted in the case of individual border crossers.

Among visa abusers from overseas, some become liable to criminal prosecution if it is determined that they obtained their nonimmigrant visas fraudulently or if they subsequently sought to adjust their status to permanent resident through fraudulent means after arriving in the United States. However, prosecution is infrequently authorized by U.S. attorneys.

35. Immigration and Naturalization Service, "FY 1983 Report of Deportable Aliens Found in the U.S.," Form G-23.18.

The actual percentage of deportable aliens who are Mexicans is not known. See Cafferty, Chiswick, Greeley, and Sullivan, *Dilemma of American Immigration*, p. 80. Warren and Passel ("Illegal Aliens from Mexico," p. 9) estimated that in 1980 approximately 50 percent of illegal aliens were Mexican nationals and that those from the Western Hemisphere, including Mexico, constituted 64 percent of the illegal population in the United States.

36. Recently, however, the news media have begun to pay more attention to other enforcement problems facing the INS in the interior. Lawrence Meyer, "The Enforcer," *Washington Post Magazine* (April 10, 1983), and Paul Dean, "INS and Its 'White-Collar' Illegal Alien Patrols," *Los Angeles Times View*, June 25, 1982.

37. For example, "Invasion from Mexico: It Just Keeps Growing," *U.S. News & World Report*, March 7, 1983, pp. 37–39.

38. There was clearly more border violence during the 1970s than the 1960s and 1950s. Yet during the 1920s and until the repeal of the Volstead Act in 1933, shootouts between patrol inspectors and liquor smugglers may have been more frequent than the gunplay that occasionally occurred between the border patrol and drug smugglers in the 1970s.

39. Whereas Gallup found only 33 percent of the public wanting legal immigration decreased in 1965, 42 percent had come to feel this way by 1977; as noted earler, both the Roper and NBC surveys of 1981 show a dramatic increase, with two-thirds of the public feeling this way since 1977.

40. See Edwin Harwood, "*Alien*ation: American Attitudes Toward Immigration," *Public Opinion* (June/July 1983): 49–51.

41. Wayne A. Cornelius, "America in the Era of Limits: Nativist Reactions to the 'New' Immigration," Working Papers in U.S.-Mexican Studies no. 3 (Center for U.S.-Mexican Studies, University of California at San Diego, 1982), pp. 6–9.

42. This is not to say that conflict is altogether absent, especially when economic interests are at stake. For example, Vietnamese and other Southeast Asian refugees who have gone into commercial fishing enterprises have run afoul of native-born American fishermen; this is due, in part, to differences in occupational codes and

practices. See Michael K. Orbach and Janese Beckwith, "Indochinese Adaptation and Local Government Policy: An Example from Monterey," *Anthropological Quarterly* (July 1982): 135–45.

43. "Stronger Policies on Aliens Favored," *New York Times*, November 15, 1983, p. A 17.

44. Harwood, "American Attitudes Toward Immigration," pp. 49–51.

45. *Interpreter Releases* 61, no. 22 (June 8, 1984): 451–57.

46. An illuminating account of how citizens will often go to the aid of deportable aliens, especially when they have "made it" in traditional American terms, appeared in the July 22, 1982, *Los Angeles Times*, "Deportation Order Threatens a Dream," Part II, p. 5. In the case described in the story, the alien and his family had absconded from a deportation hearing years earlier. By the time they had been reapprehended, they had acquired substantial equities.

47. Rian Malan, "The Necessary Alien: We All Want Immigration Reform. Just Don't Take Our Maids," *California Magazine*, December 1983, pp. 55–56.

48. Julian L. Simon, "Don't Close Our Borders," *Newsweek*, February 27, 1984, p. 11, and Julian L. Simon, "Adding Up the Costs of Our New Immigrants," *Wall Street Journal*, February 26, 1981, p. 22. Simon is almost certainly correct in claiming that illegals pay more into the Social Security system than they are collecting.

49. In one study of the Social Security and other records of aliens who had been apprehended, it was found that their mean earnings were slightly under $7,000 in 1977. David S. North, "Government Records: What They Tell Us About the Role of Illegal Immigrants in the Labor Market and in Income Transfer Programs," A report prepared for the Employment and Training Administration, U.S. Department of Labor (Washington, D.C.: New Transcentury Foundation, April 1981), p. 49.

Income and occupational data on apprehended aliens are not necessarily representative of the total illegal population because deportable aliens in less skilled blue-collar and agricultural jobs have a substantially higher risk of apprehension than deportable white-collar aliens.

50. Merle L. Wolin, "Americans Turn Down Many Jobs Vacated by Ouster of Aliens," *Wall Street Journal*, December 6, 1982, p. 16.

51. Wayne A. Cornelius, Leo R. Chavez, and Jorge G. Castro, "Mexican Immigrants and Southern California: A Summary of Current Knowledge," Research Report no. 36 (Center for U.S.-Mexican Studies, University of California at San Diego, 1982), pp. 34–49.

52. Donald Huddle, "Illegal Immigrant Workers: Benefits and Costs to the Host Country in the Context of the Immigration and Naturalization Service Raids—Project Jobs" (n.p., December 1982). Also, a letter from Donald Huddle to the author dated April 29, 1984.

53. See Franklin Abrams, "American Immigration Policy: How Strait the Gate?" *Law and Contemporary Problems* 45 (Spring 1982): 115–23.

54. Philip L. Martin, "Labor Intensive Agriculture," *Scientific American* 249, no. 4 (October 1983): 54–59.

55. Immigration and Naturalization Service, "Executive Briefing Material for FY 1985 Congressional Hearings," March 1984, p. 67a. About 90 percent of unentitled aliens were in Los Angeles County alone. It cannot be known whether all of these aliens were illegal because many who were referred to the INS for immigration status checks failed to show up.

For a review of the research evidence on welfare usage by illegal aliens see Roger Conner, "Breaking Down the Barriers: The Changing Relationship Between Illegal Immigration and Welfare," Immigration Paper 4 (September 1982). David North also reports that a substantial percentage of the group of illegal aliens whose tax and other records he analyzed received unemployment compensation they were not entitled to by law. North, *Role of Illegal Immigrants*, pp. 53–56.

However, a study conducted in San Diego County in the mid-1970s indicated that only a very small percentage of illegal aliens were receiving aid from the Department of Public Welfare. See Manuel Villalpando, "A Study of the Socio-economic Impact of Illegal Aliens on the County of San Diego" (A Research Report by the Human Resources Agency, County of San Diego, January, 1977), p. xxi.

56. There is evidence that Mexican immigrants in California produce a substantial fiscal deficit because of their lower wages compared with other immigrant groups. Thomas Muller, *The Fourth Wave: California's Newest Immigrants* (Washington, D.C.: The Urban Institute Press, 1984), pp. 17–21.

57. The findings of the San Diego County study suggest that the incidence of crime among Mexican illegal aliens is low. There are two problems with the data, however. As noted earlier, the base illegal alien population cannot be known with certainty. Also, police classifications of violators as illegal aliens may contain inaccuracies. Villalpando, *Socio-economic Impact*, p. 72.

The INS misses many illegal aliens who local police recognize as illegal aliens, either because they had been released before the INS learned about them or because INS officers were not available to interview and apprehend them.

58. Donald Huddle's survey of 200 illegal aliens apprehended in Houston in 1982 revealed that only 50 percent had, by their own admission, any taxes deducted from their wages. However, this may be partly due to the fact that most of his sample was weighted toward construction and landscaping workers. Letter from Donald Huddle to the author, April 29, 1984.

A survey conducted in 1981 and 1982 among undocumented Mexican women in Los Angeles revealed that 73 percent of the women reported income tax and Social Security deductions from their pay. Rita J. Simon and Margo de Ley, "The Work Experience of Undocumented Women Migrants in Los Angeles" (n.p., n.d.), p. 11.

59. Mary Garcia Castro, "Women in Migration," *Migration Today* 10, no. 3/4 (1982): 28–29.

60. Immigration and Naturalization Service, "Executive Briefing Material for FY 1985 Congressional Hearings," March 1984, p. 86a.

61. Nevada state law imposes strict regulations on the employment of casino workers. Illegal aliens are barred from working in casinos, and new job applicants must be cleared by the INS if they are believed to be aliens.

62. Jerome H. Skolnick, "Fed Up with the Feds," *California Magazine*, November 1983, pp. 58, 60. On the other hand, Chief Davis stated that, although his department would not assist the INS in area control operations, his officers would continue to assist them in their investigations of organized alien smuggling and other criminal violations.

63. See Sheldon L. Maram, "Hispanic Workers in the Garment and Restaurant Industries in Los Angeles County," Working Paper no. 12, Program in U. S.-Mexican Studies, University of California at San Diego (October 1980), pp. 91–97.

However, in a survey of illegal aliens apprehended in Chicago in 1983, it was found that only 16 percent had wages below the federal minimum wage level. Most of these were restaurant workers, and the low wages were not necessarily in violation of federal law in all cases. Barry R. Chiswick, "The Employment and Employers of Illegal Aliens: The Survey and Analysis of Data" (Unpublished manuscript, July 1985), p. iii.

64. Julius Rivera and Paul W. Goodman, "Clandestine Labor Circulation: A Case on the U.S.- Mexico Border," *Migration Today* 10, no. 1 (1982): 25.

65. Simon and Ley, "Undocumented Women Migrants," pp. 11–13.

66. Select Commission on Immigration and Refugee Policy, "The Final Report and Recommendations of the Select Commission on Immigration and Refugee Policy to the Congress and the President of the United States," *U.S. Immigration Policy and the National Interest* (Washington, D.C., April 1981), pp. 41–42.

67. Foreign policy realities were also partly responsible. The barrier to Chinese immigration was dropped during the early 1940s, less because of a sudden liberalization in public attitudes toward Orientals than because of the fact that China was our ally against Japan.

Although the acceptance of large numbers of displaced Europeans during the 1940s was motivated partly by humanitarian concerns, the realities of the cold war and our competition with the Soviet Union doubtless helped liberalize our policy toward refugee admissions, in sharp contrast with the callous attitude exhibited by the State Department toward refugees from Nazism during the 1930s.

68. For a discussion of aliens' rights under the law through the early 1950s, see Milton R. Konvitz, *Civil Rights in Immigration* (Westport, Conn.: Greenwood Press, 1953). For a review of legislative changes through the mid-1960s, see E. P. Hutchinson, *Legislative History of American Immigration Policy, 1798–1965* (Philadelphia: University of Pennsylvania Press, 1981). See also Schuck, "Immigration Law," pp. 30–33.

69. See Schuck, "Immigration Law," pp. 14–75.

70. See Edwin Harwood, "The Crisis in Immigration Policy," *Journal of Contemporary Studies* 6, no. 4 (Fall 1983): 47–52.

71. "The participation model . . . thus rejects the view that the individual's formal status as citizen or alien fully determines the answer to all questions about her rights. Instead, the participation model asserts that, to the extent that aliens assume and ably discharge the wide range of responsibilities normally associated with citizenship, the government must grant aliens rights that render the alien's status functionally close to

that of the citizen." From "Immigration Policy and the Rights of Aliens," *Harvard Law Review* 96 (April 1983): 1463.

Professor Schuck views this change in the legal premises underlying the judiciary's challenge to the INS's administration of the law as reflecting a new communitarian value system, which has superseded the older individualistic contractual premises that undergirded classical immigration law. What is happening to immigration law is not a de novo development of constitutional theory but merely the extension of principles that have already been applied to tort law as well as other areas of public law. Schuck, "Immigration Law," pp. 81–90. (Schuck is not among the advocates of the participation model of alien rights.)

72. The Hesburgh Commission clearly favored some form of employer sanctions provision but was deeply divided on the issue of requiring a new and more secure form of identification. There was no consensus on the system whereby employers would verify a worker's status. Select Commission on Immigration and Refugee Policy, "Final Report and Recommendations," p. 61.

73. The increased urbanization of the illegal Mexican population is now well documented. See Reynaldo Baca and Dexter Bryan, "Mexican Undocumented Workers in the Binational Community: A Research Note," *International Migration Review* 15, no. 4 (Winter 1981): 737–47. Also, Cornelius, Chavez, and Castro, "Summary of Current Knowledge," pp. 7–22.

74. The Supreme Court's decision in *Plyler* v. *Doe* affirmed that the children of illegal aliens have a right to free public education, partly on the ground that children, after all, cannot be held responsible for the violations of their parents. See *Plyler* v. *Doe*, 457 U.S. 202 (1982). But this distinction, as Schuck notes, may be difficult to maintain in the future. As Schuck points out, "the Court failed to explain why denying educational benefits to an innocent child differs from the denial of other government benefits to her undocumented parent, upon whose income and well-being the child's welfare ultimately depends." Schuck, "Immigration Law," pp. 54–55.

CHAPTER TWO

1. The INS has jurisdiction for all Title 8 criminal offenses in the United States code. These relate specifically to immigration offenses, such as entering without inspection or harboring and transporting illegal aliens. Additionally, there are a number of Title 18 offenses over which the INS can claim jurisdiction. For example, when aliens or sponsoring citizens make misrepresentations in the course of benefit applications (18 U.S.C. 1001) or when aliens fraudulently claim U.S. citizenship (18 U.S.C. 911), the INS has jurisdiction to investigate and present such cases to federal prosecutors.

2. U.S. Department of Justice, Immigration and Naturalization Service, "FY 1985 Authorization and Budget Request," January 1984, p. 11.

3. Lawful residents are officially designated *lawful permanent residents*, but they are

also referred to variously as *immigrants, lawful resident aliens, permanent resident aliens,* and *green-card holders,* among other terms.

Unlike aliens entering for short periods with nonimmigrant or diplomatic visas, lawful permanent residents are entitled to remain and work in the United States for as long as they choose. They enjoy most of the welfare and other social benefits to which citizens are entitled but not the right to vote or hold certain elective offices. They are barred by executive order from holding certain federal jobs. In some states, they are barred from holding state jobs that the courts have ruled are political in nature. Unlike native-born citizens, they are also subject to expulsion in the event they are convicted of alien smuggling or other crimes involving moral turpitude. (Naturalized citizens may be subject to expulsion if their naturalization was obtained as a result of material misrepresentations made to the government at the time they applied for visas.)

4. A special INS task force acknowledged the problem of delays and inconsistencies in adjudications in 1976. U.S. Department of Justice, Immigration and Naturalization Service. "Report of the Adjudications Task Force" (May 1, 1976), p. 3.

5. Immigration and Naturalization Service, "Report of Field Operations: FY 1982," Form G-23.5.

6. Immigration and Naturalization Service, "FY 1985 Authorization and Budget Request for the Congress," January 1984, pp. 28, 29.

7. In the case of relative visa petitions involving children, determinations of eligibility under American law may depend on assessments of the child's status under the complex marriage law of a foreign state. See, for example, *Matter of Cherismo,* Board of Immigration Appeals Interim Decision 2956, February 9, 1984.

8. Unlike many other aliens who may have to wait years for an available immigrant visa before they can enter, immediate relatives who are spouses or dependent children of United States citizens can adjust their status as immigrants without having to wait for an available quota preference visa. Parents of U.S. citizens who are 21 years of age or older can also be immigrated without having to wait for a preference visa.

9. Of the 12 million visa visitors during 1980, only 10.5 million were recorded as having left. However, most of the 1.5 million shortfall was probably due to inadequate record keeping by the commercial air carriers and the INS. John Crewdson, *The Tarnished Door: The New Immigrants and the Transformation of America* (New York: The New York Times Book Co., 1983), pp. 31, 136.

10. Immigration and Naturalization Service, "Executive Briefing Material for FY 1985," March 1984, p. 7.

11. There are 33 different grounds for exclusion, including insanity, narcotic addiction, sexual deviation, mental retardation, prostitution, membership in a Communist Party organization, and involvement in acts of political persecution directed against others.

12. The fraudulent procurement of a visa is a felony offense (8 U.S.C. 1546); however, like most immigration felonies, it is rarely prosecuted.

13. Jerry L. Mashaw, *Bureaucratic Justice: Managing Social Security Disability Claims* (New Haven, Conn.: Yale University Press, 1983), pp. 56–57. Noting that when Social Security disability insurance claimants appealed to the federal courts, 46 percent

of the disability denials were reversed or remanded, Mashaw observed: "[the] statute is clearly relevant, but which statute: the one perceived by SSA [Social Security Administration]; by the House Subcommittee on Social Security; or by the federal courts?" p. 57.

14. For a discussion of how an expanding application of due process and equal protection theories have begun to involve the federal courts in other public law fields, along with the dilemmas this poses for social policy, see Jerry L. Mashaw, *Due Process and the Administrative State* (New Haven, Conn.: Yale University Press, 1985).

15. Abraham D. Sofaer, "The Change-of-Status Adjudication: A Case Study of the Informal Agency Process," *Journal of Legal Studies* 1, no. 2 (June 1972): 382–85. Some examiners admitted that congressional inquiry cases were expedited and that the alien had a better chance of approval. In his research on Social Security disability claims, Mashaw claims that congressional inquiry cases were more apt to be expedited than others. Mashaw, *Bureaucratic Justice*, pp. 135–136.

INS officers I interviewed conceded that, when there was congressional interest in a benefit application, it was apt to be expedited. Many officers resented the fact that congressional influence was sometimes used to expedite applications.

16. Mashaw, *Bureaucratic Justice*, pp. 41–42, 195.

17. In 1983, the immigration courts were transferred from the INS's administrative jurisdiction to a separate Department of Justice office, the executive office for immigration review—a move that was motivated partly to ensure that the immigration judges would be completely independent in their adjudicatory function.

18. The use of legal sanctions by law agents for situational social control purposes has been noted by other scholars. See, for example, Maureen Mileski, "Courtroom Encounters: An Observational Study of a Lower Criminal Court," *Law and Society Review* 5 (1971): 473, 504–505, 523. Also, Jerome Skolnick, *Justice Without Trial: Law Enforcement in a Democratic Society* (New York: Wiley, 1966), pp. 94–95, 106–108.

19. Immigration and Naturalization Service, "FY 1983 Report of Field Operations," Forms G-23.18 and G-23.8. The apprehension figure used in calculating the percentage does not take into account the approximately 5,000 technical violators. Most are crew members who become deportable because their ships fail to leave port within 29 days of their arrival.

20. In 1960, the border patrol apprehended 29,000 aliens; this was 41 percent of all INS apprehensions. In 1964, the border patrol accounted for 50 percent of all INS apprehensions. By 1971, the patrol accounted for 72 percent of all apprehensions, and by 1983, patrol apprehensions were almost 90 percent of all apprehensions. The shift in the percentage is due almost entirely to the surge in Mexican EWI apprehensions during the 23-year span.

My estimates were based on a comparison of data on border patrol arrests provided by Donald Coppock, "History of the Border Patrol" (n.p., n.d.), with other available INS sources. Immigration and Naturalization Service, *1980 Statistical Yearbook* (n.p., n.d.), pp. 85, 86 and Immigration and Naturalization Service, "FY 1983 Report of Deportable Aliens Found," Form G-23.18.

21. Letter to the author from Mr. Lawrence D'Elia, Office of the Chief Immigration

Judge, executive office for immigration review, April 20, 1984. Nationwide, in fiscal year 1983, the immigration judges handled an average of 5.35 cases per day. See the solicitor general's petition for certiorari in *INS* v. *Lopez-Mendoza*, 705 F.2d 1059 (9th Cir. 1983), filed with the Supreme Court September 22, 1983. This petition is digested in *Interpreter Releases* 60, no. 43 (November 10, 1983): 844.

22. Albert W. Alschuler, "Plea Bargaining and Its History," *Columbia Law Review* 79, no. 4 (1979): 34–35, 42; also, Hans Zeisel, *The Limits of Law Enforcement* (Chicago: University of Chicago Press, 1982), pp. 39–44, 140–41. Zeisel's findings from a study of felony cases in New York City indicate that defendants convicted after a jury trial could expect to receive sentences that were double in severity those given to defendants who pled guilty.

23. *Interpreter Releases* 61, no. 10 (March 13, 1984): 195. However, some aliens and their attorneys are assessed costs and damages for abusing the court with excessive motions and delay. Thus clearly frivolous delaying tactics do carry some risk for alien plaintiffs. See, for example, *Chour* v. *INS*, 578 F.2d 464 (2d Cir. 1978).

24. Under the Refugee Act of 1980, any alien present in the United States, whether legally or illegally, may request political asylum. The standard is the same for asylum applicants as for refugees applying from abroad: namely, a showing of well-founded fear of persecution on account of race, religion, nationality, membership in a particular social group, or political opinion. If denied asylum by an INS district director, the alien may raise the claim anew in a deportation hearing. As with most other statutory relief and benefit provisions, denials of asylum claims have provoked heated and continuing litigation. The several issues still to be unresolved include the proof burden an applicant must meet to establish a well-founded fear of persecution and whether the well-founded-fear standard requires the same evidentiary showing (objective as well as subjective factors) as the earlier standard for withholding of deportation under Section 243(h), which required the alien to show a clear probability of persecution if returned home. Also, there is the issue of whether membership in a broad social class (such as the urban working class) that is subject to terrorism (by nongovernmental terrorists) might qualify an alien for asylum relief.

For a discussion of these controversies, see Deborah E. Anker and Michael H. Posner, "The Forty Year Crisis: A Legislative History of the Refugee Act of 1980," *San Diego Law Review* 19 (December 1981): 9–89; Christopher T. Hanson, "Behind the Paper Curtain: Asylum Policy Versus Asylum Practice," *New York University Review of Law and Social Change* 7 (Winter 1978): 107–41; and Deborah Anker, "Defining a Social Group," *Immigration Journal* (January-March 1983): 15–16.

25. There are a number of bizarre quirks in the provisions of the INA, including some that are clearly antiquated. Thus synthetic, chemically fabricated drugs, such as amphetamines or angel dust, are not included for purposes of establishing an alien's excludability on a narcotics charge because, when the law was first written, only natural narcotic substances or substances derived from natural drugs, such as opium, were listed.

26. This pattern was more prevalent while I was conducting my field work during 1981 and 1982. With the implementation of the new case management system in July 1983, investigators are spending less time on dual-action cases they judge unlikely to

lead to benefit denials or prosecutions. See Immigration and Naturalization Service, "FY 1985 Authorization and Budget Request for the Congress," January 1984, pp. 19–20. In fiscal year 1982, 82 percent of all cases received by investigations were completed compared with 70 percent in 1983. Now, however, cases are no longer listed as received if they fall below the threshold criteria of acceptance (seriousness and likelihood of success).

27. For a discussion of the factors that make criminal prosecution of INA violators more likely see Edwin Harwood, "Arrests Without Warrant: The Legal and Organizational Environment of Immigration Law Enforcement," *University of California, Davis, Law Review* 17 (February 1984): 513–19, 542–46.

Deportation processing (along with the discretionary grant of voluntary departure and return) is the main civil action taken. However, the INS also initiates some other civil actions, including the seizure of vehicles used for smuggling, collection of fines, and disbarment proceedings against attorneys.

28. Government regulators prefer to take actions that lead to voluntary compliance agreements and consent orders on the part of violators because of the substantial costs of litigation. Eugene Bardach and Robert A. Kagan, *Going By The Book: The Problem of Regulatory Unreasonableness* (Philadelphia: Temple University Press, 1982), pp. 40–42.

CHAPTER THREE

1. The border patrol has served other important functions over the years. For example, during World War II, it assisted in guarding aliens in detention camps and worked with the military to guard the eastern coastline against Axis saboteurs and spies. And during the early 1960s, it was given responsibility for preventing the smuggling of guns from the United States to anti-Castro rebels. See Donald Coppock, "History of the Border Patrol" (n.p.,n.d.), pp. 12, 19.

2. U.S. Department of Justice, Immigration and Naturalization Service, "FY 1983 Report of Deportable Aliens Found," Form G-23.18. At any given time, however, there are only about 400 patrol agents on duty at the southern land border.

3. For a discussion of new technological developments in linewatch surveillance, see "Technology Helps the Border Patrol," *INS Reporter* (Winter 1981–82): 10–11.

4. The border patrol has on occasion cut sign on felons being pursued by local law enforcement.

5. Immigration and Naturalization Service, "FY 1985 Authorization and Budget Request for the Congress," January 1984, p. 16.

6. In the old days, the patrol would use brush-rollers pulled behind a van to drag dirt roads at night. Then they would return the next morning to look for foot traffic and work from there. Some agents claim they had a reasonably good idea of their catch ratio (the number of illegals caught in relation to the number crossing over) because they could compare their count of the tracks made during the night against the number of aliens they chased down.

Roads are still dragged on occasion. When the agents know there is a group somewhere out in the desert, they can drag ravines or roads in a cross-hatch pattern ahead and to both sides of the group to determine the group's direction. As they move in on the group, they drag closer and closer to them until they are found and the apprehensions accomplished.

Sign cutting is more than pursuing foot tracks. Agents look for man-made disturbances in foliage (branches bent or broken in certain ways), overturned rocks, and the like. At night they can spot human traffic by playing their flashlights over grassy areas where the dew has been disturbed. One investigator volunteered that sign cutting training had come in handy once while pursuing an alien in snow across the rooftops of apartment buildings in Chicago.

7. Immigration and Naturalization Service, "FY 1985 Authorization and Budget Request," p. 16.

8. Ibid., p. 15. Immigration and Naturalization Service, *1980 Statistical Yearbook* (n.p., n.d.), p. 116.

9. "Invasion from Mexico: It Just Keeps Growing," *U.S. News and World Report*, March 7, 1983, p. 38.

10. Immigration and Naturalization Service, "FY 1983 Report of Deportable Aliens Found," Form G-23.18.

11. Some studies of the illegal Mexican population in southern California estimate that 40 percent are female. See Reynaldo Baca and Dexter Bryan, "Mexican Undocumented Workers in the Binational Community: A Research Note," *International Migration Review* 15, no. 4 (Winter 1981): 737–47.

12. According to one survey of illegal Mexican aliens, many Mexican males leave their wives and children behind in Mexico because of the lower cost of living there. Among married men whose wives lived in Mexico, a majority said they would continue to remain in Mexico by preference even if they could secure legal documents. Baca and Bryan, "Mexican Undocumented Workers," p. 744.

13. Nationwide, Mexican female apprehensions were only about 13 percent of all Mexican apprehensions. Immigration and Naturalization Service, "FY 1983 Report of Deportable Aliens."

14. To approach and question them, INS officers must have reasonable suspicion that individuals are aliens. To forcibly detain someone, they must have reasonable suspicion that that person is an illegal alien. To carry out an arrest, they must meet the higher probable cause standard of illegal alienage. For a discussion of the constitutional requirements, see Edwin Harwood, "Arrests Without Warrant: The Legal and Organizational Environment of Immigration Law Enforcement," *University of California, Davis, Law Review* 17 (February 1984): 527–39.

15. This road is called *memo lane*. Everytime a van is hit, the agents have to write up a memo. Sometimes the rocks hit their marks and patrol agents are seriously injured.

16. Immigration and Naturalization Service, "FY 1985 Authorization and Budget Request," p.17.

17. For the account of one case of an alien returned to the border by mistake, see John Hummel, "The Road North: Undocumented Workers and the Border Patrol," *Santa Cruz Weekly*, March 30, 1982, p. 8.

18. The Supreme Court ruled in *U.S.* v. *Brignoni-Ponce*, 422 U.S. 873 (1975) that vehicle searches required specific articulable facts that reasonably warrant suspicion that the vehicle contains illegal aliens. However, INS officers at the immediate border and its functional equivalent (which all the circuit courts except the ninth interpret to include fixed checkpoints) were exempted from having to meet this standard.

19. See Harwood, "Immigration Law Enforcement," pp. 542–46.

20. Category I smugglers are those who have fully developed ring organizations that include recruiters, guides, transporters, destination brokers, and safe houses and who (1) transport in excess of 250 aliens or earn more than $50,000 per month, (2) smuggle aliens involved in criminal activities, such as drugs, prostitution, hostage, and ransom situations, (3) smuggle infants, (4) smuggle terrorists, subversives, or organized crime figures, (5) smuggle for businesses dependent on illegal alien workers or businesses with chain stores throughout the United States, or (6) are corrupt high-ranking foreign or domestic officials.

Category II smugglers are those who (1) transport 100 to 250 aliens or earn $25,000 to $50,000 per month and have accomplices in their organization or (2) are labor contractors who recruit in interior or border areas and transport aliens over substantial distances.

Category III are independent free-lance smugglers who harbor or transport illegal aliens into the United States and whose relationship with those smuggled is commercial (for gain).

Category IV includes nonprofessionals who smuggle relatives, household employees, or workers in their business. Typically, they do not smuggle as a means of gainful employment. U.S. Department of Justice, Immigration and Naturalization Service, "Investigations Case Management System" (July 1, 1983, mimeographed), pp. 25–26, 30–31.

21. The agents sometimes use the term *probable cause* when they are actually referring to the lower reasonable-suspicion standard. Thus patrol agents need probable cause to make an arrest, which they can do once they have determined there are illegal aliens in a car; but they only need reasonable suspicion that illegals might be in a car to flag it down.

22. Immigration and Naturalization Service, "FY 1985 Authorization and Budget Request," p. 22.

23. Until recently, only a very small percentage (1 to 3 percent) of southern border arrests were of OTM aliens, mainly from Central America. The smuggling of aliens from the Caribbean Islands along the northern border appears to be on the rise, due perhaps to the widely known fact that the border patrol has many fewer officers stationed there. Michael Winerip, "Smuggling of Aliens By Canadian Route to U.S. Is Increasing," *New York Times*, May 1, 1983, pp. 1, 40.

24. For a discussion of how lower-echelon officials must adjust policies to cope with their day-to-day working environment, see Michael Lipsky, *Street-Level Bureaucracy* (New York: Russell Sage Foundation, 1980), pp. 84–86.

25. A good example of how professional skill can be sharpened to meet a higher constitutional standard (rather than used to circumvent the standard) is the *Cortez* case

involving a smuggler apprehended in Arizona. The case was decided in favor of the government after going on appeal to the U.S. Supreme Court. *United States* v. *Cortez*, 449 U.S. 411 (1981). In this case, several patrol agents had been tracking footprints leading from an area near the border to an east-west running highway on an Indian reservation. On different occasions, they found one "chevron" print repeatedly among other tracks, which suggested to them that that print belonged to the smuggler. When they finally stopped the van that was carrying the load, there was nothing about the vehicle per se or the behavior of the occupants inside that would normally have provided adequate probable cause for a stop, which fact the defendant used to challenge the constitutionality of the seizure.

But the agents claimed they had obtained sufficient probable cause because they had developed inferences based on a series of deductions. They had first staked out the area near where they believed the aliens were being picked up by truck. Finally, on one night they observed a truck heading down the road in the direction of the place they had tracked the footprints earlier. They measured the time that elapsed after the truck passed their observation post and estimated the truck's speed. When it returned in the opposite direction, they could establish that it must have stopped at the suspected load point, which was in a desolate area. The location of the stop ruled out travel on normal business at night. After stopping the truck and finding illegal aliens, they examined the shoes of the driver and found the chevron sole, which matched the prints they had observed at the pickup point. They knew they had their man.

Although the smuggler's conviction in the district court was overturned by the ninth circuit court of appeals on the ground that the agents lacked adequate probable cause to stop the truck, the Supreme Court reversed the ninth and upheld the conviction. Moreover, the justices expressly noted that the officers had applied their enforcement skills in a highly professional manner.

CHAPTER FOUR

1. U.S. Department of Justice, Immigration and Naturalization Service, "FY 1983 Report of Field Operations," Forms G-23.15 and G-23.21, and "FY 1983 Report of Deportable Aliens," Form G-23.18. To obtain the ratio of hours per arrest for city patrol, the "industry and other" arrests listed in the G-23.18 form were combined with the "in institutions" arrests total. The problem, however, is that the arrest classification statistics do not necessarily coincide with the statistics on officer hour by patrol function.

The comparable function of the CIs in the cities (which was called *area control surveys* until mid-1983) required approximately 4.5 officer hours per arrest.

2. Immigration and Naturalization Service, "FY 1983 Report of Field Operations," Form G-23.21.

3. Although I am writing in the present tense, it should be kept in mind that these generalizations pertain to 1981 and 1982. Under the case management system, the CIs assigned to employer surveys do not seek to maximize arrests of working aliens as much as they seek to put pressure on businesses notorious for employing illegals. Im-

migration and Naturalization Service, "Investigations Case Management System" (July 1, 1983, mimeographed), p. 21.

4. By contrast, in welfare agencies, positive errors (such as granting benefits to ineligible or marginally eligible applicants) mandate some level of eligibility screening because they impose monetary costs on taxpayers. But it is not at all clear whether unapprehended illegal aliens impose costs on taxpayers; in any case, they impose no internal costs on the INS. For a general discussion of the theoretical issues involved in the trade-off problems welfare agencies confront in minimizing positive and negative errors when adjudicating benefit claims, see Mashaw, *Due Process in the Administrative State* (New Haven, Conn: Yale University Press, 1985), Chapter Three.

5. That false claims are infrequent is suggested by the fact that the investigations branch reported 3,200 false citizenship claims and 2,600 false claims to lawful resident status in fiscal year 1982. Immigration and Naturalization Service, "FY 1983 Report of Field Operations."

However, it is hard to know what percentage of false claims made in the field are reported in the statistics. Not all are. False claims to border patrol agents are not included in the annual report of field operations statistics.

6. Under the open field doctrine, patrol agents do not need ranchers' consent to enter their property, although they cannot inspect dwellings on the property without consent or the curtilage area by their homes. (Within 25 miles of the border, they can go through yard areas on residential and farm properties.) *Hester* v. *U.S.*, 265 U.S. 57 (1924). The open field doctrine has been upheld by other decisions that have declared that the Fourth-Amendment ban on unreasonable seizures and searches extends only to dwellings and people, not to open land.

7. See James Eisenstein, *Counsel for the United States: U.S. Attorneys in the Political and Legal Systems* (Baltimore, Md.: Johns Hopkins University Press, 1978), pp. 197–98. However, most declinations of prosecutions are due to other more compelling factors, including caseload pressures and the attitudes of federal judges toward certain kinds of offenses.

8. This generalization, however, is disputed by many INS officers.

CHAPTER FIVE

1. However, the morale problems that many CIs experience arise primarily from the fact that the law is not taken seriously, as they view the matter, and that often the INS's priority appears to be one of expediting services to aliens rather than locating and sanctioning violators. See George J. Weissinger, "Law Enforcement and the Immigration and Naturalization Service: Resolving an Apparent Contradiction" (Ph.D. diss., New York University, 1982), pp. 191–201.

This problem was exacerbated during the mid-1970s because of the Carter administration's lower priority for INA interior enforcement under Commissioner Lionel Castillo.

2. The new policy initiated under the case management system in 1983 screens

out cases that are unlikely to result in successful action and also gives higher priority to cases involving serious INA violators and businesses notorious for employing illegal aliens. U.S. Department of Justice, Immigration and Naturalization Service, "Investigations Case Management System" (July 1, 1983, mimeographed), p. 3.

3. Many other federal regulatory agencies depend on "mailbag" tips for initiating investigations, although this is not always because of legal requirements but rather because of the information cost of obtaining leads to work on their own initiative. See Robert A. Katzmann, *Regulatory Bureaucracy: The Federal Trade Commission and Antitrust Policy* (Cambridge, Mass.: MIT Press, 1980), pp. 27–88. Katzmann found that Federal Trade Commission attorneys in the Bureau of Competition preferred mailbag cases because they involved conduct violations by easily identified businessmen and hence were easier to work up for prosecution, unlike the "structural" cases involving large corporate entities whose market impacts could only be discerned through very time-consuming economic and other investigations. Immigration and Naturalization Service officers, however, rely on tips mainly to meet the legal requirement for a warrant. They always know where they can go if they just want to make additional area control apprehensions. Some agents dislike working on the basis of tips because they feel they are being used by individuals who have called in the tip not because of "patriotic" concern over aliens who are breaking the law or displacing citizen workers but because of personal grudges against employers.

4. In a case that arose in Washington, D.C. (*Blackie's House of Beef*), the District of Columbia Circuit Court of Appeals overturned a district court ruling that would have required INS officers to have a particularized description of the persons being sought (either names or a detailed physical description) before a warrant could be issued. The appellate court ruled instead that INS officers were not required to meet the standards of a criminal search warrant but could obtain administrative warrants that do not require named persons if other information is available to establish probable cause that illegal aliens are working in the firm. *Blackie's House of Beef* v. *Castillo* 659 F.2d (D.C. Cir. 1981). As Stuart Bernsen notes, the circuit court, in effect, created a hybrid civil administrative warrant based on an intermediate level of probable cause. Using the balancing-approach doctrine of constitutional analysis, the court reasoned that the probable cause requirements of the Fourth Amendment should conform to the reasonable demands of administrative practice. See Stuart Bernsen, "Fourth-Amendment Warrant Standards for Immigration Search of Business Premises for Undocumented Aliens: A New Hybrid Probable Cause?" *Rutgers Law Journal* 13, no. 3 (Spring 1982): 607, 617.

5. Peter H. Schuck, *Suing Government: Citizen Remedies for Official Wrongs* (New Haven, Conn.: Yale University Press, 1983), pp. 59–81.

6. In other raids I witnessed in other parts of the country, it was not clear to me whether the officers did prior sorting of workers who remained at their workstations. My impression was that they would briefly question most workers as they moved down the rows of sewing machines.

7. For a discussion of situational social control in the context of immigration law enforcement, see Edwin Harwood, "Arrests Without Warrant: The Legal and Organ-

izational Environment of Immigration Law Enforcement," *University of California, Davis, Law Review* 17 (February 1984): 522–27.

8. This observation is based on a conversation I heard between several of the officers, who may only have been speculating on the reasons for the decision to break off the survey and go back downtown.

9. According to one study of illegal Hispanic restaurant and garment workers in the Los Angeles area, most are not temporary migrant workers but have established permanent or semipermanent residence in the United States. Sheldon L. Maram, "Hispanic Workers in the Garment and Restaurant Industries in Los Angeles County," Working Papers in U.S.-Mexican Studies, no. 12 (Center for U.S.-Mexican Studies, University of California at San Diego, October 1980), p. xiv.

10. In the fall of 1983, the Department of Justice published in the *Federal Register* a new rule that would make the no-work rider mandatory for all bonds. It is incumbent on the alien to apply to the district director for work authorization pending the outcome of a hearing. Aliens with citizen or lawful permanent resident relatives who are dependents or who have other substantial equities are likely to be authorized to work. *Interpreter Releases* 60, no. 43 (November 10, 1983): 856–58.

What is uncertain is whether the new rule will make much of a difference. The INS already has the authority to impose no-work riders in almost all cases. That it currently chooses to exercise this discretion with considerable leniency should make one question why the service would be any less lenient under the new rule. Consider this: if aliens with no-work riders on their bonds are rearrested during an employer survey, their cash bonds would not be forfeited, but they could be placed in detention at government expense. And if they have family members, they may have to be detained too. The INS simply does not have the detention capabilities and funds to detain more than a small fraction of apprehended aliens. Thus the likely effect of the new rule, assuming it withstands court challenges, will be to produce additional paperwork in the form of routine requests to district directors for work authorization.

11. See Schuck, *Suing Government*, pp. 68–75. It is also possible that an officer might claim a fear of a legal action or an administrative reprimand as a ready-to-hand justification for dropping a case that would be a waste of time because of the investigation required.

12. It is reasonable to assume that, with the inauguration of the case management system, investigator morale may have improved because officers are less likely to work cases that will not have a discernable enforcement payoff.

13. The ninth circuit has ruled that INS officers should read the *Miranda* warning to most, if not all, violators simply because of the fact that a criminal violation is involved and an incriminating response will be elicited from the person even though the EWI offense is routinely waived under the blanket declination policy. (The *Miranda* warning is not required when there is only the possibility of a civil proceeding, which is the case for most visa abusers.) *United States* v. *Mata-Abundiz*, 717 F.2d 1277 (9th Cir. 1983).

14. My assessment of the dilemmas facing the Washington, D.C. office is reinforced by observations that were arrived at independently by a journalist who stud-

ied that office later. See Lawrence Meyer, "The Enforcer," *Washington Post Magazine*, April 10, 1983, p. 12.

15. Based on oral communication to the author by several officers.

CHAPTER SIX

1. Although ASU officers are nominally under the supervision of the assistant district director of investigations (in district offices) or the sector border patrol chief, they have their own budget and separate policy guidelines. Thus, operationally, they are really under the authority of regional and central office officials.

2. This applies mainly to the fraud; antismuggling; and CINS units. Although the general unit may pursue aliens who abscond before or after hearings, much of their work is unrelated to what the CIs view as the most meaningful kinds of enforcement. In general, it entails less satisfying work.

3. As a "person" under the constitution, the alien has the Fifth-Amendment right to refuse to talk to any officer, whether from the INS or another law enforcement agency. However, if the INS has sufficient probable cause to think someone is an alien (and refusal to talk might be taken as an articulable fact along with others), that person could then be held for a deportation hearing at which point that individual would have to answer questions about immigration status or risk being deported, which is why INS has the leverage to get aliens to talk in most cases.

According to Section 287 of the INA, INS officers have the power "without warrant" to "interrogate any alien or person believed to be an alien as to his right to be or to remain in the United States." Committee of the Judiciary of the U.S. House of Representatives, *Immigration and Nationality Act* (Washington, D.C.: U.S. Government Printing Office, 1980), Section 287, pp. 96, 97.

4. Since the fall of 1983, background checks are no longer done for benefit and relief applicants unless there is other evidence pointing to criminal activity or an immigration judge specifically requests an investigation at the time of an alien's hearing.

5. However, in general, *good moral character* has come to be defined in the majority of situations as an absence of criminal convictions.

6. Investigators interviewed by George J. Weissinger, who wrote his Ph.D. dissertation on his investigations unit in New York, also reported this. See George J. Weissinger, "Law Enforcement and the Immigration and Naturalization Service: Resolving an Apparent Contradiction" (Ph.D. diss., New York University, 1982), p. 127.

7. Drunk drivers, although a major concern to the public, are often a problem for police agencies because of the time it takes an arresting officer to process a single drunk driving case, along with the fact that drunk drivers are apt to be on the road during hours when police are often busy with more serious problems. As a result, police may simply neglect to pull over a car whose driver they suspect may have been drinking or, if they do pull the car over, may release the driver if they feel another officer will be left uncovered during the time they are processing that driver. See Herman Goldstein and Charles E. Susmilch, "The Drinking-Driver in Madison: A Study

of the Problem and the Community's Response," Vol. II (University of Wisconsin Law School, July 1982), pp. 67–70.

8. For a discussion of the threshold criteria applied by federal prosecutors in cases involving INA offenders, see Edwin Harwood, "Arrests Without Warrant: The Legal and Organizational Environment of Immigration Law Enforcement," *University of California, Davis, Law Review* 17 (February 1984): 542–46.

9. U.S. Department of Justice, Immigration and Naturalization Service, "FY 1983 Report of Field Operations," Form G-23.21.

10. What distinguishes 1811 federal investigators and agents is that they are "physicals" and make arrests; 1810 federal investigators, such as Securities and Exchange Commission and Internal Revenue Service investigators, do not arrest law violators.

For a discussion of the sources of role strain experienced by the investigators in one district office, see Weissinger, *Law Enforcement and the Immigration and Naturalization Service*, pp. 125–39.

Although FBI work is perceived by INS investigators as more glamorous, as it is by the public at large, what INS officers fail to realize is that the FBI's special agents often spend considerable time on unglamorous and routine investigatory tasks— among them investigations of thefts on government property, crimes on Indian reservations, and stolen goods in interstate commerce. See James Q. Wilson, *The Investigators: Managing FBI and Narcotics Agents* (New York: Basic Books, 1978), pp. 128–33.

11. See Harwood, "Immigration Law Enforcement." The U.S. attorneys' threshold standards can vary considerably among districts because of caseload pressures, the prevalence of more serious kinds of crimes in a particular area, attitudes of judges and juries, and the like. Indeed, the INS is not alone in experiencing a high declination rate. Even the FBI turns in cases that are sometimes declined. As a result, most federal agencies prescreen their cases based on what they know the prosecutors are likely to take.

For an illuminating account of the various factors affecting prosecutorial discretion, see Robert L. Rabin, "Agency Criminal Referrals in the Federal System: An Empirical Study of Prosecutorial Discretion," *Stanford Law Review* 24 (June 1972): 1036–91.

CHAPTER SEVEN

1. Section 212(a)(19) of the INA provides that an alien is excludable (inadmissible) for entry if the person has obtained or sought to procure a visa by fraud or willful misrepresentation of a material fact. However, there are waivers for visa fraud in the case of aliens who are applying on the basis of a family relationship to a citizen or lawful resident.

2. Like many police officers who may exaggerate the dilemmas posed by a legal order they view as increasingly hostile to the goals of enforcement, it is possible that INS investigators also exaggerate the obstacles put in the path of their investigations

Notes to pages 153–176

by the courts. In suspected sham marriage cases, if the petitioners had earlier agreed to withdraw their petitions and had admitted to INS officers that theirs were marriages of convenience, then they would carry the proof burden in establishing that their marriages were bona fide if they decide to re-petition. See *Matter of Laureano*, Int. Dec. 2951, Decided by the Board of Immigration Appeals, December 12, 1983.

3. Documentary evidence may prove that the couple made misrepresentations, but they are unlikely to be prosecuted for the misrepresentation. In *Matter of McGee* (2782), a 1980 Board of Immigration Appeals case, it was decided that, if there is evidence suggesting that the petitioner and the petitioner's alien spouse have a bona fide marriage, then their misrepresentation of having lived together when they did not is not material.

CHAPTER EIGHT

1. According to one account, federal officials candidly admitted that they have been restrained because they want to avoid the spectacle of having immigration officers dragging refugees out of churches, which might increase public support for the sanctuary movement. See Ari L. Goldman, "Churches Becoming Home to Central American Exiles," *New York Times*, April 1, 1984, p. E-9. On the other hand, the INS has presented for prosecution some cases involving religious workers who have smuggled aliens for ideological or moral reasons rather than for gain.

2. In the case of the Department of Justice's Antitrust Division, the division's attorneys are able to resist efforts by legislators to influence their investigations. This is, in large part, because of the strength of the professional antitrust bar, which includes both private antitrust practitioners as well as government attorneys. Suzanne Weaver, "Antitrust Division of the Department of Labor," in James Q. Wilson, ed., *The Politics of Regulation* (New York: Basic Books, 1980), pp. 146–50.

3. Jerome H. Skolnick, *House of Cards: Legalization and Control of Casino Gambling* (Boston: Little, Brown, 1978), pp. 310–30.

4. James Q. Wilson, "The Politics of Regulation," in Wilson, *Politics of Regulation*, pp. 376–78.

5. Colin S. Diver, "A Theory of Regulatory Enforcement," *Public Policy* 28, no. 3 (Summer 1980): 262–77.

6. Ibid., p. 264.

7. Eugene Bardach and Robert A. Kagan, *Going By the Book: The Problem of Regulatory Unreasonableness* (Philadelphia, Pa.: Temple University Press, 1982), pp. 25–57, 200–209.

8. Jerry Mashaw noted the double-bind that adjudicators of Social Security disability insurance claims faced. "In oversight, budget and legislative hearings, Congress has alternately berated SSA [Social Security Administration] for its unresponsiveness to claimants and for its laxity in letting them on the rolls." Jerry L. Mashaw, *Bureaucratic Justice: Managing Social Security Disability Claims* (New Haven, Conn.: Yale University Press, 1983), p. 20.

Welfare agencies may respond to political demands for tightened screening by increasing the hurdles applicants must pass at the initial stage of intake, especially if the agency expects it may encounter legal difficulties and higher costs in removing ineligible or marginally eligible beneficiaries later. As Mashaw notes, the cost of tighter screening up front may be born by eligible welfare applicants who are deterred from applying by the increased hurdles and hassles. In the case of ineligible aliens who receive INA benefits because of inadequate screening by examiners or because of the difficulties officials believe will arise in sustaining denials (in the case of aliens who will contest), the cost may be born by aliens still abroad because of the reduced pool of available visas.

9. Indeed, the literature suggests that ceteris paribus legal immigrants impose fewer welfare costs than comparable groups of citizens and that they experience more rapid upward economic mobility. See Barry R. Chiswick, "The Economic Progress of Immigrants: Some Apparently Universal Patterns," in Barry R. Chiswick, ed., *The Gateway: U.S. Immigration Issues and Policies* (Washington, D.C.: American Enterprise Institute for Public Policy Research, 1982), pp. 119–58. Julian L. Simon argues that the tax and other economic contributions of immigrants yields "a high rate of return" to native citizens. Julian L. Simon, "The Overall Effect of Immigrants on Natives' Incomes," in Chiswick, *Immigration Issues and Policies*, pp. 314–38.

10. According to one INS examiner I interviewed, the INS tends to rein in on benefit grants during hard economic times but eases up when economic conditions improve.

11. See Thomas Muller, *The Fourth Wave: California's Newest Immigrants* (Washington, D.C.: Urban Institute Press, 1984), pp. 17–21.

12. Much of the frustration investigators experience arises not just from their perception of public indifference toward enforcement against administrative violators but also from their feeling that the INS gives service toward alien benefit applicants higher priority than enforcement against violators. See George J. Weissinger, "Law Enforcement and the Immigration and Naturalization Service: Resolving an Apparent Contradiction" (Ph.D. diss., New York University, 1982), pp. 125–39.

13. Michael Lipsky, *Street-Level Bureaucracy* (New York: Russell Sage Foundation, 1980), p. 139.

14. Ibid., pp. 18, 19.

15. See Edwin Harwood, "Arrests Without Warrant: The Legal and Organizational Environment of Immigration Law Enforcement," *University of California, Davis, Law Review* 17 (February 1984): 540–47.

16. In its 1980 report to Congress and the president, the U.S. Commission on Civil Rights criticized the INS severely for civil rights violations, unreasonable delays, and unfairness in benefit adjudications among other acts of malfeasance and nonfeasance. Although some of the criticisms were undoubtedly valid, the report lacks balance and objectivity. One gets the clear impression that the commission had been co-opted by the immigration law bar and civil rights activists. See U.S. Commission on Civil Rights, *The Tarnished Golden Door: Civil Rights Issues in Immigration* (Washington, D.C.: U.S. Government Printing Office, 1980).

17. The INS must hold smuggled aliens as material witnesses when defendants charged with alien smuggling can make a satisfactory showing that their testimony will assist their defense. *United States* v. *Valenzuela-Bernal*, 458 U.S. 858, 102 S. Ct. 3440 (July 1982).

18. Many important lower-court decisions were running against the INS during the 1970s and early 1980s. For a discussion of why some lower federal courts were becoming less deferential to the political branches of government on immigration matters, see Peter H. Schuck, "The Transformation of Immigration Law," *Columbia Law Review* 84, no. 1 (January 1984): 34–73.

19. *Lopez-Mendoza* v. *INS*, 705 F.2d 1059 (9th Cir. 1983); *INS* v. *Lopez-Mendoza*, 468 U.S. 1032, 104 S. Ct. 3479 (No. 83–491, July 5, 1984). The Board of Immigration Appeals had earlier ruled (*in re: Sandoval*) that the exclusionary rule did not apply in civil deportation hearings.

20. *INS.* v. *Delgado*, 52 U.S.L.W. 1162 (U.S. April 24, 1984).

21. When I asked several officers to spell out some of the articulable facts suggestive of illegal alienage for other nationality groups, they were hard pressed to think of attributes of behavior and clothing that would distinguish illegal from lawfully resident (or naturalized citizen) members of the group. One pointed out that Poles are known to carry a distinctive type of lunch sack and to walk to work in small groups, but the officer emphasized that it was much harder to know whether they were illegally here based on those facts alone.

22. *Jean* v. *Nelson*, 727 F.2d 957 (February 1984). Until the early 1980s, the attorney general's policy had been to grant parole to most aliens being held pending exclusion hearings. However, this was before the Mariel boat lift and the dramatic upsurge in the arrivals of Haitians by boat in southern Florida. At the time the Haitians were being detained, INS policy had shifted. Excludable aliens were henceforth to be detained unless compelling reasons could be shown why parole should be granted.

23. In the Haitian Refugee Center case, which was initially brought in the Southern District of Florida, 353 of the 1,700 Haitians released on parole failed to appear for hearings. As of June 1984, all but about 67 had been located. Letter to the author from Richard N. Ulrich, Special Assistant to the Deputy Commissioner, INS, June 27, 1984.

Although 353 abscondees, approximately 20 percent of the total number of detainees, may not seem large, it is possible that others might have decided to abscond after exhausting all remedies for relief.

24. Many lawyer-advocates are apparently well aware of the advantages of political asylum as a strategy for gaining their clients additional time. See Michael S. Teitelbaum, "Political Asylum in Theory and Practice," *The Public Interest*, no. 76 (Summer 1984): 74–86.

25. For a discussion of Simpson-Mazzoli's legislative career, see Harris N. Miller, "The Right Thing to Do: A History of Simpson-Mazzoli," in Nathan Glazer, ed., *Clamor at the Gates: The New American Immigration* (San Francisco: Institute for Contemporary Studies, 1985), pp. 49–71.

26. Efforts by the federal government to control the sale and distribution of fire-

arms to felons and other high-risk groups have similarly been handicapped by inadequate identification requirements for gun dealers. See Franklin E. Zimring, "Firearms and Federal Law: The Gun Control Act of 1968," *The Journal of Legal Studies* 4, no. 1 (January 1975): 133–98.

27. Very few employers have been prosecuted under state laws that bar employment of illegal aliens. When there have been successful prosecutions, the fines have been trivial. Wayne A. Cornelius, "Simpson-Mazzoli vs. The Realities of Mexican Immigration," in Wayne A. Cornelius and Ricardo Anzaldua Montoya, eds., *America's New Immigration Law: Origins, Rationales, and Potential Consequences* (San Diego: Center for U.S.-Mexican Studies, University of California at San Diego, 1983), pp. 142–43.

28. As a number of commentators have pointed out, the INS would face numerous difficulties in trying to enforce employer sanctions. See Cornelius, "Realities of Mexican Immigration," in Cornelius and Montoya, *America's New Immigration Law*, pp. 139–49.

A study by the general accounting office also found employer-sanctions laws in other countries to be ineffective deterrents to illegal immigration. United States Congress, "Information on the Enforcement of Laws Regarding Employment of Aliens in Selected Countries," A report by the U.S. General Accounting Office, August 31, 1982.

29. *Congressional Record—House*, June 20, 1984, pp. H 6166–70.

30. Nor are these the only problems. I have examined other problems that the INS is likely to confront in trying to enforce employer sanctions. Among other things, in sharp contrast to support given other regulatory agencies that monitor employers, tough enforcement by the INS will not be strongly supported by the public. Without postpassage backing from unions or other watchdog groups, INS's employer-sanctions effort could be subject to the same harassment that has been directed against its area control operations. See Edwin Harwood, "Enforcing the Immigration Law: Now and After Simpson-Mazzoli," in Lydio F. Tomasi, ed., *In Defense of the Alien*, vol. 7 (New York: Center for Migration Studies, 1985), pp. 51–59.

31. Zimring, "Firearms and Federal Law," p. 161.

32. Ibid., p. 147.

33. For a brief review of how litigation over amnesty might develop, see Thomas Heller and Robert A. Olson, "Legal Dilemmas in the Amnesty Provisions of the Simpson-Mazzoli Bill," in Cornelius and Montoya, eds., *America's New Immigration Law*, pp. 115–21.

34. David S. North and Jennifer R. Wagner proposed a slightly different version of this idea several years ago. They suggested that aliens entering on nonimmigrant visas be required to purchase nonrefundable round-trip tickets. David S. North and Jennifer S. Wagner, "Enforcing the Immigration Law: A Review of the Options" (A report prepared for the Select Commission on Immigration and Refugee Policy, June 1980), p. 32.

35. Herbert L. Packer, *The Limits of the Criminal Sanction* (Stanford, Calif.: Stanford University Press, 1968), pp. 277–82.

36. Jerry Mashaw notes that regulation becomes much less cumbersome and much

more effective to the extent that the agency moves away from judicial and administrative proceedings and toward licensing as the means of control. Jerry L. Mashaw, "Regulation, Logic, and Ideology," *Regulation* (November/December 1979): 46.

Under a tariff system, illegal immigrants would effectively be licensed to perform certain kinds of jobs in exchange for a fee.

37. For a fuller discussion of this possible policy alternative, see Edwin Harwood, "How Should We Enforce Immigration Law?" in Glazer, *Clamor at the Gates*, pp. 80–91.

INDEX